BLACK WATCH

BLACK WATCH

The Inside Story of the Oldest
Highland Regiment in the British Army

JOHN PARKER

headline

First published in 2005
by HEADLINE BOOK PUBLISHING

John Parker would be happy to hear from readers with their comments
on the book at the following e-mail address:
jv.parker@btinternet.com
www.john-parker.co.uk

2

ISBN 0 7553 1348 8

Cataloguing in Publication Data is available from the British Library

Typeset in Times New Roman by Palimpsest Book Production Limited,
Polmont, Stirlingshire
Printed and bound in Great Britain by
Mackays of Chatham plc, Chatham, Kent

Headline's policy is to use papers that are natural, renewable and recyclable products and
made from wood grown in sustainable forests. The logging and manufacturing processes are
expected to conform to the environmental regulations of the country of origin.

HEADLINE BOOK PUBLISHING
A division of Hodder Headline
338 Euston Road
London NW1 3BH

Every effort has been made to fulfil requirements with regard to reproducing
copyright material. The author and publisher will be glad to rectify any omissions
at the earliest opportunity.

www.headline.co.uk
www.hodderheadline.com

Contents

INTRODUCTION

This work had been in progress for some months when, in November 2004, the Black Watch became engaged in battle, fighting on two fronts. The battalion itself was operating in the most dangerous area of Iraq, after the Americans called for assistance in trying to bring some order to the shambles of the 'peace' prior to the Iraqi elections. The Black Watch duly responded with a performance that an American general described as 'awesome' in undertaking demanding work around Baghdad, where five of their men were killed and seventeen were wounded.

It was during the Baghdad deployment that battle opened up on a second front, in London. There, news finally emerged from the Ministry of Defence that this historic regiment was to be disbanded and merged with other Scottish units into a single regiment. Old soldiers and Black Watch supporters charged to the south in a last-ditch bid to save the regiment they loved. They had been campaigning for months against the rumoured changes, but it appeared that this one battle the Black Watch were destined to lose, and that is much against the grain.

Their story is among the richest in spectacle, longevity, drama and courage in British military history, an epic journey for tens of thousands of Highlanders which now has a foot in five centuries. What emerged from a relatively small guarding force to help keep the peace in the braes of Scotland in the late seventeenth century went on to expand into the Highland Watch, then the Black Watch, and thereafter to fight for the British in virtually every major war between then and now, involving a cast of characters ranging through Bonnie Prince Charlie, Napoleon, George Washington, the Kaiser, Hitler and Saddam Hussein.

The Black Watch made a name for themselves because their soldiers, from the outset, were rather special – definitely a breed apart. And while in the beginning their English masters in London regarded them as cannon fodder, like so many other regiments in the British army at that time, the Black Watch quickly showed them the difference. They may well have been at the front of the infantry assault, but they were not getting knocked over at the same rate as others in the line. In their very first battle, the Black Watch asked to be allowed to fight in their own way and, having proved the point, their soldiers were seldom out of the front line of successive British campaigns from then until the present day. It is a brilliant story of what became a battle of will over adversity – all that the British generals could throw at them, in fact, and that was plenty. Although the Scottish exclusivity was lost in the nineteenth century, the Black Watch have remained a tribal group sustained by discipline and pride.

If nothing else, that will be most apparent in the ensuing pages in which their stories are examined with the added colour and drama from many first-hand accounts and records drawn from the regiment's own archives and photographic collections, along with other sources, dating from the earliest days to modern times. The author therefore wishes to record his sincere thanks to all those who have assisted in the compilation of this account, and especially Regimental Archivist, Mr Tom Smyth, at the Black Watch Museum at Balhousie Castle, Perth. As with other books in this series, the author also once again received excellent assistance from the staff of the Imperial War

Museum's Sound Archive and Department of Documents in accessing their vast collections, as listed in the Bibliography, for material that brings real insight to the story. Unless otherwise stated, all photographs in the plate sections are courtesy of the Black Watch (Royal Highland Regiment), who also hold the copyright to those illustrations.

CHAPTER ONE

Beginning with a Mutiny

The Black Watch, senior among Scotland's historic Highland regiments, derives from the tradition of Independent Companies raised by King Charles II in 1667 when the Earl of Atholl was instructed to enlist as many men as necessary to secure peace and pacify the unruly Highlands, formally designated under that seal as the 'shyres of Inverness, Nairn, Murray, Banff, Aberdeen, Mairnes, Angus, Perth, Clackmannan, Monteith, Stirling and Dumbarton'. The 'peace' they were meant to keep was initially infighting and lawlessness among the population of the Highlands of Scotland, and especially to halt the raids on the Lowlands and cross-border sorties into England. Across an unforgiving landscape, long-established families, each controlling their clan and own section of the Highland territory, were capable of raising substantial forces of well-armed and well-equipped fighting men. Such was the prowess of the Highlanders that they had long become renowned across Europe and the Baltic as mercenaries, a tradition that had built since Scots marched under the standard of Joan of Arc in 1429 and continued on down the centuries.

In the seventeenth century Scottish mercenaries were active in the Thirty Years War, and almost 10,000 Scots are known to have served under Gustavus Adolphus of Sweden alone, in his campaigns in support of the Protestants in Germany. Other groups fought for the French, Dutch, Norwegians and Russians regardless of cause or religion. As Cannon's *Historical Record of the British Army* (1845) records in somewhat romantic tone:

> ... inhabitants of various countries have acquired celebrity in different ways; some in the fine arts, others in manufactures, commerce, agriculture, and maritime enterprise, and the Highlanders of Scotland have been conspicuous for the possession of every military virtue which adorns the character of the hero who has adopted the profession of arms. Naturally patient and brave, and inured to hardship in their youth in the hilly districts of a northern climate, these warlike mountaineers have always proved themselves a race of lion-like champions, valiant in the field, faithful, constant, generous in the hour of victory, and endued with calm perseverance under trial and disaster. Led by a native ardour for military fame, they have sought renown in distant lands, where they have been celebrated for martial achievements, and their services have been eagerly sought after by foreign potentates and by renowned generals who have admired and commended their intrepid bearing in moments of terror and danger, calculated to appal the bravest troops. For many centuries a band of Scottish warriors formed the bodyguard of the sovereigns of France, who confided in their valour and fidelity during periods of great danger. The famed 'Scots Brigade', in the service of the United Provinces, is celebrated in the military annals of the sixteenth, seventeenth and early part of the eighteenth centuries, for all the qualities of a valuable corps; and the prowess of the numerous Highland regiments was proclaimed by the voice of fame through all the countries of Christendom.

True enough in every respect, but to the English the Highlanders were heathens and cut-throats. Poets and writers, on the other hand, regaled

6

their readers with romantic stories and verse about bright-eyed young men dashing through the heather, displaying their artistry with assorted weapons strung about their person, such as blue-bladed broadswords flashing afore them like flames, or their wizardry with pistols and muskets, dirks and axes.

Before going on to the later development of the Black Watch, some background into the complexities of Highland loyalties at the time is necessary. The majority of Highlanders spoke Gaelic, although many in what then passed as the middle classes of the clan system also spoke both English and French, and the use of Latin was not uncommon either. Apart from soldiers, black cattle and fish were the main exports from the Highlands, and there was also a hefty local trade in weaponry of all kinds. This in part resulted from the arms carried by returning mercenaries, causing considerable inter-Highland warfare and lawlessness that various kings and politicians tried to eliminate, but failed dismally. James VI of Scotland inadvertently perpetuated the problem by granting writs of Fire and Sword to various clan chiefs, giving them power to administer their own local justice, a power that was often turned to the holder's advantage. Even the army was unable to make any serious inroads into Highland misdemeanours, and the battalions of southern troops posted to garrisons at Fort William, Bernera or Ruthven often became virtual prisoners in their own barracks. It was at that point that Charles II issued his commission to the second Earl of Atholl, authorising him to raise independent companies of clansmen to keep 'watch upon the braes'.

By the end of the seventeenth century there were a number of such companies, usually captained by clan gentry leading their troop of 'Highlanders cloathed in their ancient, proper, Caledonian Dress and armed all with Broad Swords, Targets, Guns, Side-pistols and Durks, alias Daggers'. They were known as the Watch but operated without proper regulations and little military training, which of course meant, human nature as it is, that some of their leaders and their men were not averse to a spot of corruption and blackmail. Perhaps the only dividing line in their operations was that of religion, which leads us to another area of conflict that simmered in the Highlands, and which in turn was to have a profound effect on the eventual course in history to be pursued by the Black Watch. The Scots' long-standing clashes with the English veered hopefully towards some kind of resolution when their own King James VI, whose rule they had enjoyed since 1567, acceded to the throne of England as James I in 1603. Subsequently, a number of schemes for union with England were raised throughout that century, but all failed. The English saw little to be gained and the Scots had no wish whatsoever to become the junior nation in an alliance.

The idea was further downgraded on the arrival of James II of England (James VII of Scotland), whose reign as the first Catholic monarch since Mary Tudor was welcomed with sedition and rebellion. He was forced to abdicate in the 1688 rebellion against his rule. At this point the English Parliament asked James's daughter Mary and her husband, William of Orange from the Netherlands, to act as regents until James's newly born son, James Francis Stuart, was raised in the Protestant faith to take the throne on his coming of age. William refused these terms and insisted on having the Crown along with his wife. Parliament agreed, thus sowing the seeds of subsequent Jacobite uprisings (Jacobite from the Latin word for James, Jacobus) to restore the Stuart line to the thrones of Scotland and England.

The erstwhile monarch's son and heir, the would-be James III of England and James VIII of Scotland, was left hoping for the call of his nation, and Louis XIV of France declared his recognition of him as the rightful heir to both the English and Scottish thrones. The English Parliament would not have it, and by an Act of Settlement passed a decree to thwart the Stuart claims, thus ensuring that the Crown would pass to Sophia of Hanover, a cousin of Charles I, or her heirs, leading to the eventual arrival of the Hanoverian Georges and the present line of succession. The English also proposed threatening legislation with the Alien Act of 1705, which decreed that unless Scotland began immediate negotiations for a union, the Scots would be treated as aliens in England, thus destroying the country's trade. Consequently, the Scottish Parliament had little alternative but to acquiesce and eventually passed the Act of Union, so that Scotland

and England were effectively to become one country. On 28 April 1707 the Scottish Parliament held its last session – until it was restored in 1999. Meanwhile, the Jacobites were seething, waiting and hoping for the return of their king.

The independent companies of the Watch went about their business until further murmurings of discontent began to arise when Queen Anne died in 1714, to be succeeded by the Elector of Hanover, George I. Staunch Jacobites and their Catholic allies across the British Isles and in France still championed their alternative monarchy, and less than a year after the formation of the new British Parliament the exiled pretender James VIII of Scotland sailed towards the Scottish coast supported by a strong force of French troops to attempt to reclaim the throne.

They were met by an even larger force of English ships and subsequently returned to France without incident. The Jacobite cause in Scotland, stirred by this event, continued to campaign for James's return, and on 6 September 1715 the sixth Earl of Mar, John Erskine, declared himself for the Jacobite Pretender and left Braemar with a 3,500-strong force to head south to meet up with the Jacobites in England. By the end of the month, his army had expanded to more than 10,000 men, and he took over Inverness with little opposition, providing a springboard for the capture of much of eastern Scotland. His advance was halted by a surprise assault led by the pro-Hanoverian Duke of Argyll at the head of an army of fewer than 4,000, with a final showdown in what became known as the Battle of Sheriffmuir, near Dunblane, Perthshire. Although the battle was indecisive, the Jacobites lost the impetus. By the time James came ashore in Scotland later that year, the prospect of him reviving his claim to the Scottish throne once again slipped away and he sailed back to France, never to set foot in Scotland again. That Jacobite rebellion, known as the Fifteen, had a severe effect on the Highlands of Scotland, where the clans were to suffer immediate and harsh restrictions, regardless of which side they supported. Among the most forbidding in terms of livelihood and tradition was a law that came into immediate effect, banning all Highlanders from owning, manufacturing or carrying arms. Search parties were inaugurated to enforce these measures, which carried quite draconian punishments. Anyone found in possession of a claymore, the traditional weapon of the Scottish Highlands, could be arrested and sent overseas to serve in the redcoat regiments. This was, of course, not merely the stripping of arms; it was an assault on a way of life that the Hanoverian law-makers around the throne would pursue with unswerving harshness, eventually aimed at crushing the Highland clans and especially – although by no means exclusively – the Jacobite supporters. Major-General David Stewart of Garth, an officer of the Black Watch and an early historian, provides an intimate portrait of the initial effects of these new laws, although, as we will see, much worse was to follow:

A Highlander would fight to the last drop of his blood at the command of his Chief, and if he thought his honour, or that of his clan, insulted he was equally ready to call for redress and to seek revenge; yet with this disposition and though generally armed few lives were lost except in general engagements and skirmishes. This is particularly to be remarked in their personal encounters, duels and trials of strength. A relation of mine, the late Mr Stewart of Bohallie, afforded an instance of the Highland character. He was . . . one of the best swordsmen of his time . . . in his youth [he] had been hot and impetuous and as in those days the country was full of young men [who] had ample opportunity of proving the temper of their swords and their dexterity in the use of them. Bohallie often spoke of many contests and trials of skill, but they always avoided, he said, coming to extremities and were in general satisfied when blood was drawn. His swords and targets gave evidence of the service they had seen. On one occasion he was passing from Breadalbane to Loch Lomond through Glenfalloch in company with James Macgregor, one of Rob Roy's sons. As they came to a certain spot Macgregor said: 'It was here that I tried the mettle of one of your kinsmen!' Some miles further on, he continued: 'Here I made another of your blood feel the superiority of my sword

... and here,' said he, when in sight of Ben Lomond in the country of the Macgregors, 'I made a third of your royal clan yield to the clan Gregor.' My old friend's blood was set in motion by the first remark; the second, as he said, made it boil; however, he restrained himself till the third, when he exclaimed: 'You have said and done enough, now stand and defend yourself and see if a fourth defeat of a Stewart will give victory to a Gregarach.' As they were both good swordsmen it was some time before Macgregor received a cut on the sword arm, when, dropping his target, he gave up the contest.

The Highland Watch – forerunner of the Black Watch – was disbanded and disarmed along with the rest of the Highlands in the wake of the Fifteen. However, it quickly became apparent that peacekeeping and disarming were unenforceable without wholesale policing of the Highlands by government troops. A whole unsatisfactory decade passed before determined action was initiated from London, calling for a full investigation and total disarming of the Scottish Highlands. By then, George II was on the throne, and perhaps spurred on by the recent news of the birth of an infant destined to become Bonnie Prince Charlie, he called for a full report on Highland activity. The task was handed to General George Wade, an astute and straight-talking Irishman. He coupled this with proposals for a massive road- and fort-building programme that enabled deeper penetration of countryside largely inaccessible up to that time. He also quickly discovered that attempts to disarm the Highlanders had not only failed in the past but had been turned to profitable industry in that old weapons and obsolete muskets specially imported from Holland had been exchanged for a government bounty for surrendering arms, while their plentiful supply of modern weapons were kept hidden.

The upshot was that Wade was authorised to form six Independent Companies of Highlanders under Simon, 11th Lord Lovat, Sir Duncan Campbell of Lochnell and Colonel William Grant of Ballindalloch, who all held the rank of captains. The force of around 500 men was raised mostly from clans supposedly loyal to the Hanoverian government, although not, as it turned out, exclusively so. In fact, Simon, Lord Lovat, a wily old rogue, had been involved in talks with the Earl of Seaforth in 1719 about a new Jacobite uprising but had then turned on him, informed the king and snatched some of the earl's land. As will be seen, Lovat was also involved in the later and final Jacobite rebellion in 1745, with his own men fighting at Culloden, resulting in his own arrest and execution.

The new Watch companies came into being in 1725 and were required to wear a 'government-approved' uniform tartan that was dark in colour and is thought to have inspired the name given to them locally as *Am Freiceadan Dubh*, the Black Watch. Wade's own report on the situation makes clear the intent that the six companies were to be used to bring calm to the troubled Highlands, and for that reason some would suggest that the colour of the tartan was not necessarily the reason they were called the Black Watch, but that they had 'black hearts' for siding with 'enemies of true Highland spirit'. The sensitive nature of the deployment of men recruited from within the area was clearly an issue that Wade approached with some thought. His report of 1724 certainly makes clear that recruitment for the companies was to be among 'such Highlanders as are well affected to His Majesty's Government and commanded by officers speaking the language of the country, subject to martial law, and under the inspection and orders of the Governors of Fort William and Inverness, and the officer commanding His Majesty's forces in those parts. That the said companies be employed in disarming the Highlanders, preventing depredations, bringing criminals to justice, and hinder rebels and attained persons from inhabiting that part of the kingdom.'

The latter aspects seemed to be as much related to religion as to rebellion and criminality, in that the majority of recruits acknowledged their affiliation to the Protestant rather than the Catholic cause, and by that affiliation were seen as enemies of the Jacobites. But Cannon's *Historical Record* does go to some lengths to establish that men drawn from both persuasions served together in the Black Watch without rancour or malice:

These six companies were employed in enforcing the disarming act, in overawing the disaffected, in preventing reprisals and plunder between rival clans and the depredations of the mountaineers on their more peaceable neighbours of the plains ... The officers were taken from the clans of Campbell, Grant, Munroe etc. which had embraced the principles of the 1688 rebellion, but many men were from the clan of Athole and those of Perthshire which adhered to the opposite interest.

One aspect that appeared to be fairly standard was that the men were all drawn from families who were 'landholders and persons in good circumstances' – in other words from relatively well-to-do families. They were accustomed to being attended by gillies, who in turn often joined up with them and continued to serve their masters. Dress for the six companies was standardised in style as well as colour. The kilt of that era was a weighty plaid, twelve yards long. The upper part was thrown across the left shoulder and held in place with a brooch, while the lower part was belted around the middle to hang just above the kneecap. A short jacket was worn of green, blue or black cloth, along with a flat blue bonnet and a large goatskin purse or sporran. In addition to the 1725 government issue of a light musket, bayonet, broadsword and cartouche box, they carried a dirk and a Highland steel pistol, and, in some cases, a *targaid*, or shield. Sergeants also carried a Lochaber axe.

Each company employed a piper, because the Highlanders refused to march without the bagpipe. The companies took on the air of being rather more than mere soldiers, and the men would have been insulted to be compared with an English redcoat. Many of them did not even consider themselves soldiers. 'There was much affinity with their ancient usages, so that their services seemed merely that of a clan, sanctioned by legal authority,' wrote General Stewart. 'Furthermore, a member of the Watch could walk abroad as his ancestors had done, carrying his arms about him.'

One boasted of carrying the arms his father had used in the charge at Sheriffmuir. And so in every respect these were men apart, their purpose to keep the peace in the mountains, always destined for service in Scotland, or so they believed. The Black Watch companies, under regimentation proposed by Major Scipio Duroure in 1731, were distributed across an extensive area of countryside and for years hence performed their duties in a manner that earned the respect of the people they were keeping watch over. The Black Watch were so successful that it at last dawned on the military masters in the south that there lay in the far north a huge reservoir of potential soldiers who could be turned out for England. This proposal was rejected in the military hierarchy, still suspicious of Highlanders. Even so, eyes had settled on the Black Watch, admired by army officers for some years despite their unorthodox approach to soldiering. Some were anxious to bring them into the main arena, while others were less enthusiastic, preferring to keep the Highlanders where they were, and in their place. In reality there could be no comparison with the average English battalion, filled by press gangs or men bought out of country jails. Persuaded to some extent by this argument, George II ordered the incorporation of the six companies of the Black Watch into a regiment, to be augmented to ten companies. The formal warrant, dated 25 October 1739, was issued, addressed to Colonel John, Earl of Crawford and Lindsay:

> Whereas we have thought fit that a Regiment of Foot be forthwith formed under your command, and consist of ten companies, each to contain one captain, one lieutenant, one ensign, three serjeants, three corporals, two drummers, and one hundred effective private men; which said regiment shall be partly formed out of six independent companies of foot in the Highlands of North Britain, three of which are now commanded by captains, and three by captain-lieutenants . . . The regiment shall commence and take place according to the establishment thereof. And of these our orders and commands, you, and the said three captains and three captain-lieutenants commanding at present the six independent Highland companies, and all others concerned, are to take notice, and yield obedience thereto accordingly.

This elevation to regimental status meant that the Highlanders would lose the independence they had enjoyed under their own commanders for the first decade of their existence and, worse, threatened to take them out of their beloved Highlands for ever, to become part of the general establishment of the British army, governed by unfamiliar rules and regulations that might well challenge the loyalty of the young Scottish soldiers. The question was: did the Black Watch realise that by this action George II could now call on the new regiment for duty in wars that might keep them overseas for years at a time? This, as we will see, was soon to become a vital issue.

In May 1740, 850 officers and men of the new regiment, which had been given the title of the 43rd of Foot (later promoted to the 42nd Regiment of Foot) and wearing scarlet jackets with buff facings, assembled at Aberfeldy for inspection. The arms they carried were largely their own property, many of which were family heirlooms and bore the scars of past Highland wars. For the next fifteen months they remained on the banks of the Tay and the Lyon, trained and exercised by their lieutenant-colonel, Sir Robert Munro of Foulis. They had to learn from scratch the military methodology of marching by files, by platoons, by companies and in battalion order, and to march on the centre or wheel to the right and left about, to learn each tap of a grenadier drum and to obey its permutations without hesitation.

As the winter of 1741 set in, the companies were dispersed among the garrisons of the Great Glen, their training over, and there continued the duties they had signed up for, generally on the understanding that they would not leave Scotland. For the British army, however, there was no such understanding, and at that time Britain was becoming deeply involved in the War of the Austrian Succession (1740–48), the country's first major conflict for twenty years. The army had been seriously neglected, its officers and men largely untrained in harsh combat. Hence, when the time came, strong fighters like the Black Watch were nothing short of a godsend to George's military ambitions.

In 1743 the regiment were ordered to march to London to be

reviewed by the king on Finchley Common, blissfully unaware that he usually reviewed his regiments immediately before they went abroad. The men of the Watch believed the king wanted to take a look at his newest regiment in kilted attire. After all, hadn't he earlier asked to see a Highlander in full dress and armed to the teeth? Two soldiers were selected and sent to London: John Campbell and a handsome MacGregor, known as Gregor the Beautiful. They were brought to St James's Palace to appear before the king and an audience of scarlet-coated, gold-laced and white-cuffed officers who included his son, the Duke of Cumberland, soon to command his army in Flanders. Also present was the creator of the Black Watch, George Wade, who was now a field marshal. Campbell and MacGregor gave an energetic exhibition of exercises with the broadsword, and the delighted monarch presented each with a guinea. They silently forgave him the insult, so the story goes, and handed the coins to a porter as they left.

Now the whole regiment were heading south. They set off in high spirits from Inverness for their 600-mile march. For the first few days the spirits of the Highlanders were high as crowds turned out to watch them go, marching to their pipes and drums through the towns and villages en route to the border and into England. They pushed on into territory where few Highlanders had ever been seen, and as they penetrated deeper into the English countryside they were often jeered rather than cheered by English townsfolk.

Then a greater bombshell: as they marched on down the Roman road towards London, they came upon a shabby bunch of soldiers marching in the opposite direction, several of them clearly ill and pallid. There were just sixty men in the party, Scottish Lowlanders, and all that remained of a battalion of the Royal Scots which had just returned from the West Indies, where they had been sent to fight the Spanish. The Royals, the 1st Regiment of Foot, had served since the mists of time, in consequence of which they bear to this day the nickname Pontius Pilate's Bodyguard. As the oldest Regiment of Infantry in the British army, they also had the traditional, if dubious, honour of the being the Right of Line, and therefore to be the first in any conflict. Now, as they sat at a country inn by the Roman road, the Royal Scots told a story that put the fear of God into the unworldly Watch, whispering the drama to make the most of their stories, although a straightforward factual account would have been worrying enough. They were inspired no doubt by the contempt the Lowlanders harboured for Highlanders, especially these healthy young soldiers, in all their finery, marching to see the king.

Where were their comrades? the Highlanders asked. Killed in action? Well, yes, many had been torn to shreds by round shot and sword, but most lay in yellow fever graves in the West Indies from where these bedraggled survivors had recently landed. The Highlanders had already heard tell of the Caribbean islands from stories of relatives and ancestors transported, most never to be seen again. It was the nightmare of all soldiers and criminals alike to be sent there. The British colonies in the Caribbean were strategically important and spice-rich. They had to be protected from competing nations, and so the English poured soldiers into the islands to secure trade. The death toll had been horrendous and continued to be so, with more than 40,000 soldiers dying in the last decade of the eighteenth century alone from fever, cholera, malaria and other rampant tropical diseases.

And now, in the tavern on the Roman road, the Royal Scots drew them closer. Confidentially, they said, they knew for certain that the 43rd Regiment of Foot, the Black Watch, would replace them in the West Indies. Ships were waiting in London to take them straight away, and beware, said the Royals, beware of the ships, the transports. They were filthy and disease-ridden, back from one crossing and setting out again having ditched dozens of bodies over the side on the way home. One more thing, said the Scots before getting on their way, 'If your officers die from the fever, or abandon their men for other reasons, you Highlanders will be sold as slaves'.

By now, the men of the Black Watch also knew that the review by the king was not a special honour but proof that they were to be sent out of the country. As they marched on towards the review ground, bitterness, anger and nervousness gripped them, and they were to face yet one more disappointment. The king had not bothered

17

to wait to review them. He had already left for Flanders. Even so, there was considerable interest in their arrival, especially from the London journals. One, incidentally, had already published the news that the Black Watch, Britain's only kilted regiment, would soon be in service in King George's War in Flanders, and that many ladies in society were excited at the prospect of seeing the somewhat 'barbaric, bare-shanked peculiarities of their dress'.

Many such ladies, along with a complete cross section of the people of London making up thousands, came to the review on Saturday 14 May on Finchley Common. Field Marshal Wade deputised for the king at the review, and the proceedings began inside a formation of two troops of dragoons and a company of the Third Guards forming a square to hold back this vast crowd, anxious to witness the unusual spectacle. On the periphery, all kinds of vendors, musicians, jugglers, singers, pickpockets and assorted entertainers turned the event into a noisy carnival, the like of which the Highlanders had never seen.

Nor had the Londoners seen the like of the Highlanders, as they marched and drilled in all their finery, and the reaction of the population was not always complimentary. At the end of the review the companies were brought together to receive orders just delivered from the office of the Secretary of War: in five days hence they were to march to the Isle of Dogs to prepare to board transports already anchored in the Thames for an overseas posting. No other details were given, although later that night one of their officers did tell a corporal that he believed they were bound for Flanders, news that everyone except the rank and file seemed to know.

Over the next forty-eight hours the men were reaching a fever pitch of anxiety. Some were openly talking about going home, marching back to Scotland, and all felt an injustice was about to be meted out to them, and being 'gentlemen soldiers', by and large, they were torn between accepting their plight and leaving. They met in small groups discussing the situation, some arguing that they had every right to march back to Scotland because the British army had reneged on its agreement. General Stewart explained:

When the Highlanders entered the King's service they considered themselves a contracting party in the agreements made with the government, from whom they naturally expected the same punctual performance of their engagements, as well as some degree, at least, of the kindness and attention which they and their fathers had met with from their ancient and hereditary chieftains. [With] the terms which had been expressly stipulated with His Majesty's officers violated, the Highlanders warmly resented such unexpected treatment.

It was an impossible situation, especially for the inexperienced Highlanders whose entire lives as soldiers had been spent among their own people. Now, split up in separate billets, collective action became difficult, but word was sent by runners that there were definite proposals that they should return home forthwith. In their naivety, the leaders of those in favour of returning home apparently argued that if sufficient numbers joined a protest that they believed was a valid one, the authorities would not dare to take any action. The majority, however, while angry and dispirited, accepted their plight, but on the night of 17 May a total of 120 men decided that they'd had enough. Under cover of darkness they moved out of their separate encampments to begin their march back north in two groups. They planned to march by night and to rest by day, and did so with complete military precision and discipline.

When their departure was discovered, 600 men of the 3rd Foot Guards and 50 riders from the Horse Grenadiers were dispatched from Barnet, while, further north, 19 troops of dragoons quartered at Northampton, Huntingdon, Leicester and Loughborough were put into the countryside to search their own areas. The runaways had been reduced in number, a handful giving up just north of London but the rest moved at a remarkable pace: within no more than seventy-two hours they had covered almost seventy miles, settling for the night in a forested area called Ladywood, three miles east of the village of Sudborough on the road to Oundle, Northamptonshire. It was ironically just six miles from

19

Fotheringhay Castle, where Mary Queen of Scots was beheaded on 8 February 1587.

Although well positioned for a fight if it came to it, some of the runaways were already having second thoughts. At first light on 21 May, one of their leaders went towards a nearby hamlet, but on the periphery of the wood he met and startled a local resident, explained what they were about and asked if he would convey a message to the local Justice of the Peace. The countryman agreed, and shortly Major John Creed, a former soldier who had fought in Flanders and Spain, arrived on horseback and met the leaders of the runaways. They explained that they were prepared to surrender on their own terms, which would include a free pardon for all. Creed agreed to deliver their message and galloped off to Oundle, where he wrote a note concerning his discovery of the 'gentlemen Highlanders' and instructed the town constable to go at once to the nearest officer of the dragoons to state that Creed was in negotiation with them. Creed also wrote to his employer, James, second Duke of Montagu, a King's Regent and one of the country's largest landowners whose Boughton estate in Northamptonshire covered a vast area. Unbeknown to Creed at the time, an employee of the duke had spotted the Highlanders earlier in the day while patrolling the grounds and had reported the fact to Major Charles Otway, of the Duke's Carabineers, quartered near Kettering. He in turn alerted the dragoons, and from that moment the Highlanders' fate was sealed. The dragoons were already closing in, from the north, west, east and south, although no further action was taken until the arrival of Brigadier-General Blakeney, who was galloping over from the Forest of Rockingham where he had been leading the search in that area. Now in command of the situation at Ladywood, he sent Captain John Ball into the woods to continue the negotiations begun earlier by Creed and to gain intelligence of the lie of the land. Ball reported back that the Highlanders had chosen an excellent spot to defend themselves . . . 'a large ditch four or five feet high, with a forest hedge thereon in manner as near could be like an half moon . . . with a strong and thick wood behind . . . and on each end of the half moon they had planted twenty men . . . and in the body about seventy men. The rest were to guard a high gate that led into [their hide].'

Blakeney realised that the description Ball had given him meant that for the time being further negotiation would be better than a battle. Ball returned to the hide and persuaded at least some of the men to give themselves up. They followed him out, then others came, and finally all began to make their way through the undergrowth, dropping their weapons as they came into Blakeney's camp – ninety-eight men in all. One other who had died had been buried at the soldiers' camp. Ball was given the task of escorting them into custody, first marching to the nearby town of Thrapston, then on to Northampton, and finally back to London, where, after passing the gauntlet of jeering crowds, they were locked in the Tower with eight others who were picked up at various points on their journey. Of the rest, nine were known to have made their escape to the safety of the Highlands and three others were never heard of again. The captives now faced the death sentence unless, as Ball had suggested, the king agreed to show them mercy.

The king, then in Hanover, was duly informed of all that had happened, and the Highlanders were kept in the Tower on bread and water until his pleasure was known. On 2 June a messenger returned with a note indicating that the king's mercy could be extended 'but an example of severity should be made of the most guilty'. The next day the trial began in the cramped surroundings of the house of the Deputy Lieutenant of the Tower, Adam Williamson, with the Reverend Campbell, a Scottish minister, acting as interpreter for the seventy-nine men who spoke only Gaelic. He noted in his diary later that they believed to a man that on no account would they be required to serve outside Scotland, yet in court each relied for his defence on a statement that Reverend Campbell maintained was written out for them by a stranger who came to visit, the last sentence of which simply stated: 'Our unhappy conduct was owing solely to our ignorance and credulity.'

The trial descended into farce, as the president of the court martial and the twelve senior officers who sat with him rattled through the evidence, dispensing up to fifteen men each day. Campbell did his best to translate the proceedings but admitted it was asking too much for a proper summation. As one of them protested: 'I did not desert. I only wanted to march back to my own country. I will not be transported to the plantations like a thief and a rogue.'

Each of the 107 was brought before the court to be sentenced. They heard the same words, agonisingly repeated: *Guilty of mutiny and desertion, and the sentence is death by firing squad.* A great deal of unexpectedly angry reaction from the public and the newspapers erupted immediately and was further fanned by reports that the whole business had been inspired by Jacobite spies who persuaded the men to desert, an allegation that had been ignored by the court but which remained in play for many years to come. In the Highlands, special arrangements were ordered by the Secretary of War to 'hinder depredations and secure the peace', although the likelihood of trouble subsided when the Secretary of War announced three days later that the king had shown mercy on the men, and that all but three were to be saved from the firing squad and exiled to serve with regiments in the colonies. The three harshly singled out as ringleaders of the mutiny were Corporal Samuel MacPherson of Laggan in Badenoch, Corporal Malcolm MacPherson of the same parish, and Private Farquhar Shaw of Rothiemurchus.

All made a plea for mercy, but it was ignored. On 18 July 1743 they were shot before a firing squad, a duty that fell on the Scots Guards whose regiment was at that time providing the Tower guard. 'The unfortunate men,' a Westminster journal reported, 'behaved with perfect resolution and propriety.' Of the remainder, two died while incarcerated at the Tower and twenty-six of the youngest soldiers were sent into exile for service in regular army units in Gibraltar or Minorca, which was considered to be a mitigated sentence. All the remaining men were kept locked in the Tower until September, by which time many were ill. They were transported to redcoat regiments in the Leeward Islands and to the colony of Georgia, which for many was tantamount to a sentence of death by exile or ill health.

The regiment in the Leeward Island remained as a permanent garrison for the next thirty-three years, and many hundreds of soldiers died of disease while manning it. The regiment in Georgia was also severely neglected and finally abandoned by its commander, with only 500 of the original 5,000 troops still alive. The soldiers remaining at that point eventually passed to the control of the civil administration and were never heard of again. Nor was this unhappy state of affairs restricted merely to the men. During the course of the trial, a number of their womenfolk – wives and girlfriends – had travelled to London to be near their men, and in due course those being sent to Georgia were allowed to take wives, provided they paid £5 for their transport. Several of the unmarried couples were suitably accommodated in a service conducted by Reverend Campbell, who also arranged for a barrack room to be set aside on the night they were married, with beds separated off with blankets hanging from the ceiling.

In the terrible aftermath of these events, it did not go unnoticed that those who were shot, and many of the Finchley rebels sent to the most severe climes, came from clans suspected of supporting the Jacobite cause, including the Stewarts, the MacPhersons, MacGregors, MacIntyres, MacDonalds, Robertsons and Grants. In due course a monument was erected to the collective memory of the Black Watch mutineers, if such they can be truly called, in the image of Private Shaw, and they would never be forgotten because they had accepted their punishment with dignity.

CHAPTER TWO

No Going Back

So it was true. Even as the runaways were being returned to London, the rest of the Black Watch Regiment were marched to Greenwich to cross the river and then onwards to Gravesend, where they embarked for overseas duty under the watchful eye of Wolfe's marines, thankfully not to the West Indies, for the moment at least, but to Flanders. They were destined to become part of the Hanoverian-led enterprise guided by King George II in the War of the Austrian Succession – generally known as King George's War, since it had little to do with the British Isles.

The conflict dated from 1740, when the deaths of two European monarchs, Frederick William I, King of Prussia, and Charles VI, Emperor of Austria, led to war between their successors when Prussia seized the rich Austrian province of Silesia. The French, meanwhile, invaded Bavaria and then threatened Flanders, a region dominated by Austria and the Dutch Republic. An allied army was hastily assembled to counter the French invasion, with troops from Austria and various German states, including Hanover. George II, as both King of England and Elector of Hanover, decided to send British troops to join the allies. The somewhat disjointed conflict was pursuing a slow course, and in that year of 1743 the allied army marched south to the Frankfurt region of Germany, where it was joined by George II, who led the allies in the Battle of Dettingen, fought against the French (the Black Watch were not engaged).

Two years of unproductive manoeuvring passed before the Black Watch were finally called into serious action at Fontenoy. Marshal Saxe, with a French army of 80,000 men, had besieged Tournay, and King George's second and favourite son, the Duke of Cumberland, then aged twenty-four, prepared to move against him with 50,000 men under his command. The French, well dug in in an advantageous position, commanded a four-mile battle front from the crest of a hill, where they had built a fortified redoubt with guns trained on the route of the British advance, which was first to be made through woods. Black Watch troops were among those selected for Cumberland's front-line action, with the task of charging and capturing the redoubt. They were at that moment to become the first kilted regiment called to action in Europe and were also given permission to fight in the same manner they would use in the Highlands, much to the chagrin of some of Cumberland's senior commanders. Cumberland personally reviewed the Highland Regiment and commended its appearance and discipline. But first, according to Cannon's *Historical Record*, he decided to 'test the loyalty of the Black Watch'. This was to be achieved by:

> . . . a galloping of aides-de-camp along the line of the British, and soon the Black Watch was ordered to be in readiness to aid in clearing the plain of the concealed infantry, and in covering a reconnoitring party, which was to consist of the Duke of Cumberland, accompanied by the Chiefs of the army. By this movement, it was intended that the Highland Regiment should have its loyalty put to the test by being brought in contact with the enemy immediately under his own eye. The Highlanders . . . were determined to show what, as soldiers, they were able and willing to perform.

In the early skirmishing, the Black Watch advanced with a party of Austrian hussars and 'displayed their native ardour and intrepidity' in which they utilised many of the tricks of their trade, learned in the Highlands. On one occasion a Highlander posted in front was pinned down by a French sharpshooter firing towards them. He took his bayonet and placed it on a stick fixed behind a bush. The sharpshooter saw the bayonet and continued to fire at the spot while the Scot crawled to a point where he could take aim, and brought the Frenchman down. The Highlanders were then ordered to support the Dutch in an attempt to secure the village of Veson. The Dutch troops were to attack the King of France's Household Guards positioned on top of rising ground and went on ahead, following their standard procedure of halting and firing every twenty paces. The Highlanders became thoroughly frustrated by this tactic because it gave the enemy time to fire at will and the Dutch troops were falling at every stop. Instead, the Black Watch dashed forward, overtook the Dutch and the front ranks, handed back their firelocks to the rear rank, drew their swords and quickly drove the French from their ground. When the attack was over, it was found that the Highlanders had lost fewer than a dozen men killed or wounded, while the Dutch, who had not come up at all, lost more than five times that number. At about midday a second attack was made on the enemy's positions, when the Dutch again failed, and Lieutenant-Colonel Sir Robert Munro was ordered, with the Highlanders, to sustain the British troops fighting superior numbers. Cannon's account states:

The lieutenant-colonel brought them into action in gallant style. He had obtained the permission of the Duke of Cumberland to allow them to fight in their own way. Sir Robert, according to the usage of his countrymen, ordered the whole regiment to clap to the ground, on receiving the French fire, and instantly after its discharge they sprang up, and coming close to the enemy poured in their shot upon them to the certain destruction of multitudes, and drove them precipitately through their own lines; then retreating drew up again, and attacked them a second time after the same manner. These attacks they repeated several times on the same day, to the surprise of the whole army. Sir Robert was everywhere with his regiment, notwithstanding his great corpulency, and when in the trenches he was hauled out by his legs and arms by his own men and it is observed that when he commanded the whole regiment to clap to the ground, he himself [unable to do so] stood alone with the colours behind him, receiving the fire of the enemy. The Duke of Cumberland witnessed the gallant conduct of the regiment and [also] observed a Highlander [Sergeant James Campbell] who had killed nine men, making a stroke with his broadsword at the tenth, when his arm was shot off by a cannonball. His Royal Highness applauded the Highlander's conduct, and promised him a reward of a value equal to the arm. [Sadly] . . . while the regiment was thus evincing its prowess, the French commander made a determined attack with an immense body of fresh troops, and drove back the British line, and the Highlanders were borne down by the retreating body . . . The Black Watch took part in covering the retrograde movement, in which they evinced the same native intrepidity which they had displayed during the action, repeatedly facing about and checking the pursuit by their fire. The Earl of Crawford thanked the troops which covered the retreat under his orders, telling them they had acquired as much honour in covering so great a retreat, as if they had gained the battle.

Nor was the fame of the Black Watch restricted to the battlefields. At home, their prowess was recorded in the *London Gazette* as 'heroic gallantry' and recognised throughout Britain. Similar tributes were paid later in the *Vienna Gazette*, whose writer, like most Continentals, was taken with their character, courage and dress:

The Highlanders are a people totally different in their dress, manners and temper from the other inhabitants of Britain. They are caught in the mountains when young and still run with a surprising degree of swiftness . . . they make very good soldiers when disciplined . . . [and have] an extraordinary submission and love for their officers who are all young and handsome . . . It is to be hoped that their king's laudable, though late, endeavours to civilise them and instruct them in the principles of Christianity will meet with success . . . The French held them at first in great contempt but they have met with them so often and seen them in front of so many battles that they firmly believe there are twelve battalions of them in the army instead of two.

It would not be long, however, before the army Establishment began to rein in the unorthodox methods of the Highlanders which had been so well tried and tested in their home environment. In later encounters they would first be deprived of their pistols, and then their magnificent broadswords, to be armed in conventional infantry manner with musket and bayonet. Their tactics, too, would undergo changes to fit the requirements of the commanding generals. But their remarkable endurance and speed in all aspects of attacking manoeuvres could not be faulted. No one could outdo them in the charge, and that would apply whether with broadsword or bayonet.

They were engaged from start to finish of the Battle of Fontenoy and came through it with remarkably few casualties, certainly far fewer in percentage terms than any other unit involved. Regiments had been cut to ribbons on both sides, each losing around 8,000. The Black Watch lost two officers and 30 men killed, with three officers, two sergeants and 86 men wounded, leaving more than 900 ablebodied men fit for service. They had come through their first major test in war with flying colours, yet barely had the dust settled or the wounds healed than they were on the move again.

In August they were called hurriedly back to Britain as part of a fire brigade effort to quell a crisis in their homeland: the Jacobites were uprising again, with the backing of the French, and the longrunning feud between the two royal Houses of Hanover and Stuart flared, this time to its climax. While George II was busy with his war in Europe, the Young Pretender to the throne, Charles Edward Stuart, made his move to reclaim what he believed was his inheritance. Born in Rome in 1720, he was the grandson of deposed King James II of England and the son of the Old Pretender who had twice tried to invade Scotland in order to seize the British throne, the last time in 1715. With the blessing of his father and the support of a French invasion force, he decided to make his claim and lead the House of Stuart back to power in Scotland, which could be achieved only by defeating the English.

After consultations with the French while the British were at Fontenoy, Charles made his move, landed in Scotland and raised his standard at Glenfinnan. He quickly gathered an army from the minority of Highland clans that supported him. Charles then made his way south to Edinburgh, which he entered with little resistance, and his first opponent, Sir John Cope's army of 4,000 men encountered south of the city, was brushed aside. Scotland was fleetingly in the hands of the Jacobites, and Charles did not intend to halt at the border. With intelligence from the French in regard to British troop movements, he decided he would march on into England, gathering support as he went. Meanwhile, a substantial force was already being assembled by the Duke of Cumberland, made up of his own British troops, along with Dutch and German support brought immediately from Europe.

The Black Watch were among them, but they were held back in the south of England with three other regiments to forestall any possible invasion from the French along the South Coast. The decision to keep the Highlanders in the south was not out of compassion, or indeed military strategy. Despite their showing at Fontenoy, the Hanoverians still had doubts as to whether they could be trusted to remain loyal. The Highlanders would certainly have had relatives who were on the opposite side, and that eventually proved to be the case. Some 300 men in the Black Watch had next of kin in the Jacobite army marching with Charles, and, as was the case throughout the Highlands, in some instances brother fought brother in the ensuing bitterness. Charles pressed on and within the month had reached Derby, although he picked up precious little support in England.

Worse, the French started back-pedalling wh:n the size of Cumberland's army became apparent. The Jacobites had more than 5,000 men marching ever further from home, running low on supplies and receiving little support from English Jacobites. With Cumberland bearing down on him with a rumoured 30,000 men, Charles decided to retreat to Scotland to make a stand there. In fact, the opposing force consisted of fewer than 10,000 men, but Charles did not wait to count them. He headed north, and en route managed to win another important battle at Falkirk in January 1746, when he was confronted by the courageous former colonel of the Black Watch, Sir Robert Munro of Foulis, who had been promoted to take command of the 37th Foot. Unfortunately, his new regiment did not have the flare of his old one and fled ahead of a Jacobite charge. Sir Robert and a younger brother by his side were killed by Lochiel's Camerons. They were buried in the churchyard of Falkirk and their funeral was attended not only by the 37th Foot but by many from the Jacobite army, again demonstrating the diversity of opinion that Highland people were able to live with, but which was not understood by those in the south.

Despite this success against Munro's troops, Charles's somewhat ragtag army began to suffer as the Scottish winter and a dire shortage of food and ammunition took their toll, with the French having long since reneged on their promise to send support in materials and manpower. The Duke of Cumberland pushed further north and was less than fifteen miles from the Jacobites' camp near Inverness when Charles, in foolhardy desperation, decided to strike first. He sent 1,500 of his best troops to make a night march on Cumberland's camp. They sent back a runner confirming Cumberland's over-whelming strength, and the following morning, 16 April 1746, Cumberland's army marched on to the moors at Culloden with their commander's instruction resounding in their ears: No Quarter Given.

Hugely outnumbered and totally outgunned, the Jacobites moved into position for the last act in the battle between the royal houses. When Cumberland's artillery let fly, Charles's army was shot to pieces, mauled, massacred and scattered, a scene that left 1,500 Highlanders and around 300 of the duke's men dead, a terrible slaughter – and the last land battle to be fought in Britain. Nor did the carnage end at Culloden. While London celebrated victory over the Jacobites, and the German composer Handel wrote *See the Conquering Hero Come*, the king's army moved into the glens to continue their bloody onslaught in an orgy of fire and violence, burning villages and hanging the 'rebels'. Cumberland's army had but a single mission: to quell the Highlanders once and for all.

Among the many arrested and tried for treason was one of the commanders of the Independent Companies, Simon, 11th Lord Lovat, chief of the Fraser clan, whose vast lands stretched along the Great Glen, from Inverness to the line of hills running along the River Beauly. Lovat and the Fraser clan had turned out two battalions, around 500 men in total, who were in the front line of the Jacobite army and were almost wiped out by the government second line. Although he did not take part in the battle, Lord Lovat was hunted down, taken to London and imprisoned in the Tower to await trial for treason. He was subsequently convicted and on 9 April 1747 was beheaded on Tower Hill, the last person to be so in Britain. Throughout the Highlands, revenge was to be taken without mercy on the clans who supported the Stuart bid, an offensive that for years turned into an unprecedented assault on the clan system as a whole, regardless of loyalty to Charles. New laws were eventually passed in London aimed at annihilating the principal features of Highland life, and the military – from which the Black Watch were this time excluded – patrolled the countryside over General Wade's roads to enforce them. Many of the Jacobite chiefs who survived were sent into exile and their estates forfeited to the Crown, to be administered by government agents.

All existing laws, and especially those that gave community powers to clan chiefs, were abolished. All chiefs who remained had to swear allegiance to the Hanoverian dynasty, and the total disarming of the Highlanders was resumed with exacting diligence that now went even further, aimed at the destruction of vital aspects of clan life that had developed over centuries. Even the wearing of tartan was banned, as was the speaking of Gaelic, the language of the many who spoke little or no English. They had to swear that they would not possess any gun, sword, pistol or arm whatever, never use tartan, plaid or any part of the Highland garb and acknowledge that if they did so, and were caught, they would be transported. Highlanders were scattered to far corners of the earth in what became the forerunner of the infamous Highland Clearances of future years, when landowners and government conjoined to begin the wholesale removal of tens of thousands of people to make way for sheep. Those who supported the Young Pretender could never have imagined the consequences of what transpired in the wake of Culloden and Bonnie Prince Charlie, who fled in ignominy, only to become a hero in the romantic telling of the story years later, with the added dash of alleged romance with Flora Macdonald, who helped him escape and was locked up in the Tower of London for her trouble. Charles settled in Rome as the Duke of Albany and married a princess, but they separated after less than ten years of marriage while he took to drink and died in 1788.

This diversion from the main thrust of events involving the Black Watch was, nonetheless, a vitally important era affecting every conceivable aspect of life, whether a soldier or a clansman. The Highlands remained the heartland and the main recruiting area of the Black Watch. Although the regiment had proved its loyalty under arms to King George II, this did not appear to be sufficient for a military administration unequivocally under the royal thumb. The army ruled that for the time being the Black Watch could not be trusted for service back in the Highlands, a fact that was to be hugely disproved by Highland soldiers in the decades, and then centuries, ahead.

One of the areas not affected was recruitment. New Highland regiments emerged as the British army began to take advantage of this source of fighting men. These regiments offered a haven for those wishing to continue traditions such as bearing arms and wearing a kilt, quite apart from offering an escape route from the traumas after the '45 rebellion. Also, the army meant that many other aspects of their own traditions could be maintained, including a healthy tolerance for religious belief, an aspect that was important to many at that time, as indeed was the counsel that the men could receive from a regimental chaplain.

It is worth recording that in the Black Watch at that time, no one was better able to take care of the needs of a diverse group of men, and eventually the women and children who joined them (see Chapter Five), than their chaplain of that era, the Reverend Dr Adam Ferguson, who had been at school in Dunkeld with a number of the men in the first Black Watch Regiment. Few realised at the time that they were receiving advice from a great thinker who was to become one of Scotland's foremost historians and philosophers, remembered as one of the founding fathers of modern sociology. Educated at the University of St Andrews, Ferguson was appointed to the Black Watch in 1745 and was with them around the time of their transfer to Flanders, and thus had the experience of a man who, fourteen years later, became Professor of Natural Philosophy at the University of Edinburgh and who wrote many famous works, including *The Morality of Stage Plays Seriously Considered* (1757), *Essay on the History of Civil Society* (1767), *Institutes of Moral Philosophy* (1769) and *Remarks* (1776), in which he proposed peace terms for the North Americans fighting in the American Revolution.

As a Black Watch chaplain, Ferguson was a great comfort to the Highlanders and, according to one historian of the day, 'held an equal if not in some respects a greater influence over the minds of the men than their commanding officer'. More than that – and unusually for chaplains of any regiment – he was to be found in the thick of action when the soldiers went into battle, advancing at the head of the column with a drawn sword in his hand. When first spotted in this mode by commanding officer Munro, Ferguson was ordered to the rear; when he ignored the command, he was threatened with having his clergyman's commission cancelled. He retorted angrily, 'Damn my commission!' and went back into the bloody fray.

Thereafter, and throughout his stay with the Black Watch, he continued his unique style of chaplaincy with great compassion, counselling, praying with the dying and helping with the wounded. Cannon noted: 'By his fearless zeal, his intrepidity, his friendship towards the soldiers and his amiable and cheerful manner, reproving them with severity when it was necessary, mixing among them with ease and familiarity, and being as ready as any of them with a poem or heroic tale – he acquired an unbounded ascendancy over them.'

In the months ahead, when the Black Watch faced uncertainty about their own future direction, there would certainly be a great need for the listening post that a chaplain of his stature and understanding could provide. Difficult times were indeed signposted as the Watch now began what in reality formed a series of footsteps through the entire military history of the British army, from 1745 to the present day.

Soon after being stood down from their defensive position in the South of England, their worst fears were realised. Indeed, the truth was out that King George's generals now planned to send them overseas, this time far away to North America, specifically to Cape Breton to strengthen the British defences against the French. But not far into the journey their convoy of ships was hit by gales and high seas and had to turn back. The regiment ended up weeks later in Ireland. They were then shipped to Flanders to give further support to the Austrians in the continuing skirmishes in King George's War. They were seldom called on until 1749, when they covered a British withdrawal before they themselves were pulled out and sent back to Ireland, there to remain as a garrison regiment for the next nine years, in much the same role that they performed in the Highlands.

Ireland, like their homeland, had been a battleground in the religious struggles between William of Orange and James II, leaving Protestants in the ascendancy and rigorous restrictions on Catholics, barring them from holding office of any kind or even owning land in their own country. The Black Watch came in at an especially crucial time, when, quite apart from religious considerations, trading restrictions were imposed by the Hanoverians forbidding virtually anything that might compete with English commerce. As in the Highlands, thousands were leaving the country, and in the meantime the Irish situation had been aggravated by a succession of troubling, unyielding calamities. At the time, and throughout their initial posting through to 1756, the Black Watch established a rapport with a community which normally resented the presence of British troops in no uncertain manner. This pattern of getting on well with the locals would be repeated again, and eventually, in the second half of the twentieth century, the Black Watch received regular postings to Northern Ireland and elsewhere specifically for their peacekeeping and stabilisation skills. It was clearly a particular calling that would be handed down through generations, and, as will be seen, would become particularly evident in Iraq in 2003–4.

During their time in Ireland, the Black Watch witnessed the growing pace of emigration to the colonies, later hastened by the potato famine, and joined by disillusioned Scots, Welsh and indeed a large number of English. The Atlantic shuttle to North America was undoubtedly the busiest of routes, with British sea power by then in full flow. The French were equally ambitious about increasing their colonising strengths in that region, and the antagonism between the two nations in Europe was merely replicated in the jostling for position in the New World. Major territory deep in Canada and North America fell under French control during their massive fort-building enterprises, and in several areas the British had been losing ground and some of their own fortified settlements. In the summer of 1756 a new British initiative was launched. It included a fresh assault on Louisburg, the main fortified seaport of Cape Breton, which was now once again in French hands. As a result, a large force, including the Black Watch, assembled to continue what had already become the American phase of a worldwide nine-year war (1754–63) fought between France and Britain. They embarked at Greenock in June 1756 and sailed to New York to join a 5,000-strong force under the command of the Earl of Loudon, who was supposedly to lead his men into immediate confrontation with the French army, led by the famous Marquis de Montcalm.

Unfortunately, Loudon turned out to be a poor choice to launch this renewed British campaign. He dithered for so long that many began to believe he had no intention of launching his troops into battle; some suspected his mental state, and even the French were getting bored with his inactivity. As key British forts fell to the French, the Watch were kicking their heels in Albany and remained inactive for almost a year. In January 1757 Loudon was finally persuaded to draw up a plan of attack when the weather became more favourable, urged on by the governors of Nova Scotia and New England. Even then, he confined his immediate objective to one of the lesser tasks on the road map to securing British interests, the capture of Louisburg, disregarding those who were pressing him to attack French frontier positions. Nor did he hurry. It was July before he massed his entire manpower, 30,000 soldiers, 16 ships of the line and dozens of frigates and transports. The troops were landed and were put to work immediately constructing a parade ground on a tract of rugged land, and for the next month undergoing training and staging mock fights.

Major-General Lord Charles Hay was one of the many officers who couldn't fathom Loudon's thinking and was angrily heard to reveal his displeasure to other officers, shouting: 'See how the power of England is held in chains by imbecility! Her substance is wasted by indecision! With such ships and such men as we have here, Cape Breton and its fortress, and all this eastern region, might have been a part of the British empire a month ago.' A report of his outburst was given to Loudon, who ordered his arrest for sedition and sent him post-haste to a court martial in England, where he was acquitted. Hay was right. Throughout this time, the French had been reinforcing the fortress, and when the earl learned that the enemy had one more ship than his own navy he abandoned the expedition and sailed for New York, leaving the army thoroughly nonplussed.

Fortunately, the incompetent earl's antics eventually caused the high command in London to sack him, only to replace him by another less-than-energetic commander, the ageing and corpulent General Sir Robert Abercromby to whom a level of unwarranted responsibility was being handed somewhat late in life – too late, in fact. He planned an attack on the key French fort of Ticonderoga, which lay at the southern end of Lake Champlain, part of the long inland waterway that was the main route for a British land invasion of French Canada. In June 1758 a force of British regular and American provincial troops – 15,000 men, including the Black Watch – were assembled at the head of Lake George.

The northern tip of Lake George is joined to the southern end of Lake Champlain by a five-mile strip of river marked by a mixture of rapids and swamps. The French fort stood at the point where the river enters Lake Champlain. Montcalm's regular French battalions were positioned at various points along the river, but he planned a final hurdle to the British advance should it get that far. Montcalm ordered the building of a near-impenetrable mass of felled trees, branches and thorn in front of the fort. After an initial hesitation, Abercromby decided to launch his attack, having first sent his engineer to reconnoitre the French position. He came back to report that the felled trees could be stormed by infantry assault.

Behind the fortified line stood no fewer than seven French regiments, and soon after 9 a.m. on 8 July the British and Americans began their attempt to cross the tree obstructions, with the Black Watch and the 55th Regiment of Foot held in reserve. The attack went in time and again, and throughout the day the French held them back until finally the reserve troops were launched, first utilising the 55th, which made good progress until they were badly hit by French fire at the felled forestation. The Highlanders, fired by their impatience and indignation, now charged into the felled trees using their swords to lop off the sharpened branches, and some came close enough to the rampart to hack footholds and climb it. Three times Abercromby ordered them to withdraw, and when they did so more than half their privates and two-thirds of the officers were either dead or desperately wounded. An English officer of the 55th Regiment who witnessed the attack by the Highlanders wrote:

> With a mixture of esteem, grief and envy, I consider the great loss and immortal glory acquired by the Scots Highlanders in the late bloody affair. Impatient for orders, they rushed forward to the entrenchments, which many of them actually mounted. They appeared like lions breaking their chains. Their intrepidity was rather animated than damped by seeing their comrades fall

on every side. I have only to say that they seemed more anxious to revenge the cause of their deceased friends, than careful to avoid the same fate. By their assistance we expect soon to give a good account of the enemy and ourselves. There is much harmony and friendship between us.

Lieutenant William Grant of the Black Watch left us this account of the battle:

The attack began a little past one in the afternoon, and about two the fire became general on both sides, which was exceedingly heavy and without any intermission, insomuch that the oldest soldier present never saw so furious and incessant a fire. The affair at Fontenoy was nothing to it; I saw both. We laboured under insurmountable difficulties . . . but the difficult access to their lines was what gave them a fatal advantage over us. They took care to cut down monstrous large oak trees, which covered all the ground from the foot of their breastwork about the distance of a cannon shot every way in their front. This not only broke our ranks and made it impossible for us to keep order but put it entirely out of our power to advance till we cut our way through. I have seen men behave with courage and resolution before now, but such determined bravery can hardly have been equalled in any part of the history of ancient Rome. Even those who were mortally wounded cried aloud to their companions not to mind, or lose a thought upon them, but to follow their officers, and to mind the honour of their country. Nay, their ardour was such that it was difficult to bring them off. They paid dearly for their intrepidity. The remains of the regiment had the honour to cover the retreat of the army and brought off the wounded, as we did at Fontenoy. When shall we have so fine a regiment again? I hope we shall be allowed to recruit.

Another brief account survives in the National Archives of Scotland in the form of a letter written from Lake George on 11 July 1758 by

Captain Allan Campbell. He is writing to his brother, John Campbell of Barcaldine. Much of the letter is a regretful listing of the names of officers who were killed or injured in the battle. However, Captain Campbell is pleased to inform his brother that both he and his nephew George are unhurt. His spellings and punctuation have been retained:

Dear Brother: The 8th of this mounth we had a hot Brush at the lines of Ticonderoga where we lost a Considerable number of men and officers . . . Our Regt Acquired great Glory by the good behaveour of Both men, and Officers, tho we were unsuccessfull. I have the pleasure to aquent you that Both my Nephew George and I Eskeap'd without a Scratch tho Both in the heat of the action. George is a pritty lad hes now a Lt in Coll. Gages Regt of Light Infantry, Your Son the Major was well about two mounths ago at Philadelphia we are now at the end of Lake George Encampt I have told you now all the news that can occurr to me or that I have time to write you a[s] I thought it my Duty to aquent you and my other Brothers of my being well after a Smart action. I have no time to write you more being Excesively hurried having no Body to asist me in the affairs of my Company having my three Lts Kill'd or wounded viz Lt Balie kill'd, and Lts Arch'd Campbell, and William Grant wounded, I'll Write you very fully in my nixt. My best wishes to my Sister to your family, and all our friends and I am D[ea]r.

Brother Your most affec: And Lov: Brothr while Allan Campbell

In all, the Black Watch lost 8 officers, 9 sergeants and 297 men killed, and 17 officers, 10 sergeants, and 306 soldiers wounded, which was a desperately high toll, although it was not regarded as a disaster but more as one more act of heroism by the Highlanders that came so close to altering the course of the battle. William Pitt, the Secretary of State, overseeing the progress of the Seven Years War, announced to Parliament that henceforth the Black Watch would be known as the Royal Highland Regiment, as a testimony of 'His Majesty's satisfaction and approbation of its extraordinary courage, loyalty and exemplary conduct'. Furthermore, the regiment were ordered to raise a second battalion, exclusively recruited in the Highlands, which, he assured Parliament, would 'conquer for you in every part of the world'.

Even so, there was no getting away from the fact that the French had caused immense damage to Abercromby's attacking force, and in panic he ordered a retreat to the southern end of Lake George. He was quickly replaced by General the Earl of Amherst, who was left to plan the return match, and it would be another year before the British could wrest Canada from French control. Any account of the Battle of Ticonderoga would be incomplete without mentioning the story of the mysterious circumstances surrounding the death of the Black Watch's Major Duncan Campbell of Inverawe.

Events date from 1740, when the major, then on his home turf, had agreed to conceal a fugitive running from Highlanders he was sure would kill him. When Campbell later discovered that the fugitive had murdered a cousin, he stood by his word not to hand him over to his pursuers, but did ask him to leave his property in breach of a promise he had made. That same night, the fugitive appeared in a dream to Campbell of Inverawe and said: 'I will see you at Ticonderoga.' He had never heard the name and nor had he when he arrived in North America, having served in the Black Watch for twenty years. One night in the officers' mess in Albany, Campbell told the story to his colleagues around the table after dinner. When he had finished, he made them promise to let him know at once if they heard the name. At that point, Ticonderoga had not been mentioned, but soon his colleagues learned that it was the Indian name of the fort they were to attack in July 1758. Lieutenant-Colonel Francis Grant, the commanding officer, persuaded the other officers to keep the news from Campbell, and they referred to it by its French name. On the morning of the attack, however, Campbell reported that the apparition had come to him again: 'I have seen him. He came to my tent last night. This is Ticonderoga. I shall die today.' And so he did. He was severely wounded in the battle, resulting in the amputation of his arm, but died at Fort Edward.

41

Ticonderoga thus went into the Black Watch history for that story and into a poem by Robert Louis Stevenson. Twenty years later, it was a key location in the battles relating to the American Revolution, and the Black Watch would be there in the thick of it again.

CHAPTER THREE

Indian Fighters

Now . . . the West Indies appeared on the horizon. Here the lives of so many thousands of British soldiers had been, and would continue to be, claimed by fever over and above any fighting, and all worst fears would be realised. The 2nd Battalion, the 42nd Royal Highland Regiment, formally came into being at Perth in October 1758, and in a matter of months the new recruits were heading to take possession of the French islands of Martinique and Guadeloupe. Why such tiny islands of sugar cane, silver sand and disease were considered so vital to the British ambitions in the region, when major resources were still required in Canada, could hardly be fathomed. Indeed, it turned out to be an ill-researched and wasteful expedition that achieved little apart from leaving too many of the contingent of almost 6,000 under Major-General Hopson lying in fever graves.

The force to which the new Highland soldiers had been assigned landed without serious opposition at Port Royal, Martinique, an island at the tail end of the Caribbean archipelago. Too good to be true? It certainly was, because the generals then realised that they had too few heavy guns to withstand any serious assault by the French, if such arose. So the commander of the large fleet that had carried the army across the Atlantic to this remarkably unappealing place, discounting the wondrous beaches, refused to leave his ships in the firing line without suitable defensive equipment and demanded that they sail away forthwith.

So as not to make this highly uncomfortable journey a complete waste of time and effort, a conference among the major ranks decided to contain their effort to an attack on Guadeloupe back up the chain of islands. There, initially, they met no stronger opposition than a local defender named Madame Ducharney and her small native army of African extract who put up some spirited resistance before they were overpowered by the Highlanders and Royal Marines, who then moved on to attack the French at Fort Louis in January. This task proved to be no walkover, with the French holding out for more than four months before being forced to surrender through shortage of supplies and their declining complement of troops, many dropping from sickness. The British had the same problem, and in that short space of time 1,856 of their troops were either dead or laid low with sickness and heat exhaustion, quite apart from those who were casualties in the fighting. Among the fatalities was the expedition commander, Major-General Hopson. His successor, General Barrington, finally overcame French resistance in May, and Guadeloupe was secure – for the time being.

The new battalion of the Black Watch were then put back into the ships to proceed immediately to North America, where they were required to join a force being assembled to make yet another attempt to break the deadlock at the seemingly impenetrable Ticonderoga and onward for a fresh battle with the French, with Canada as the prize. They linked up with the soldiers of the 1st Battalion who had taken a rest for a long, cold winter on Long Island to recuperate and were now to participate in the van of a three-pronged assault on the French, urged on by William Pitt in London.

He was pressing for the matter of securing Canada under the British flag to be achieved with the utmost urgency. So, while General Prideaux set out a strong defence at Niagara to prevent counter-attacks from the west, General Amherst arranged his 15,000 North American and British troops to begin the fresh assault on Ticonderoga while the brilliant thirty-two-year-old General James Wolfe was already on the road to taking Quebec, a journey that began in 1759, when he took command of the largest British naval force ever to cross the Atlantic. Assisting Wolfe were Brigadiers General Robert Monkton, James Murray and George Townsend. The flotilla from England demonstrated to the French that this time they meant business. It comprised forty-nine men-of-war – a formidable number, almost a quarter of the Royal Navy's available stock – along with two hundred transports and provision ships. After calling at Halifax and Louisburg to pick up several hundred American troops, the fleet sailed for St Lawrence on 16 June. They fooled their enemy's lookout station by flying French colours and having a Highland officer call out to them in French. Lookouts were lured to the ships and were captured by the British, who threatened to hang the men unless they showed them the safest routes through the treacherous approaches so that they could establish position on the west bank of the St Lawrence within attacking distance of Quebec.

Wolfe's great problem lay in getting his men across the river in sufficient strength to attack his enemy, safely hidden behind the natural fortress of steep cliffs stretching along the approaches to both sides of the city. General Montcalm, the French commander-in-chief of the Canadian force, believed his position to be impregnable to such an attack and had based his entire strategy on stalling the British until the winter, when the enemy ships would have to pull out or be frozen solid. Wolfe, on the other hand, had to attempt to force the Canadians and their North American Indian allies to come out and fight, and one of the tactics he used was to burn settlements to the south of Quebec, hoping to tempt Montcalm into attacking him.

The Frenchman refused to budge, so Wolfe now tried another ploy: on 30 July almost 800 grenadiers were rowed towards the shore for a direct assault but were forced to take to the water after their boats hit submerged rocks and wade the final 300 yards. Consequently, the invasion force was cut to pieces by musket and cannon fire from the French-Canadian lines. However, a second wave of grenadiers did manage to land and form ranks. Drummers tapped out the charge, and the grenadiers dashed forward, screaming, and began their attempt to scale the cliffs, only to be cut down by the dozen. When they pulled back, Indians scaled down the cliff face and added further humiliation by scalping the dead and wounded; 443 men were lost.

Montcalm was now apparently confident that the British, after such a rebuff, would pull back. Wolfe, knowing well that he had but a few weeks before the winter set in, rose from his sickbed, suffering severe fever, to plan a new assault. He ordered a survey of the cliff face beneath the Plains of Abraham at the rear of the city walls. By chance, his men discovered an opening heavily covered with undergrowth two miles west of Quebec, which contained a ready-made path to the plains at the top, although it had been hacked almost to destruction by Montcalm's men. This was Wolfe's last hope. On 13 September 1759 the general himself rode in the lead of the flat-bottomed boats carrying his attacking force, utilising a specially selected troop of twenty-four men whose task was to kill or capture the sentries at the top of the path winding up the cliff face. Behind Wolfe's boat came others carrying Highlanders[1] who were to secure the beachhead. Behind them came the remaining transports with a second wave, artillery and supplies, while British frigates stood on station from Quebec to Beauport, firing with every gun as a diversion.

---

[1] In this case the famous Fraser's Highlanders, raised by Lieutenant-General Simon Fraser, Master of Lovat, grandson of the eleventh Lord Lovat who was executed for his part in the Jacobite rebellion of 1745–6, past sins now forgiven. He was commissioned Lieutenant-Colonel Commandant and authorised on 5 January 1757 to raise a regiment of foot, designated the 78th Regiment of Foot; 2nd Highland Battalion, with a strength of forty-four officers, forty sergeants and corporals, twenty drummers, and ten companies of a hundred men each. The 78th assembled at Inverness, and when the regiment embarked at Glasgow in April 1757 it was accompanied by so many volunteers that three additional companies were authorised. When another company was added in 1758, the unit had the formidable strength of 1,542 in all ranks. It was disbanded in 1763.

The battle for Canada was finally under way, and by daylight almost 4,500 British and North American troops had reached the clifftop to form up on the open fields of the Plains of Abraham. Elements from five regiments took position in the lines across the plains, with Wolfe himself leading from the front, on the right of the line. Montcalm was alerted too late. The sound of swirling bagpipes let it be known that the British were coming, and across the plains the French commander saw before him the incredible sight of the infantrymen who had been secreted into position before dawn without a shot being fired. There they stood, waiting for a fight. It was after 9 a.m. before Montcalm assembled his defensive lines, first with a combined force of French, Canadian and Indian sharpshooters emerging from the wooded areas ahead of the plains to begin the opening volleys. Wolfe, walking his own lines, was immediately hit, a musket ball wounding his left wrist while he was comforting a captain who had been shot in the chest. The general's wound was bandaged while he walked on, directing his troops towards the opposing force, now forming under the walls of Quebec. On the opposing side, Montcalm appeared on horseback ahead of his 5,000 troops, urging them to fight for all they were worth. He then raised his sword to signal the advance, moving ahead in a formation three rows deep, giving orders not to begin firing until they were within a hundred yards.

The French had three field guns, the British one. The musket strength was more or less equal, and the weapon was similar, using a round of ammunition which comprised a charge of gunpowder and a lead ball wrapped in cartridge paper. To load, the soldier took a cartridge and ripped it open, often with his teeth, and poured some of the powder into the firing mechanism and the rest into the barrel, folded the paper and pushed it into the barrel and dropped the ball on top, forcing it down with a ramrod, carried under the barrel of the musket. Pulling the trigger caused the flint held by the hammer to strike against the pan lid, flicking it open as it did so. The spark from the flint ignited the powder in the pan, firing the charge in the barrel, releasing a streak of flame and smoke with the discharged ball to a maximum range of just fifty yards. In wet weather – as it was on that day – these muskets were unpredictable. Even so, an experienced soldier might load and fire three or four times in a minute, although loading and firing became slower because of the cleaning process required after about fifteen rounds.

Montcalm's soldiers moved ahead in a formation three rows deep and held their fire until they were within a hundred yards of the British lines. Wolfe's troops stood their ground, refusing to fire yet, their only movement coming when soldiers ran to fill up the line when a comrade was felled. At seventy-five yards, the first rank of Wolfe's lines dropped to one knee, and both ranks held their fire until the Canadians were forty yards out. Wolfe then gave the order to fire.

The scene was now a classic and intense killing contest, amid the screams, blood and gore of battle as it reached close-quarters range, the last volley being fired by both lines at just a dozen yards before the bayonet charge. The French commander was hit twice but remained mounted on his horse. He rode back for treatment but died the following morning. His opponent, General Wolfe, also in the thick of the battle, was similarly wounded. Two grenadiers carried him from the field, where he, too, died from his wounds (his body was returned to England for a hero's funeral). Wolfe's tactics had broken the opposing lines into complete disarray, and they finally turned in front of the bayonets and a charge by the Highlanders, their swords swirling. Sporadic rallies were staged, but the British pressed on, sparing few but the French officers. A final stand at buildings housing the military bakery in the centre of the valley halted the British advance long enough for many of the limping and wounded battle-field refugees to withdraw at high cost to those involved in this final episode before Wolfe's army, minus their leader, claimed victory. The governor of Quebec ordered evacuation and surrender.

Quebec had fallen, but the British had a long, harsh winter ahead before Canada was indisputably in their hands. The Black Watch were deeply involved in this final act when General Amherst's massive force began the process of locking up Ticonderoga with a siege that even the most optimistic of Frenchmen could see was a deadlock situation. The French gave up even before the 42nd began the attack proper, setting fire to their own fortress to cover their withdrawal to Lake Champlain, where a small fleet was waiting to effect their escape. Amherst pursued the retreating army but eventually returned to take up residence at Ticonderoga as winter set in.

As soon as conditions permitted, in May 1760, Amherst set out to complete his mission. The role of the Black Watch began with a march from the Hudson to Fort Oswego on Lake Ontario, where Amherst was assembling his army. The 1st Battalion of the 42nd and the 1st Guards were shipped to the head of the St Lawrence to act as advance guard, ahead of Amherst's main troop movement. Fort Levi was quickly taken, and the Highlanders moved on at a fast pace to reach Montreal in the first week of September, ahead of a pincer movement by two groups dispatched by Amherst. By then the fighting was all but over, and the British flag waved over almost the whole of eastern North America.

There still remained some unfinished business against the French in the West Indies where, it will be recalled, the new 2nd Battalion of the 42nd was dispatched with other regiments to take control of Martinique and Guadeloupe, then under French rule. The latter had been successfully achieved, but the British force was withdrawn from Martinique because there were insufficient guns to cover the British fleet in the event of an attack. With Canada secure, General Amherst was directed in 1761 to send a considerable force back to the West Indies, with a particular request that it should include the Black Watch, because the regiment's 'abstemious habits, great activity, and capability for bearing the vicissitudes of heat and cold render them well qualified for that climate'.

The island of Martinique had become especially important under the new situation in North America, and more so because it was the only one still under French control in the Windward Islands. The French had, since the previous British attempt, built up a substantial and well-equipped force, and intelligence suggested they would not be easily shifted. Consequently, in January 1762 Amherst put the Black Watch and seventeen other regiments into transports, accompanied by eight ships of the line under the command of Admiral Rodney to put some weight into the planned attack. It proved adequate this time to break down a strongly held French position which required bombardment and heavy fighting to achieve. The Black Watch force suffered fifteen killed and eighty-six wounded. Among the latter an incredible story of recovery emerged. Captain Murray was knocked down by a musket ball which entered the left side of his body under the lower rib, passed through the left lobe of his lung, across his chest and lodged in his right shoulder blade. He was assumed to be as good as dead by the surgeon who examined him and merely given what medication would make him comfortable until his life ebbed away, as was normal in such cases. But Captain Murray amazed everyone by not dying. He clung to life, his condition improved and within three weeks he was up and about. He was subsequently repatriated to Scotland, where his health further improved, although he remained for the next thirty-two years in some discomfort, unable to lie down and always sleeping in an upright position. This did not prevent him from leading a full and worthwhile life, eventually becoming a lieutenant-general, Colonel of the 72nd Regiment and ultimately MP for Perth, prior to his death in 1794.

Martinique passed safely into British hands without great cost in terms of casualties, although the West Indies situation was never a stable one, and to be administered and defended by an absentee land-lord so distant from the island was difficult, whichever side was in control. In the event, Martinique, a prized French possession (still with strong links in the twenty-first century), was destined for further changes of ownership in the years ahead. For the time being, however, the French were out, and the force that succeeded in achieving that ambition then became fortuitously available for a new mission right on its doorstep – to attack Spanish interests in the Caribbean. Spain had supported France in the Seven Years War and continued to do so as the British sought to carve France out of the majority of her North American interests ahead of negotiations that would lead to the 1763 Treaty of Paris, under which the three nations would cede some of their existing colonies to bring an era of supposed peace between them. Spain had control of Cuba, as well as parts of Florida and other linked interests to which the Caribbean was a tributary.

Havana was the service centre and collection point, as it were, for all Spanish interests in the region, as well as operating as the commercial hub of Spanish America, especially the mineral-rich regions of Peru and Mexico, where gold and silver had been, and still were being, plundered in substantial quantities. It was a hugely attractive city, of which visitors to Havana even today may still see glimpses, and was surrounded by a military presence that the Spanish believed to be impregnable. To continue the theme of Caribbean influence, the British mounted an attack through an expedition led by the Earl of Albemarle, who had under command a substantial fleet: 19 ships of the line, 13 frigates, 110 transports and an army of 11,000, which included the Black Watch and many of the regiments whose task in the taking of Martinique had just been successfully completed.

Once again, the toll of the heat and disease on the soldiers was a heavy one during the four months of military actions, when 694 men died from illness or heat exhaustion, whereas 342 were killed in action. In the case of the Black Watch, the casualty percentages were equally alarming: only eight killed in action, while eighty-two officers and men died of sickness. For those who survived, there was the reward of a share in the rich prize money, said to be worth more than £3 million. Less than a year later, however, Havana was restored to Spain as part of the Treaty of Paris in which the Americas were carved up, to provide Britain with the bulk of her Empire.

These adventures, continuous and demanding, meant that the 42nd Royal Highland Regiment, Black Watch, ranked among the most often used units in the British army around this exceedingly busy period in the Americas, and the toll had been heavy. After ten harsh months in the Caribbean, even though they had fared better than most regiments in terms of casualties through soldiering or illness, there were only sufficient surviving soldiers in the whole regiment to sustain a single battalion. They arrived back in New York in October 1762, and after the heat of Havana took the brunt of a particularly harsh winter, quartered at Albany before setting out to participate in yet another experience that was an essential part of British history in North America – battles with American Indians.

These were briefly experienced earlier in Canada, during scraps with the combined forces of the French and Indians, but there was a distinct difference in dealing with this particular enemy attacking the British forts. The soldiers had to undertake some serious training – and learn lessons from old hands at the fort – on how to fight the native Indians. In fact, they found that there were some similarities to their own tribal system and methodology in approaching and attacking an enemy.

At the time, several tribes had combined their available men to attack the British forts between Lake Erie and Pittsburgh. Fort Pitt had been hard hit. The fort stood on the fork of the Ohio River, and the region had earlier been the focal point of numerous battles between the French and the English, and both separately with the Indian population, who were striving to save their homelands. By controlling the Ohio River, the English would be able to expand their colonial power beyond the Appalachian Mountains, and the French needed the river for access to New France. Both powers had already sacrificed thousands of lives and enormous amounts of money disputing this area of land, with the native Americans in the middle, until finally an army of over 6,000 British and American colonial soldiers led by General John Forbes reclaimed the region once and for all for the British Empire on 25 November 1758.

Once General Forbes had wrested the area from the French, he renamed it Pittsborough in honour of William Pitt. Fort Pitt thereafter became one of the largest English strongholds in North America and also became the focus of increasingly successful attacks by the Indian population, to the point when the fort was under permanent siege. Only a handful of other British outposts on the frontier had successfully withstood these attacks during the conflict known as Pontiac's War.

Now, the Black Watch became a leading component of Colonel Henry Bouquet's famous Indian fighters, along with detachments from the 77th Regiment (also known as Montgomerie's Highlanders) and the 60th, which were sent to relieve the fort with a force of 978 soldiers in all, plus a train of supply wagons. Their additional task once there was to 'pacify' the native Indian warriors in what was a long-standing trouble spot for the British. Typical among these attacks was one that became known as the Battle of Bushy Run, which could have set the scene for a later Hollywood Western. The troops guarding the supply train were ambushed by the Indians as the soldiers made their way over a deep-sided, rock-strewn pass, a known ambush scene. The Indians were well hidden behind boulders and bushes that presented an almost suicidal situation for the soldiers, with the Indians attacking and then retreating before the soldiers could engage them in battle. Finally, two companies were ordered to feign a retreat, thus enticing the Indians to come out to attack the departing soldiers, only to be trapped by two more companies of soldiers hidden behind a hill. In the ensuing fight, the Indians were caught in the middle and took heavy losses, thereby lifting the siege on Fort Pitt.

The 42nd remained at Fort Pitt for more than a year, and throughout that time the Highlanders in their kilts were a lively match for the equally unorthodox and determined Indians. The regiment marched close on a thousand miles in its time at Fort Pitt, with months of skirmishing around the fort with an enemy they came to respect for his skills but remaining wary of his treachery. Their casualties were also high, and it was inevitable that some of the Highlanders fell into the hands of Indians who notoriously inflicted terrible torture on soldiers prior to killing them. One of them who escaped death left this memoir of how he and others were saved by the action of one of the Montgomerie men:

> Allan Macpherson . . . witnessing the miserable fate of several of his fellow prisoners, who had been tortured to death by the Indians, and seeing them preparing to commence the same operations on himself [and others], made signs that he had something to communicate. An interpreter was brought. Macpherson told them that provided his life was spared for a few minutes,

he would communicate the secret of an extraordinary medicine, which, if applied to the skin, would cause it to resist the strongest blow of a tomahawk, or sword, and that, if they would allow him to go to the woods with a guard, to collect the plants proper for his medicine, he would prepare it and allow the experiment to be tried on his own neck by the strongest and most expert warrior among them. This story easily gained upon the superstitious credulity of the Indians, and the request of the Highlander was instantly complied with. Being sent into the woods, he soon returned with such plants as he chose to pick up. Having boiled these herbs, he rubbed his neck with their juice and, laying his head upon a log of wood, desired the strongest man among them to strike at his neck with his tomahawk, when he would find he could not make the smallest impression. An Indian, levelling a blow with all his might, cut with such force that the head flew off to a distance of several yards. The Indians were fixed in amazement at their own credulity, and the address with which their prisoner had escaped the lingering death prepared for him; but, instead of being enraged at the escape of their victim, they were so pleased with his ingenuity that they refrained from inflicting further cruelties on the remaining prisoners.

Most of those captured by Indians did indeed suffer a terrifically painful death, and these events, aligned with those in the other casualty-strewn eleven years since the regiment had sailed for North America, meant that it had undergone a massive change in personnel through casualties of war, sickness on land and, of course, losses while at sea through scurvy, disease and storms. New personnel had been recruited, the bulk from the new battalion raised in Scotland, and through further recruitment and transfers from other Highland units already in North America. However, the plain fact of the matter was that the Black Watch needed a rest; the men were tired out, their uniforms were shabby, and many were ready to go home, especially those who still had families or who had left their women back in

Scotland. It was time to head back to home waters – although not to Scotland. They were to be posted back to law-and-order duties in Ireland, and when they heard this a large number opted to stay in America and were transferred to other regiments.

Their work in the Americas and the West Indies had been magnificent, and that it was appreciated by the Americans themselves was evident from a newspaper report in the *Virginia Gazette* of 30 July 1767:

> Last Sunday evening the Royal Highland Regiment embarked for Ireland. Since its arrival in America it has been distinguished for having undergone amazing fatigues, made long and frequent marches through an inhospitable country, bearing excessive heat and severe cold with alacrity and cheerfulness. It has ensured to us peace and security; and along with our blessings for those benefits it has our thanks for that decorum in behaviour which it maintained here, giving an example that the most amiable conduct in civil life is in no way inconsistent with the character of the good soldier.

They arrived back in the autumn of 1767, first to Cork and then on to Dublin, where the regiment remained for the next three and a half years, time spent on recuperation and the enlistment and training of badly needed recruits. The Highlands of Scotland were scoured for new men, and great efforts were clearly made to continue and uphold the traditions on which the original Black Watch regiment were based: hardy young men with strong family connections, generally well educated and preferably with Gaelic as their first language, although not necessarily so. It is apparent from many accounts that despite their losses during the quarter of a century since the Black Watch had left Scotland on that fateful march to London, the original concept of their regiment – albeit one born to keep the peace in the braes – had barely altered. Eric Linklater provided one of the most apt descriptions at this point in the regiment's history:

Manners were those of a well-conducted village, there was no crime in their companies, and their stature, at a standard height of five feet seven inches – in the grenadier company they were taller – was well above the average of the entire army . . . [there was] a stubborn retention of the character that had marked the independent companies from which the soldiers were, in a sense, descended. In language, habit and behaviour they were naturally conservative. The men appear to have lived well, and were able to save a little money which they spent on improving the faded uniforms in which a careless Government was content to clothe them.

The clan spirit had evolved into the regimental spirit, and for the time being they clung dearly to ideas formed long ago in the heartlands of a people whose traditions were already being trampled under the so-called march of commercial progress, which translated in Scotland to the accelerating Clearances of the Highlands that began with Hanoverian revenge after Culloden. The characteristics outlined above remained unquestionably the lifeblood of the regiment and sustained the men through their many horrific experiences – and would continue to do. General David Stewart of Garth, one of the most quoted observers of Highlanders through his 1822 study into their character, manners and history, stated that:

> . . . in forming his military character the Highlander was not more favoured by nature than the social system under which he had lived . . . he acquired a hardihood which enabled him to sustain severe privations. As the simplicity of his life gave vigour to his body, so it fortified the mind. Possessing a frame and constitution thus hardened, he was taught to consider courage as the most honourable virtue, cowardice the most disgraceful failing.

Many young men could already foresee the future – one of a disintegrating way of life in the Highlands – and regimental life with like-minded fellows seemed to many a very acceptable alternative. A number of Highland regiments were now competing with the Black Watch for both men and honours, although the 42nd remained a popular choice for new recruits and, as we have seen, the regiment had emerged as a significant contributor to the military prowess of the creators of the British Empire, and would continue to do so.

As a batch of new recruits arrived in Ireland for their indoctrination into the traditions of the regiment, a more arduous task fell to their lot – that of moving to support the civil authorities in Belfast in 1772, to stand between Catholics and Protestants in ongoing troubles, as well as offering direction for the civil authorities, to put it politely, in seeking to bring moderation into the tactics used during an increasing number of property disputes between tenants and their landlords. As already noted from previous encounters in Ireland, the Black Watch were among the most successful of all the British regiments sent to that country, and with Gaelic speakers on both sides succeeded in bringing calming influences to bear regardless of religious beliefs. It was therefore with a genuine feeling of loss among the Irish when the Black Watch's tour of Ireland came to an end in 1776 when they returned to Scotland. They were needed for sterner stuff elsewhere . . . as America embarked on its Revolution, or War of Independence.

CHAPTER FOUR

Defeating George Washington

And so to revolution . . . and with it came a return across the Atlantic for the 42nd Royal Highland Regiment, Black Watch, when the thirteen colonies of the British Empire on the eastern seaboard took control of their own destiny and launched the United States of America, determined to end rule from London. The reasons were economic, or at least the issue of taxation was the one that finally drove the wedge into general discontent and widened it to one of talk of rebellion. By decree in 1764, the king, whose country was in dire financial straits after the Seven Years War, signed a new law that ultimately placed a heavy burden of taxation on the American colonies. Over the coming decade, many who felt it unjust were drawn to the cause of an already vocal movement of American patriotism against the so-called mother country.

The most famous event on the road to conflagration was the Boston Tea Party of 1773, which resulted in George III resorting to a policy of coercion towards Massachusetts, and the promptness of involving the Black Watch into the proceedings that followed will be evident from the summary of events below. The fact was that the British would need all the troops they could lay their hands on, and although the Highlanders were always among the first to be selected in such situations, the army recruiters would also be trawling the prisons, poor houses and 'refuse of the streets' attempting to fill the numbers needed this time for their general infantry.

The Black Watch, up to strength and in good mettle, were prime material under such circumstances, and, like his father before him, George III was apparently keen to see them included at the earliest moment. In fact, their contribution, though welcome, could provide only a fraction of the required manpower, as events in America stumbled through mismanagement to the inevitable course of events that followed, a battle of wills between the Americans and the mother country. First blood was drawn at the Battles of Concord and Lexington. In Massachusetts, the then seat of the crisis, each town began to enlist a third of its militia in minutemen organisations to be ready to act. On 10 May 1775 George Washington somewhat reluctantly accepted the position of commander of the patriotic forces. He was in favour of attempting to achieve a peaceful resolution, which came from the patriots by way of what was known as the 'Olive Branch Petition', expressing a desire for the restoration of harmony between Britain and her colonies issued in the summer of 1775. This was rejected out of hand by the British, and later that month General Gage, Governor of Massachusetts, received limited reinforcements from England, bringing his total force to 6,500 rank and file.

The major military operations of 1775 and early 1776 were not around Boston but in Canada, which the Americans tried to add as a fourteenth colony. Canada seemed a tempting and vulnerable target. To take it would eliminate a British base at the head of the familiar invasion route along the lake and river chain connecting the St Lawrence to the Hudson. In late June 1775 Congress, getting no response to an appeal to the Canadians to join in its cause, instructed Major-General Philip Schuyler of New York to take possession of Canada, a task in which he failed.

However, across the thirteen states support was growing among Americans towards renouncing the British Crown, which indeed occurred in the spring. All royal governors were ousted, and patriots replaced British authority in the colonies by makeshift governments. In July 1776 the most important document in American history was adopted by the new American Congress: the Declaration of Independence. (Incidentally, it has been said that almost half the signatories to it were of Scottish descent.) By then, the Black Watch were in transit, under the command of Lieutenant-Colonel Thomas Stirling. They left Greenock, along with a detachment from Fraser's Highlanders, in mid-April 1776, although the initial omens were not good. The transports in which they were travelling were tossed and buffeted by storms in the Atlantic during the ten-week journey, although all but one of the ships rode out the gales and made it successfully to the other side after a horrendous crossing.

The one that didn't was full of Black Watch soldiers, but her misfortune was not one that caused the ship to be lost – quite the reverse. As the ship's captain temporarily lost sight of the rest of the fleet, a predator in the shape of an American privateer crew boarded her and claimed the ship as their prize. They promised the soldiers they would not be harmed provided they did not attempt violence. This was red-rag-to-a-bull talk, and naturally the Highlanders responded by lulling the privateers into a false sense of security before making their move, recapturing the ship and sailing on to America. They made it safely to Jamestown, Virginia, unaware that the state was among those supporting the rebel cause. They were immediately taken into custody again, but made a tempting offer of freedom and money if they deserted and joined the rebel cause. Not one accepted, and they remained prisoners for two years before they were exchanged for captives from the patriot force and rejoined their own unit.

The build-up of British troops was going ahead. Nine thousand landed on Staten Island on 8 July 1776 – four days after independence was declared. They were under the command of General Sir William Howe, who had taken over from Cage and had been awaiting the arrival of the fleet under the command of his brother, Admiral Lord Richard Howe, bearing British regulars, including the Black Watch, Fraser's Highlanders and 8,000 German mercenaries from the principality of Hesse, who became known as Hessians. They arrived on 3 August, and by the end of August General Howe had 32,000 troops under command, 18,000 short of the number he had asked for but still the largest army ever raised for an overseas operation by the British government.

General Washington was doing his best to train and prepare his vastly inferior army, but he was also hampered by the British control of the sea lanes around New York with a fleet that included ten ships of the line, twenty frigates, and a dozen bomb-ketches positioned close to Washington's greatest concentration of troops, which amounted to fewer that 8,000 men on Long Island. Washington's whole effective force, for manning batteries, securing passes and occupying posts, some of them 15 miles apart, did not then exceed 11,000 men, and most of them were poorly armed militia and a regiment of artillery without skilled gunners and equipped with old iron field-pieces. Washington's pleadings for additional volunteers from the states were answered by the arrival of patriotic yeomanry, a similarly ill-equipped force but which swelled his army to 17,000 men.

On 22 August General Howe began transporting troops across the bay from Staten Island to Long Island, while Washington began digging in around Brooklyn Village. Black Watch companies were among 15,000 troops landed on the west end of Long Island over the coming four days, along with the Germans. Under the command of Sir Henry Clinton and Lord Cornwallis, they began moving toward the Bedford and Jamaica passes, to gain the rear of the Americans. The Americans on the left did not see the danger until the British had gained their flank and launched a persistent attack. From the redoubt on Brooklyn Heights, Washington saw many of his troops killed and captured, the latter to suffer in what local historians describe as 'the loathsome British prisons in the city of New York and the prison-ships nearby'.

On 26 August a company from the Black Watch moved on Jamaica Pass and seized the five American guards there, allowing the British to advance behind American lines undetected until they reached the settlement of Bedford, where they opened fire. The American troops were forced back into Brooklyn Heights, and Washington withdrew across the East River to Manhattan. Howe, in the meantime, moved to outflank him again and on 13 September began to move his army across the East River to Kips Bay, again with Black Watch companies involved for what became known as the Battle of Harlem Heights. In this encounter, the British infantry took a mauling from Colonel Thomas Knowlton's Connecticut Regiment but, as the British began digging in, Washington decided to withdraw north to White Plains, with the British in pursuit. He had lost New York City.

An account of the incident, under the headline 'The Black Watch in New York', provides an amusing description of the arrival of the troops in Manhattan:

The first annual concert ever held within the limits of Central Park, New York, took place on Sunday, 10th September, 1776, about sunset. Perhaps it might be more correctly termed a musical contest, as will appear. It was held on that elevated plateau, near the present northern boundary of the Park, where the line of 106th Street, between 7th and 8th Avenues, would cross it, if produced. During the afternoon a Hessian Regiment had encamped on the plateau. Their tents were pitched around. Evening parade had just been dismissed. And, as was the custom of the commander, the Yager Regimental Band were about to close the day with some choice selections from their repertoire, Meister Carl Spitzig was the bandmaster. He stood beside a rough music-desk. Down his back hung a very long and very stiff Hessian queue. He looked on the music-page before him, and raised aloft his violin bow. He brought it down with a quick sweep, and the band began Mozart's grand serenata, 'Ascanio in Alba'.

The serenata floated in grand measures on the evening air, every phrase rendered with artistic taste, every note true in time and tune. Suddenly, Meister Carl's sharp ear detected a flaw. Something was wrong. He looked suspiciously at a flute. Then he shook his bow at a bassoon. Meister Spitzig was getting excited. Again he poised his bow in the air to begin, and then brought it down with a gesture of despair. He had caught the discord. Yes, there it was, floating on the breeze, echoing up a glen – the skirl and drone of approaching Scotch bagpipes! 'Sackpfeifen!' cried the Colonel. 'Ach, Himmel! Mein Oberst! Ya, die Sackpfeifen!' cried Meister Carl.

The pipes drew nearer, playing a warlike pibroch. Presently the black plumes [bonnets] of a Highland regiment were seen above the bushes, and then the measured tramp of men was heard. The column of Highlanders entered upon the plateau, and marched to a position on the right. Deploying into line, about a hundred paces to the eastward, they stacked arms and promptly broke ranks. Some sat down to supper upon the banks; others, wrapped in their plaids, sought rest on the ground. This was the Forty-second Regiment, or Royal Highlanders, already then, for thirty-six years, renowned in the annals of the British army as the Black Watch. They were uniformed in jackets of a dark and rusty red with dark blue facings, and wore broad black belts. Tartan plaids and kilts, bare legs, checkered hose and bright buckled brogs, Glengarry caps, muskets and bayonet and dirks – all the national costume of Highlandmen they had, except their former basket-hilted broadswords and their pistols. These had been taken from them that morning, on the grounds – so the history of the regiment says – that 'they retarded the men by getting entangled in the brushwood'.

They had landed with the Hessian regiment, had been delayed in the pursuit, and at length had been ordered to take post on their right in advance. They waited for no tents, for they were accustomed to the free air and the open heath. The men were scattered around in moody silence. They were not tired, but, what was worse, they were discontented, and were becoming demoralised. For the first time in its history the regiment had been deprived of its distinguishing national weapons, and, as the men considered, without sufficient reason. It was not the first time the Forty-second had met with injustice, and had resented it. Remembering former difficulties, their results, and their final adjustments, the commissioned officers wisely retired to their own quarters, leaving the men to work off their discontent for the evening.

In November 1776 the last position the Americans held on Manhattan Island around Fort Washington was under attack, with the Black Watch to the fore – and, indeed, noticeably so in all demanding assignments in this series of battles. Early on 15 November the Americans rejected a call by General Howe for the fort to surrender. American positions were then bombarded by British artillery batteries across the Harlem River and by the frigate *Pearl* ahead of a three-pronged assault by British forces. Among skirmishing, a hard fight developed as the 42nd landed on the east side, forcing the remaining American troops in that area to fall back to the fort, where they were given no option but to surrender.

The British side suffered 450 casualties, of which 320 were Hessians and 81 were from the Black Watch. The Americans suffered 2,900 losses, most of whom were prisoners. American defeats had thus followed in succession at Long Island, Harlem Heights and White Plains, although Washington did manage to register one success at the end of a dismal first year of battle, with a Christmas-night crossing of the Delaware to capture Trenton. This was followed shortly after by a victory at the Battle of Princeton, and Howe retreated to New York while both armies went in search of winter quarters prior to the launch of the spring campaign.

In the event, General Howe seemed none too keen to get on with it. He waited until June 1777 before putting his troops back into action with an unproductive feint into New Jersey utilising the German mercenaries and the Black Watch in the lead. Then, when his supply line fell behind, he made an about-turn back to New York, where he proceeded to engage a two-pronged plan for the remainder of the year, with his own army destined to head south to capture Philadelphia, while General Burgoyne's Army of the North would march down from Canada to capture Albany, isolating New England and thereby hoping to force a surrender of Washington's army.

Washington's intelligence in early July reported that Howe's army was moving down the Atlantic coast, and it could hardly have been a secret: the movement entailed another logistical nightmare for the British, loading and sailing a 265-ship armada – the largest ever assembled in America – filled with 17,000 troops, 3,000 horses, weapons and supplies at New Jersey for a 32-day journey to land at the head of Maryland's Elk River. Hundreds of horses and a number of men died on what was a thoroughly distressing and uncomfortable journey, which took far longer than anticipated. Worse, the disgorging of the ships was delayed because of the Elk River's shallow, muddy waters, which meant that the largest ships had to unload further from the planned site. It was well into August before the monolith got under way, while in London the general was facing heavy criticism for having 'wasted' half the fighting season.

Howe also hoped to find a large contingent of loyalists waiting for him, but none came. And so, with this massive, trundling line of troops, cannon and supply train, he had to begin his march on Philadelphia to the north, at that point unaware that Washington had in the meantime moved his army of 11,000 men overland to Wilmington, Delaware, twenty miles south of Philadelphia, and the same distance from where Howe had landed. Then, as the two armies prepared for battle, a terrible storm struck, the deluge of rain severely damaging their ammunition and turning roads into muddy morasses. British Captain John Montresor wrote: '. . . the order for marching was countermanded . . . The roads heavy and the horses mere Carrion, the soldiery not sufficiently refreshed and the greater part of their ammunition damaged . . . The guards [alone] had sixteen thousand cartridges damaged by the storm.'

It was 28 August before the British began their move forward, and the loyalists, who should have been there to meet and guide them, were still nowhere to be seen. Instead, one account noted that 'the countryside was hauntingly unpeopled . . . officers found deserted fields and farms where cattle and horses had obviously pastured recently'. Without the promised guides, Howe sent a party under General Cornwallis to reconnoitre ahead, a group that included a company of the Black Watch. As the snaking line progressed, however,

66

the weather improved and a contemporary diarist recorded: '[It was] beautiful to see . . . as they came in sight on the river slope west of the town, with their scarlet coats, their bright guns and bayonets gleaming in the rays of an early August sun.' After sixteen days of uncomfortable marching, the first battle of the Philadelphia campaign of 1777 began on the morning of 11 September, led by General Howe, who personally took command of Cornwallis's column of redcoats. The Americans and British were now face to face on opposite sides of the creek. But the British kept busy. Howe sent out a party from the 42nd to scout, under the leadership of Captain Johann Ewald. Then the British launched a furious attack. While the Continental Army fought valiantly, they were overwhelmed by the sheer weight of the British opposition and fell back to new defensive lines. The fighting here was the fiercest of the entire battle. The American line gave way five times, ever re-forming, but was pushed further back.

But gradually the tide turned as the British fell victim to the vagaries of their massive supply line, especially after France entered the war in 1778. Spain declared war on England in the next year and Holland followed suit. The latter two countries did not support the American states and even France put more troops into the West Indies. Now, overstretched and having to guard against the invasion of the home shores, the British weakened their efforts in America. Even so, the British were able to maintain an army that was usually superior to Washington's, but with the Royal Navy also weakened and over-worked, Britain was unable to sustain the demands of the incredible supply line that was gradually disintegrating. As the war ground on to its conclusion, the 42nd moved to Halifax, Nova Scotia in October 1783 where a large number of men took their discharges to remain in Canada. A Black Watch 'colony' was established on the Nashwaak River, New Brunswick while the regiment moved on to Cape Breton and the island of St John in 1786. They finally left Canada to return to England in 1789, having been abroad for thirteen years. They remained in Tynemouth to dispel the effects of the sea journey and illnesses before travelling to Edinburgh for a brief leave and to take in desperately needed recruits.

Finding new men of the standard to which the Black Watch had become accustomed was already becoming a problem for the recruiting officers. As the serving soldiers themselves discovered on their return, the Highlands of Scotland were being bled of their youth and vigour by the demands of the British army. The whole way of life of the region was in the process of changing for ever. Although the Highland Clearances did not begin in earnest for another twenty-five years, emigration to America, Canada and other colonial countries had been picking up pace in spite of the wars across the Atlantic. The phenomenon that in time placed large Scottish communities in virtually every place to which British ships travelled was a response to a number of factors that, as already noted, began in the aftermath of the 1745 rebellion and were followed in an era of improved agricultural practices resulting in part from the roads that General Wade constructed for his policing of the Highlands at the time of the formation of the Black Watch. Nor was it only the poorest among the community who set out for a new life. The relatively prosperous leaseholders who were facing increasing rents from the lairds as farming techniques improved were among those heading for distant shores, in many cases the very clansmen from whom the regiment had been recruited in the first place. An account of a gathering of would-be émigrés at Killin, Stirling, in the late 1770s tells us:

Here convened about thirty families making in all about three hundred people. Early the next morning the whole company was called together by the sound of bagpipes and the order of their march was settled. Men, women and children had all their proper stations assigned. They were all dressed in their best attire; and the men armed in the Highland fashion. Many of them were possessed of two or three hundred pounds and few of less than thirty or forty; which at least showed that they had not starved upon their farms. They were a jocund crew and set out, not like people flying from the face of poverty but like men who were about to carry their wealth, their strength and a little property to a better market.

These were people disillusioned with changes in their homeland, and they hoped to re-create the old ways in new settlements abroad, ignoring scare stories about poor conditions put about by the lairds and government officials as they tried to stem the flow. But in fact it became a self-feeding exodus, as letters home told of a prosperous new life, once they had overcome the initial hard labour of clearing forests and building their homes. The military was especially badly hit through the shortage of recruits and joined forces with the lairds in their propaganda to discourage emigration. Later, as conditions changed again and sheep farming became the predominant industry in the Highlands, resulting in the eventual Clearances of smallholders and crofters, emigration became a wholesale movement out of the glens.

There was already growing discontent in the Highlands over these conflicting issues when, in 1790, the Black Watch began patrols in the areas of the old Independent Companies, again to keep the peace. They spent the next eighteen months or so patrolling the vast acreages, including Ross and Cromarty, from the east coast to the west coast, where their immediate problem of filling their regimental complement was aided by the Marquess of Huntly, who had recently raised an independent company of young Highlanders and turned them over to the regiment in 1791. Their pedigree was superb, organised as they were by a family whose leader three generations earlier had stood by the king during the Civil War and had been executed by Cromwell. There was still much Highland heritage about the place, and the Black Watch, now renowned and revered for their exploits in the service of the Hanoverian kings of England, as some still preferred to call them, maintained an uneasy kind of peace. But trouble elsewhere was already in the wind, and coincidentally in Flanders, the place where the Black Watch gained their first experience of real fighting back in 1745.

CHAPTER FIVE

Wars, Wives and Widows

This time, Flanders was the scene of the first exchanges in what eventually became a new war against an old enemy with a new face. Initially, the movement of troops was no more than a protective measure against the ambitious revolutionary forces in France following the overthrow of Louis XVI and the abolition of the monarchy in 1791. France was now at odds with the monarchical and dynastic governments of the rest of Europe, which subsequently gave way to full-blown war. It was a conflict that would last for twenty-three years, passing through all its critical phases, first under what became known as the French Revolutionary Wars between 1792 and 1802, followed by the Napoleonic Wars, 1803–15, a succession of tumultuous and famous battles in which the Black Watch would be engaged throughout.

The encounters began in August 1792, when a joint Prussian-Austrian force crossed into France and began marching towards Paris to rescue the deposed monarch. The troops were halted at Valmy by the French regular army and by revolutionary volunteers. The battle was won by regular French artillery units, which simply bombarded the invading troops to an excruciatingly bloody halt. This was

71

followed by gains in the Netherlands, where other French forces pushed back the Austrian army at the Battle of Jemappes. In January 1793 the revolutionary government in Paris executed King Louis and Marie-Antoinette, an act that raised the stakes and stirred Britain and other European nations into sending a coalition army, which turned out to be an infamously disjointed effort, with each country working to its own agenda.

The revolutionary council in Paris responded with an act that would change the face of warfare for ever, by passing new laws of *levy en masse*, by which all Frenchmen between the ages of eighteen and twenty-five were to make themselves available for military service. At a stroke, the French were able to assemble the first-ever conscript army and began to amass a force of over 200,000 men. By then, the invading armies of Prussia and Austria were already being pushed back across the border. The Black Watch became involved the following year, when Britain sent an army under the overall command of the Duke of York, second son of George III, whose Chiefs of Staff had sent him on a task in which he was to fail ignominiously. He was supposedly marching to rescue the Austrian army, which was in trouble against the French at Fleurus, but ran into severe opposition himself. Noted as the first time in which aerial reconnaissance was employed, with the French using military balloons, the Austrians' 52,000 regulars were met by 75,000 troops, many of them conscripts, and a 6-hour battle ended as a major reverse for the coalition.

As the Austrians retreated, York's army, badly equipped and ill led, faced a desperate situation as it made a fighting retreat, so a second British contingent under the command of the Earl of Moira, whose regiments included the Black Watch, was dispatched in haste to Ostend. Moira's orders were to defend the town to maintain an open port, but the day he arrived, 26 June, coincided with the defeat of the Austrian army at Fleurus. Moira saw at once that Ostend was now worthless and, by a hazardous march, made his way to Alost (Aalst), where he met up with the retreating first contingent of the British army under the Duke of York. The British army, unsupported by its allies, was pushed back into Holland, while the Austrians pulled out of the fight altogether, leaving the defence of Holland to the British and Dutch. Moira himself returned to England at the end of July, but his troops remained in the Netherlands under the Duke of York, who now faced an incredibly difficult situation. The haste at which the whole army had been deployed meant that supplies of virtually every commodity were running on empty: the artillery units had guns but no drivers, the medical cover was virtually non-existent and the troops were clothed in summer wear, with no supplies for the oncoming winter.

Meantime, the Duke of York was still going backwards, retreating as far as Bremen, and in the onset of the coldest of winters the British troops were falling by the wayside as a result of their wounds, sickness and bad food, finally dying from the cold. The following contemporary account provides an enlightening description of the plight of the Black Watch and their colleagues of the many regiments that formed this unfortunate British force:

The Duke of York quitted the command of the army on the 6th of December, 1794, and returned to England; a sufficient indication that even the British ministry had given up the cause of Holland as desperate. The state of the army was extremely bad, even while the duke, by his presence, controlled, in some degree, the rapacity of the inferior agents, and prevented, as far as the exertions of one man in the midst of a corrupt system could, the unpardonable neglect which prevailed in every department. But he was no sooner departed, and the army placed under the command of a foreigner, than the grossest abuses were committed. Perhaps there never was a period when the supplies to the troops cost such enormous sums to the nation, and there certainly never was a war in which the army was so destitute. Warm clothing supplied by the patriotic contributions of the English nation, by some mismanagement or corrupt practice, many of the wretched, suffering victims, never received any advantage. The condition of the sick was deplorable beyond all

73

precedent; and, when a man was ordered for the hospital, the common expression throughout the army was, that he was 'sent to the shambles'.

The account picks up the story along with horrific scenes as the weather closed in and deaths began to be counted in their hundreds:

... poignant sufferings during this retreat would form a tale whose lightest word would harrow up the soul, and make the blood run cold with horror. [The sick and wounded] constantly removed in open wagons, exposed to the intense severity of the weather, to drifting snow and heavy falls of sleet and rain, frequently without any victuals till the army halted, and then but scantily provided; littered down in cold churches, upon a short allowance of dirty straw, and few of them enjoying the comforts of even a single blanket to repel the rigorous attacks of the night air, it is no wonder that they expired by hundreds, martyrs to the most unpardonable neglect. The multitudes who sank into the arms of death, oppressed with cold and fatigue, are beyond calculation. Some of the sufferers were mounted behind the cavalry, and even behind some of the officers, whose humanity on this occasion reflects honour on their character; but many more were left behind, dead or dying, or buried under the drifts of snow. The 16th of January 1795 was a day more peculiarly marked by distressing scenes than any other during the retreat. The troops were on that morning put in motion at daybreak, with the view of reaching Loonen, a village distant about twenty-three miles. Owing to the uncommon severity of the weather, and the snow, which lying deep on the ground, was drifted in the faces of the men by a strong easterly wind, they were so worn down by fatigue that it was thought advisable to halt some of the regiments at two neighbouring villages, about nine miles short of their destination. The whole of the British could not, however, be possibly accommodated; and it was left to the discretion of commanding officers of corps to continue the march, or to take up such situations as they could meet with on the road.

Some of the regiments proceeded even after sunset with their baggage and field-pieces; and, consequently, were entirely dispersed, as it was impossible to trace out any pathway over the dreary common. Great numbers of men, unable to bear up against the fatigue they had undergone, and several women and children, were frozen to death in their attempts to discover the road which their battalion had pursued. [One] regiment was so scattered that no return whatever of its strength could be given next day, and the few straggling parties that joined gave a very melancholy account of the main body.

An officer of the Guards who was ordered to reconnoitre ahead the next morning was thus able to appraise the desperation of the men in this lumbering, retreating train and particularly the dreadful consequences of the preceding night's march, especially among the womenfolk who travelled with the soldiers. His account was written down for posterity:

On the morning of the 17th, I was sent upon a particular duty, to trace out a road over the common, by which the army and artillery might safely proceed to Loonen. When the party marched it was scarcely light and, as day broke in upon us, the horrible scenes that it revealed afforded a shocking proof of the miseries of a winter campaign. On the common, about half a mile off the road, we discovered a baggage cart, with a team of five horses, apparently in distress. I galloped towards the spot and found the poor animals were stiff but not dead, the hoarfrost on their manes plainly showing that they had been there all night. Not perceiving any driver with them, I struck my sword repeatedly on the covered tilt, inquiring at the same time if there was any person in the cart; at length a very feeble voice answered me, and some one underneath appeared to be making an effort to rise; a pair of naked, frost-nipped legs were then advanced, and the most miserable object I ever beheld sunk heavily to the ground, the whole of his clothing so ragged and worn that I can scarcely say that he was covered; so stiff and frozen was the miserable wretch that he was by no means capable of moving. He informed me that his regiment had lost its road; and, in turning to another, he found his horses incapable of clearing his cart from the ruts; and that himself and his two comrades were left behind, to proceed in the best manner they could. The two men he spoke of were lying dead in the cart, having all three endeavoured to communicate to each other a degree of warmth by creeping close together. We placed the miserable survivor upon one of the horses of his team, and led him forward to join his battalion; by that means his life was preserved; yet I fear but for a season for, when placed in the hospital, his toes dropt off frost-bitten, and we could not proceed a hundred yards without perceiving the dead bodies of men, women and children, and horses, in every direction.

One scene made an impression on my memory which time will never be able to efface. Near another cart, a little further on the common, we perceived a stout-looking man and a beautiful-looking young woman with an infant about seven months old at the breast, all three frozen and dead. The mother had most certainly expired in the act of suckling her child, as with one breast exposed, she lay upon the drifted snow, the milk, to all appearance, in a stream drawn from the nipple by the babe, having instantly congealed. The infant seemed as if its life had but just been disengaged, and it reposed its little head on its mother's bosom, with an overflow of milk frozen as it trickled from the mouth. Their countenances were perfectly composed and fresh, resembling those of persons in a sound and tranquil slumber.

About fifty yards further in advance was another dead man, with a bundle of linen and a few biscuits evidently belonging to the poor woman and child; and a little further was a horse lying down but not quite dead, with a couple of panniers on his back, one of which contained, as we discovered, the body of another child, about two years of age, wrapped up in flannel and straw. This, as we afterwards heard, was the whole of one family, a sergeant's wife, her brother and children. The man found with the horse and bundle had remained behind to assist them. During a march, thus memorable for its miseries, he had just gained sight of a distant hamlet, where they might have obtained shelter from the inclemency of the weather, when his strength failed him and, as the battalion passed the spot, the troops were witnesses in their turn of this melancholy scene.

During this dreadful winter, as many as 4,000 among the regiments died from exhaustion, cold or battle wounds, yet the Black Watch, wearing their traditional plaid kilts, suffered just twenty five casualties from battle or the weather during the period of this assignment, which lasted from June 1794 to April 1795. At that point the Black Watch were withdrawn temporarily from the war in Europe because, although they did not know it yet, they were to become part of another force being assembled to take on the French elsewhere, a task that would take them back to the dreaded West Indies.

A closer examination of the aspect of the womenfolk of the regiment may be helpful in view of the references above to the deaths of women and children. Highlanders' wives, widows and camp followers were generally well known to be women of remarkable stamina, and some of such character that they made their way into the accounts of battles of that era. British army regulations did not encourage their soldiers to marry, especially those in lower ranks. Regimental commanders were given some leeway in regard to allowing marriage, but as a general rule at the time only six out of every hundred men were allowed to have wives 'on strength', meaning that they could live in the barracks, were given free rations and, in some cases, arrangements were made to educate their children.

Few barracks provided separate married quarters for the lower ranks, and usually areas in large barrack rooms or tents were partitioned with blankets or some other temporary arrangement. Some men carried their own tents for privacy, and when babies were born the arrangements for birth were generally primitive and quite lacking in privacy. Those 'official' wives who subsequently became widows, as many did, were given the opportunity to find another husband within the regiment; failing that, they had to leave and make their own arrangements.

Many soldiers did have wives who were 'off strength' and were given no privileges at all, and who were not allowed, officially at least, to accompany their husbands on their travels, although this did not necessarily stop them. As camp followers, groups of these unattributed women and children would set up tents or buildings on the edge of the military encampments in conditions that were, to say the least, harsh. The women consisted of wives, unmarried girlfriends or plain no-bones-about-it camp followers – in other words, resident prostitutes. In the Black Watch, the rules had always been fairly strictly observed, and those who wished to wed could do so only with their commanding officer's approval, and that included a personal inspection of the bride-to-be, and there also had to be a vacancy within the annual quota of allowed marriages. Officers were a class apart in every sense, since most of them had formal marriages in their home surroundings; some of these wives would travel with their husbands, but there was no hard-and-fast rule because it was often easier for an officer to take home leave, even from North America.

During campaigns, accommodation for soldiers' wives was always scarce, and a wife might end up sharing a tent with her husband and half a dozen of his colleagues. The wives also established themselves in working for the regiment and actually served a necessary function on campaigns where they were hired by the army, for a pittance, to wash, cook, mend uniforms and act as nurses. Many became long-service wives, sometimes having two or three husbands within the regiment after widowhood, and there are colourful descriptions of some who made it into print. One soldier's wife in the 42nd was recalled in writings left by the Reverend John Grant, minister of Tamintoul, Moray:

In personal respect and fortune at the head of the inhabitants [of Tamintoul] must be ranked Mrs M'Kenzie, of the best inn at the sign of the horns. This heroine began her career of celebrity in the accommodating disposition of an easy virtue, at the age of fourteen in the year 1745. That year saw her in Flanders, caressing and caressed. Superior to the little prejudices of her sex, she relinquished the first object of her affection and attached herself to a personage high in the military department. After a campaign or two spent in acquiring a knowledge of man and the world, Scotland saw her again; but wearied of the inactivity of rural retirement she then married and made her husband enlist in the Royal Highlanders at the commencement of the war in 1756. With him she navigated the Atlantic and sallied forth on American ground in quest of adventures, equally prepared to meet her friends, or encounter her enemies in the fields of Venus or Mars as occasion offered. At the conclusion of the war she revisited her native country. After a variety of vicissitudes in Germany, France, Holland, England, Ireland, Scotland, America and the West Indies her anchor is now moored on dry land in the village of Tamintoul. It might be imagined that such extremes of climate, so many rugged paths, so many severe bruises, as she must have experienced in her progress through life, would have impaired her health, especially when it is considered that she added twenty-four children to the aggregate of general births, beside some homunculi that stopped short in their passage. Wonderful, however, as it may appear, at this moment she is as fit for her usual active life as ever; and except two or three grey hairs vegetating from a mole upon one of her cheeks, that formerly set off a high ruddy complexion, she still retains all the apparent freshness and vigour of youth.

There was a particular incident involving a soldier's wife who tended the wounds Black Watch Colonel Graham received in the West Indies in 1797. General Stewart, in his sketches of the Highlanders, stated that she was a woman of uncommon character:

She had been long a follower of the camp and had acquired some of its manners. While she was so good and useful a nurse in quarters she was also bold and fearless in the field. [On one occasion] . . . when an attack was to be made, I directed that her husband, who was in my company, should remain behind to take charge of the men's knapsacks, which they had thrown off to be light for the advance up the hill, as I did not wish to have him exposed to danger on account of his wife and family. He obeyed his orders and remained with his charge, but his wife, believing herself not to be included in those injunctions, pushed forward to the assault. When the enemy had been beaten from the third redoubt, I was standing giving some directions to the men and preparing to push on to the fourth and last redoubt, when I found myself tapped in the shoulder and turning round saw my Amazonian friend standing with her clothes tucked up to her knees; and seizing my hand she exclaimed: 'Well done, my Highland lads! See how the brigands scamper like so many deer . . . Let us drive them from yonder hill.' On inquiry I found that she had been in the hottest fire cheering and animating the men and when the action was over she was as active as any of the surgeons in assisting the wounded.

Other contemporary accounts also praise the fortitude of the women-folk, and especially in the area of acquiring goods en route. They were, said one report:

capital foragers, occasional looters and as full of *esprit de corps* as the men, and bore the fatigues of a campaign with patient fortitude . . . I knew well an old lady who used to tell with pride how, when a sudden order to march came, while the linen of the men she washed for was in the tub, she took advantage of the fact that she was billeted on a wood merchant to make a roaring fire, and succeeded in giving every man his dry shirt as he stood on parade, emerging like Wellington at Fuentes d'Onor, undefeated by the difficulties of the situation. She gave brandy to the wounded in the ensuing engagement, made her husband's breakfast before the fight of the next day, and ended her eventful life as the respected hostess of a hotel in Argyllshire.

There is little doubt, however, that life for the womenfolk travelling with their husbands on campaigns was generally incredibly harsh and dangerous. Sergeant James Anton, in his 1842 book *Retrospect of a Military Life*, based on his service in the Black Watch, wrote:

Perhaps the reader may be desirous to know how the women following the army on an hostile campaign bear the hardships to which they are exposed [which are] anything but pleasant and would be unsupportable, were it not that each sees her neighbour suffering as much as herself. Her bed is generally the damp ground; her threadbare mantle, which envelopes her bundle by day, serves for a sheet by night, and her husband's blanket for a coverlet. Accustomed to such usage as this, she can scarcely meet with worse when absent. Indeed, the kindly manner in which the benighted women were received at the quarters of any of the corps cantoned in the houses by the way, was highly creditable to the army, and sometimes rendered the wayfarers more comfortable than they would have been with their respective regiments, seeing that they found shelter within a house.

On occasions this care for the women brought some amazing stories. One recounted by Sergeant Anton told of a soldier's wife who was in the latter stages of pregnancy at a time of a long withdrawal of her husband's unit during the Peninsular Wars, hotly pursued by the French. When the woman went into labour during the march, there was no alternative but to leave her by the wayside to be attended by the French, who were then close behind. The child was indeed safely born and was attended by a French medical officer, while all around the war continued. She was eventually sent forward again and reunited with her husband. There were other stories of women less fortunate, one relating to a woman carrying an infant in her arms during a retreat across a river:

> The bridge, which the enemy had been endeavouring to break down, [was] damaged ... and in passing through, the men supported each other as well as they could, so as to prevent them falling. The wife of a sergeant of one of the regiments attempted to pass on a donkey, with a child in her arms, and owing to some sudden stumble or slip of the animal, the child gave a start and dropped into the stream. The distracted mother gave a shriek, leaped after the infant, and both were swept off by the rapid current, in the presence of the husband, who plunged into the water in hopes to recover them, but they were gone for ever, and he himself was with difficulty rescued. After this accident, the women who were following the army remained until the bridge was so far repaired as to enable them to pass over.
>
> My poor wife ... was detained, along with several other women, on the left bank until the bridge was repaired. While this was doing, one of the women belonging to the regiment begged her to take charge of a little ass-colt, with a couple of bundles, until she should go back to make some purchases; she complied, and before the other returned, the bridge was repaired. She [set off] driving the colt before her but before she got to the further end, the stubborn animal stood still and would not move a foot. Another regiment was advancing, the passage was impeded, and struggling to get out of the way, determined to leave the animal, when a grenadier lifted the colt in his arms, and carried it to the end of the bridge. My poor wife thanked him with the tear in her eye, the only acknowledgement she could make for his kindness.

In relating experiences on a later campaign in the war with France, Sergeant Anton did express views on the issue of wives and camp followers which, at the time, might well have been considered controversial. He told of how a restriction was placed on the number of women who could travel with the regiment and how a number were ordered to remain in Ostend and thus fend for themselves:

[Two days later] they found their way to the regiment [then in Ghent]; they were conveyed back to the same place from which they had escaped, and there closely watched. Yet, in a week or two, they eluded the vigilance of the sentries, and joined their husbands once more, and as no official reports were made to their prejudice, they followed the fortunes of their husbands during the campaign, along with those who boasted the privilege. It may not here be improper to remark that, on all occasions of troops being dispatched to the scene of expected hostilities, women should not be permitted to accompany them. If an exception is made in one single instance, it only gives room for pressing, and almost irresistible applications from others, and throws the performance of a very painful duty, namely, that of refusing permission, on the officers commanding companies. Every private soldier conceives that he has as good a right to this indulgence for his wife, as the first non-commissioned officer in the regiment, and certainly he is right. She will prove much more useful than one who, instead of being serviceable, considers herself entitled to be served, assumes the consequence of a lady without any of the good qualifications or accomplishments of one, and helps to embitter the domestic enjoyments of others, by exciting petty jealousies that otherwise would never exist. It is generally the case, in selecting women to follow the army to a foreign station, that choice is made of those without children, as they are considered more capable of performing the services that may be required of them, than those encumbered with a family. This, though just as regards our wants, is not so with respect to many a well-deserving woman, who is thus cast on the public, or left to her own exertions, which too often fail her in the endeavour to support herself and children, while the childless woman is selected, and profits from that circumstance.

I am no great theorist, but I am certain that much might be done to obviate the necessity of soldiers' wives being burdensome to the public, by adopting proper means for their support. Why should not the soldier contribute part of his pay towards the maintenance of his family at home? In fact, it ought to be stipulated that he should do so, before permission is given him to marry. If no women were permitted to accompany the army (I mean on a hostile campaign, for I see no objection that can be made to the women being permitted to follow their husbands in times of peace, wherever their regiments might be stationed), the married men might earn more than their daily pay, by washing for the officers and non-commissioned officers, and to any of the single men who are not inclined to wash their own linen, and thus be enabled to make the larger remittances. The fixing of a residence, also, for his young family ought to be held out as a stimulus for this arrangement.

Sergeant Anton pointed out that in the 42nd at that time a woman who was permitted to accompany her husband received a half-ration free; a child over seven received one-third rations, and one under seven a quarter of a ration. Those who were not permitted to accompany their husbands received no rations. 'I must also remark,' he added, 'that on foreign stations, where this allowance is made to the women and children, it will be found that the least necessitous are the first to apply, and the first to be placed on this benevolent list. I have seen privates' wives, with three or more children, without rations while the wives and children of sergeant-majors, and quartermaster-sergeants, were getting them.'

All these women were following the regiment in the period now under review and would have experienced the full drama of this era of Black Watch history, of which fresh and unwelcome demands were about to emerge.

On their return from France in June 1795, the men were quartered at barracks in Royston, Hertfordshire, and on the day of George III's birthday a box was delivered to the Commanding Officer containing red feathers as an award for outstanding gallantry. This formed the basis of the Red Hackle that was to be worn in the men's bonnets in perpetuity. The Red Vulture feather was later confirmed to be worn exclusively by the 42nd Royal Highland Regiment, and indeed it does today. At the time, though, the cynics among them might have wondered what George III was up to, because whenever he (or at least those who made the approach and the decisions in his name) was being nice to the Black Watch, it was usually a prelude to some particularly difficult assignment. And, sure enough, one came very quickly thereafter.

Barely had the Black Watch reconditioned themselves and their equipment after the débâcle in the Netherlands than their officers were placed on almost immediate alert, to be ready to move at forty-eight hours' notice. The regimental commanders were also delighted to accept a large intake of new recruits. They came from other Highland units that had been disbanded, providing the Black Watch with considerable extra strength, sound in the knowledge that they were like-minded soldiers maintaining the Highland influence. They would soon be tested. Major-General Sir Ralph Abercromby, one of the Duke of York's commanders in the ill-fated First Coalition against the French revolutionaries, was now charged with taking an army of no fewer than 25,000 for immediate action in the West Indies to add weight to a force already attempting to maintain British interests there. Battles were already in progress. As soon as war with France was declared in February 1793, the French had moved to take possession of islands under British control. A force of 7,000, commanded by Lieutenant-General Sir Charles Grey, sailed on 26 November but did not reach Barbados until early January 1794. Although Grey met with early success, a combination of yellow fever and the need to place troops in several island locations quickly reversed the advantage. As the commander himself recorded, his troops were 'quite exhausted by the unparalleled services of fatigue and fire they had gone through, for such a length of time, in the worst climate'.

Then, as what was known locally as the 'sickly season' took hold, the men started falling ill at an alarming rate. At the garrison of Basse-Terre, for example, only 470 men out of 2,249 were fit for duty by September, while at Saint-Domingue, where 4,000 men had landed, more than 2,200 died from either battle wounds or sickness – mostly the latter – and thus the campaign had gone from early success to a pending disaster. As the British hold weakened, a number of islands in the West Indies rose in revolt against the British, and by March 1795 the situation had become critical. The power struggle for the commodity-rich islands was a crucial element in the overall battle for supremacy between Britain and France, given that whichever nation held sway in that region had control of its valuable resources of sugar, spices, rum, coffee, cotton and cocoa.

At this point the Black Watch and other regiments became part of Abercromby's expedition to save the day. They would be supplemented by German and Swiss mercenaries. With remarkable speed, 23 battalions of British infantry and 340 ships were assembled at Southampton and Cork to begin this huge operation. But time was lost in supplying the vessels, and then severe weather – which became known in the south as the Great Storms of 1795–6 – virtually scuppered the relief effort before it had begun. Although some of the transports set sail in October, many were scattered at sea and others did not finally get under way until January 1796. Those attempting to sail faced huge problems as the weather deteriorated, and the Black Watch were in the thick of it. There were 500 of the regiment's men on one ship that collided with another and had to return for repairs. Several other ships were driven back by furious gales from the south-west, tossed around like matchwood. Many men were drowned. The fleet was reassembled in the first week of December, but the vessels were held back by continuing severe weather and it was the end of January before a mere fifty ships could sail. They did not reach the West Indies until late March. Even so, some did not complete the journey. These included five companies of the Black Watch under

Lieutenant-Colonel Dickson on board one ship that limped into Gibraltar, where they were forced to remain. Five other companies aboard the ship *Middlesex*, which was among those that got away in October, did reach Barbados in the first week of February and were put straight to work.

In spite of these incredible reverses, the British commanders managed to assemble their brigades of mixed and matched regiments, first landing on the island of St Lucia, where the Highlanders found themselves serving in a brigade commanded by one of Glasgow's most famous soldiers, General Sir John Moore, who, apart from his outstanding military record, became best known for imploring Robert Burns to pen his autobiography. Under Moore's outstanding leadership, the tide was turned in this ill-starred expedition, and within two months the British had secured the surrender of the French garrisons on the island, aided in part by the high sickness tolls that the French were also experiencing.

From there, the Black Watch sailed on to the island St Vincent side by side with, among others, one of Britain's oldest regiments, the Buffs (Royal East Kent Regiment, 3rd Foot), created in 1572. Moore's brigade quickly quelled the opposition, or at least he thought he had when 800 of them surrendered. But they later broke out of the stockade and teamed up with some 5,000 local irregulars and continued to keep the British occupied until September. The combined efforts of the Black Watch and the Buffs gradually bore down on the French and reclaimed most of the territory that had been occupied. Even so, the cost to Abercromby's army as a whole was substantial, largely through illness. War Office records for 1796 showed that just over forty per cent of European soldiers died within a year of arriving in the West Indies, not counting those who had been swept overboard or died of scurvy en route. For the British army, this translated into 264 officers and an incredible 12,387 men who died of yellow fever or other diseases. It was a national scandal that had been left unattended too long. Some efforts were made in the immediate wake of those astounding figures by attempting to keep British soldiers out of areas where the disease was most prolific, but it would be another six years or more before the death rate began to show a slight decline.

This was achieved to some extent by passing the risk to non-British soldiers, such as men of African birth or descent who were rescued from captured slave ships and 'invited' to join local militias. Others excluded from the figures were mercenaries largely from Germany and Switzerland, along with Dutch, Irish and not a small number of French who were opposed to the revolutionary council in Paris. Manpower was also supplemented by the British army recruiting condemned prisoners, deserters and prisoners of war into militia groups while at the same time attempting to build up local defence forces, including some strong Afro-Caribbean units.

The 42nd added to its strength by taking in men from the 79th Highlanders who had served for two years in Martinique and were allowed transfer to the Black Watch just before they were released from duties in the West Indies. Although they had fought in several places where yellow fever was virulent, the Highlanders escaped heavy losses through disease and they arrived without a single sick man on board. They landed at Portsmouth on 30 July 1797 and were marched to Hillsea barracks, where they spent just a few weeks before embarking for Gibraltar to join the five other companies whose journey to the West Indies had been interrupted by the storms. They had remained on the Rock and had been put to work on various kinds of manual labour that went towards improving the somewhat neglected British naval base there.

Now, reunited, they were assigned to capture the island of Minorca, in November 1798, a task achieved virtually without opposition. The Spanish commander, whose garrison far outnumbered the invaders, surrendered immediately, believing the British force to be far greater than it was. The possession of Minorca was important. It was to be used as a rendezvous point for a large force about to be deployed through the Mediterranean to aid Britain's allies: for the relief of Genoa, and to form a blockade of the French garrison at Valletta on the island of Malta, which in the event became the first stage of a far more important engagement.

CHAPTER SIX

Fighting Napoleon

The next move was the third instalment of the French wars in which the Black Watch became involved. While they were away in the Caribbean, that young military genius Napoleon Bonaparte had invaded Egypt. He was then trapped inside his prize by Nelson, who made a daring and dramatic assault on the French fleet anchored in Aboukir Bay in 1798, sinking or capturing thirteen of Napoleon's seventeen ships. Napoleon himself abandoned his army to further his political ambitions in Paris in 1799, leaving his troops *in situ* to hold their ground. In London, the presence of the French in Egypt was considered a threat to British control of the eastern Mediterranean, and subsequently to India. Through diplomatic channels, dialogue was exchanged with the Turks on how best to eject the French from their present residency.

At the other end of the Mediterranean, Sir Ralph Abercromby was moved to Gibraltar to gather his army to link up with a Turkish contingent and ultimately launch a joint invasion of Egypt to defeat the remaining French force. It was a task, according to London assessments, that could be achieved with some ease. Intelligence reports put the French army at just 12,000 men. Easier said than done: on the way, a number of British ships damaged by bad weather began leaking and had to put in to the British naval dockyards at Valletta, and weeks of waiting for repairs meant that by the time the convoy anchored in what was then Marmorice Bay on the west coast of Turkey towards the end of 1800, many troops had been struck by illness. The British land forces amounted to 13,234 men and 630 artillery, but the efficient force, discounting those who were sick, was only 12,334. The fleet sailed in two divisions for Marmorice, the first arriving on 28 December and the second four days later. Having received the Turkish supplies, which were, it was noted, 'in every respect deficient', the fleet again got under way on 23 February, and on the morning of 1 March the white sandy coast of Egypt came into view. The fleet anchored in Aboukir Bay – on the spot where the Battle of the Nile had been fought nearly three years before – and almost immediately a violent gale sprang up, which continued without let-up for six days. Two other aspects of the situation came as something of a disappointment – if not shock – to Abercromby. First, he discovered that all drinking water for his army would have to be supplied from the ships, and secondly the small French army that London had mentioned turned out to be almost three times as large as the predicted number: 32,000 in total, plus several thousand native troops.

Finally, in the early hours, fifty-eight flat boats were on their way, but as daylight came up they were spotted by the French gunners. The sailors rowed on towards the shore under a heavy hail of grape- and case-shot. Major-General Sir John Moore's brigade, which included the Black Watch, led the way, beating off a swirling assault by cavalry. The British soldiers were cheering loudly as they stormed the beaches and formed a line without themselves firing a shot until close at hand to take on the incoming cavalry. Then they marched forward under fire from 2,500 muskets, climbed a steep treacherous slope and drove off the French front line at the point of their bayonets. Scattered fire was kept up for a time by the enemy's second line in the small sand-hills, but then they fled in confusion on the advance of the troops. The Guards, having landed on ground nearly on a level with the water, were immediately attacked, the first by cavalry, and the 54th by a body of infantry, who advanced with fixed bayonets. Sir John Fortescue's *History of the British Army* records:

> The finest performance of the day was that of the 42nd . . . [who] were the first to land and formed under heavy fire and repulsed the horsemen by their volleys. The Highlanders then advanced, with the 58th in support, and drove the infantry opposed to them out of the sand-hills, and captured three guns.

In what was described as 'this brilliant affair' by Fortescue, the British had 4 officers, 4 sergeants and 94 rank and file killed, among whom were 31 Highlanders, and 26 officers, 34 sergeants, 5 drummers and 450 rank and file wounded, of whom 151 were from the 42nd. Despite these heavy casualties, the Black Watch regrouped with the rest of the assault force to meet a last-ditch charge by the French cavalry. The initial fighting was watched from the flagship of the fleet by the commander-in-chief, Abercromby, who was anxious to be at the head of his troops. He decided immediately to go ashore and, on reaching land, 'leaped from the boat with the vigour of youth . . . Taking his station on a little sand-hill, he received the congratulations of the officers by whom he was surrounded, on the ability and firmness with which he had conducted the enterprise.' The rest of Abercromby's men began their advance on Alexandria, twelve miles away. The ensuing battles were fought on several fronts, and casualties were heavy. In one incredible foray, the Black Watch barely escaped annihilation, as Stewart of Garth's account of the incident clearly demonstrates:

> Orders were given to drive the enemy back, which were instantly performed with complete success. Encouraged by the commander-in-chief, who called out from his station, 'My brave Highlanders, remember your country, remember your forefathers!', they pursued the enemy along the plain, but they had not proceeded far when General Moore, whose eye was keen, perceived through the increasing clearness of the atmosphere,

fresh columns of the enemy drawn up on the plain beyond with three squadrons of cavalry, as if ready to charge through the intervals of their retreating infantry. As no time was to be lost, the general ordered the regiment to retire from their advanced position, and re-form on the left of the redoubt. This order, although repeated by Colonel Stewart, was only partially heard in consequence of the noise of the firing; and the result was, that whilst the companies who heard it retired on the redoubt, the rest hesitated to follow. The enemy, observing the intervals between these companies, resolved to avail themselves of the circumstance, and advanced in great force. Broken as the line was by the separation of the companies, it seemed almost impossible to resist with effect an impetuous charge of cavalry; yet every man stood firm. Many of the enemy were killed in the advance. The companies, who stood in compact bodies, drove back all who charged them, with great loss . . . It is extraordinary that in this onset only thirteen Highlanders were wounded by the sabre, a circumstance to be ascribed to the firmness with which they stood, first endeavouring to bring down the horse, before the rider came within sword-length, and then dispatching him with the bayonet, before he had time to recover his legs from the fall of the horse.

Enraged at the disaster which had befallen the elite of his cavalry, [the French commander] ordered forward a column of infantry, supported by cavalry, to make a second attempt on the position; but this body was repulsed at all points by the Highlanders. Another body of cavalry now dashed forward as the former had done, and met with a similar reception, numbers falling, and others passing through to the rear, where they were again overpowered by the 28th. It was impossible for the Highlanders to withstand much longer such repeated attacks, particularly as they were reduced to the necessity of fighting every man on his own ground, and unless supported they must soon have been destroyed. The fortunate arrival of the brigade of Brigadier-General Charles Stewart, which advanced from the second line, and formed on the left of the Highlanders, probably saved them from destruction. At this time the enemy were advancing in great force, both in cavalry and infantry, apparently determined to overwhelm the handful of men who had hitherto baffled all their efforts. Though surprised to find a fresh and more numerous body of troops opposed to them, they nevertheless ventured to charge, but were again driven back with great precipitation.

Later, Abercromby himself was caught in the mêlée and Private Dowie, in his unpublished diary, made a note of the scene: 'Sir Ralph engaged with three of the enemy, cutting before and behind like a youth of twenty. One of our grenadiers named Barker, having spent his ammunition, charged his piece with loose powder from his cartouche, fired his ramrod, and killed one of them, while Sir Ralph struck down another, and the third made off.' The general was already badly wounded but remained on the battlefield until the French had been repulsed, leaving 1,000 dead on the field, with another 200 taken prisoner.

Abercromby died of his wounds a week later, but his army had made a rapid advance, forcing the French to withdraw and seek an 'honourable peace'. Within the month, Alexandria was in British hands, and by September the whole of Egypt was under British control. Fortescue went on to further praise the Highlanders, who, he said, stood 'pre-eminent for a steadfastness and gallantry which would be difficult to match in any army'. Word of their contribution travelled far and wide, and the battles of Aboukir Bay and Alexandria won them honours and fame – but at considerable cost. When Alexandria was won, only 315 men of the Black Watch regiment were fit for duty, having been more exposed than any of the other regiments engaged. In sustaining the brunt of the battle their loss was nearly three times the aggregate amount of the loss of all the other regiments, more than half of whom were never called on in the initial stages when the bulk of the fighting occurred. As a tribute to the battles for Aboukir and Alexandria, the Sphinx was added to the Regimental Arms.

And so, with the French subdued, the Black Watch were among those units to embark for Southampton, from where they marched to Winchester barracks. There, a number of the men came down with a contagious fever, of which Captain Lamont and several privates died. They were, therefore, not at their best when in May 1802 the regiment was marched to Ashford, Kent, to be reviewed by George III before marching on for a posting to Edinburgh. En route they were met in many towns and villages by well-wishers bearing gifts of food and drink and when, finally, Edinburgh came in sight, they saw that thousands of people had walked out some distance from the city to meet them and accompany them to the castle. They remained in their new quarters, 'giving way', as one report put it, 'too freely to the temptations to which they were exposed, by the hospitality of the inhabitants, till the spring of 1803'. This restful interlude was to end all too quickly.

The uneasy peace, which had been declared between Britain and France with the Treaty of Amiens signed on 27 March 1802, soon showed signs of collapsing. In May the following year, the war was renewed. Having brought a number of European nations to heel, Napoleon Bonaparte, First Consul of the French Republic, once again set his sights on Britain. These ambitions became more threatening when, in May 1804, he took the title of Emperor of the French and in the same month was crowned King of Italy in Milan.

In Britain, moves were already afoot to increase the overall strength of the British army by forming battalions for the internal defence of the nation. Finding volunteers who would commit to a lifetime's service was overcome by introducing a form of conscription by ballot for what was to be called the Army of Reserve, and it was under this scheme that a 2nd Battalion of the Black Watch was formed in 1803. The names of those selected for service were drawn from parish rolls, although there was a get-out clause. Those conscripted were able to name a substitute and, while a wealthy man might pay someone else directly to take his place, a number of societies were formed whereby eligible males could take out a type of insurance. If the insured person's name was pulled out of the ballot, a substitute was guaranteed to be found. These societies mushroomed and were especially prevalent in Perth to handle the business of buy-outs from Highlanders. Many of the new recruits for the 2nd Battalion of the Black Watch were therefore substitutes, and for the first time there was a real dilution of the Highland spirit in that when the new battalion came into being, a survey of the roll revealed that 230 of its 1,343 additional men were substitutes. These new battalions would operate only within the United Kingdom, and so, when the 2nd Battalion left the barracks in 1804, they were sent to Ireland. Later, a £10 bounty was offered to those who volunteered for the regular army, although in this case they were offered a limited seven-year service, where previously there had been no choice but to sign on for life.

Napoleon, creating his own massive armies through conscription, had begun to prepare for the invasion of the British Isles, assembling nearly 2,000 ships between Brest and Antwerp and concentrating his Grande Armée at Boulogne. To land that force on the coast of Britain against the might of the hugely superior Royal Navy would be suicidal. Napoleon had to secure control of the English Channel, and in December 1804 he induced Spain to declare war on Britain. Immediately, French and Spanish squadrons massed in the Antilles to lure the British squadron into these waters. The defeat of the British there would roughly equalise the Franco-Spanish navy and the British in the ensuing battle for the Channel.

The plan was a most famous failure. On 21 October 1805 Napoleon's consortium was met by Nelson and destroyed off Cape Trafalgar. Nelson himself was, of course, killed in this greatest of naval battles. The danger of invasion was lifted, and the British now had freedom of movement at sea. In response, Napoleon tried to induce capitulation by stifling the British economy, and very nearly succeeded, by closing all of Europe to British merchandise. He ordered the confiscation of all goods coming from English factories or from the British colonies and condemned as fair prize not only every British ship but also every ship that had touched the coasts of England or its colonies. England's old ally, Portugal, refused to comply, so Spain allowed French troops to cross the borders and occupy Lisbon. At the same time, Napoleon usurped the Spanish monarchy and anointed Joseph Bonaparte their new king, causing immediate insurgency across the nations. The British government was prepared to offer only limited help in what eventually became the ongoing saga of the Peninsular Wars, which can only be summarised below in pursuit of the story of some classic activity by the Highlanders.

Major-General Sir Arthur Wellesley (later the first Duke of Wellington) was dispatched to Portugal to lead an army of 30,000 to put the invaders to flight in the Battle of Vimiero on 21 August 1808. He might well have achieved a total surrender but for orders from on high not to pursue the French. Consequently, the army in that region lived to fight another day, and Wellesley returned to England. Now the match had to be replayed. Wellesley was replaced by two generals, who in turn were recalled, and command of the British army in Portugal eventually devolved to Sir John Moore, who immediately sent for the Highland regiments to join him. The 1st Battalion of the 42nd, which had spent the last three tedious years kicking their heels in Gibraltar, was shipped over at once, to be joined by the Gordon and Cameron Highlanders from England.

On 6 October Moore was ordered to march into Spain, a move that came as a complete surprise to him because his predecessors had made no preparations for such a march, by way of supplies, clothing or transport. Nor did he possess any information about the state of the country, or intelligence on the best route he ought to take. From his own knowledge of the area, he decided it was impossible to transport the artillery by the road through the mountains, and he decided to split his army into three divisions and to march into Spain by different routes. One of these divisions consisted of a brigade of artillery and four regiments of infantry, of which the Black Watch was one.

Moore's instructions were to send a force of 30,000 infantry and 5,000 cavalry to assist the Spanish army in the expulsion of French troops and their unwanted king. The French had amassed an army in excess of 200,000, and consequently Moore was hugely dependent on his Spanish counterparts. Most analysts would have already been talking in terms of a suicidal mission, and thus it proved. Napoleon was marching on Madrid when Moore was forced to leave Lisbon even before wagons could be found for food supplies, and he was still awaiting the guns. As he pulled together the best force he could muster, a final disaster struck. News reached him that the Spanish armies had been severely mauled by the French and that Madrid had fallen. He managed to link up with Spanish General Romana's army of 60,000 only to find the men so demoralised that they had no heart for a fight, and in any event the general refused to operate under British orders. Worse news was to follow. Having captured Madrid, Napoleon was now marching on Moore's army with 80,000 under command, travelling at a considerable pace.

A smaller French force of 18,000 under Marshal Soult was located to the north-east, and now the British faced the prospect of being surrounded by an enemy numbering almost 100,000 men against their own force, which was at best now under a third of the enemy strength. Moore decided he had no alternative but to retreat. He reversed his army in a north-westerly direction, heading for the coastal city of Corunna, where transports were to be brought forward to rescue him and his 30,000 troops and animals. And so began a nightmare march of more than 350 miles through a treacherous and mountainous landscape, in ever-declining weather, with Napoleon in hot pursuit. The 42nd, along with other regiments, took news of the retreat badly and demonstrated their feeling, according to one officer's report, with 'a disappointment [that] broke out into a murmur . . . The effect of this counter-order on our soldiers was the most extraordinary, and from the greatest pitch of exaltation and courage, at once a solemn gloom prevailed throughout our ranks. Nothing was heard but the clang of firelocks thrown down in despair.'

Moore knew from personal knowledge of the region that unless the British troops reached the mountains and beyond before the French caught up, they would be cut to pieces in a pincer movement. Napoleon aimed to beat him to it. Moore had his army marching day and night, with minimum of rest, until they reached the point of relative safety at Astorga on 31 December 1808. It was a close-run race. At that point Napoleon was just fifteen miles behind, and, once he realised that the British had escaped, the Emperor handed the pursuit to Soult and returned to Paris. Even so, Moore kept the momentum to stay ahead, a task that was impeded by the two divisions at the head of the march whose discipline had gone awry, and who were looting houses en route for wine and plundering stores of shoes, clothing and food intended for the divisions in the rear of the fleeing column.

Consequently, when the rear came up, their shoes and clothes ragged and worn, they found insufficient stores and replacements. Hundreds of men had to brave the bitter weather ahead across the mountainous ranges in broken shoes, or none at all. The road was also littered with pack animals that had died of exhaustion, as well as men, women and children who could not keep up with the pace Moore had set. This unfortunate and dejected mass reached the north-west coast at Corunna on 11 January, and Moore now found one more disappointment waiting for him. The ships he had ordered to evacuate his army had not arrived, and a massive bottleneck of troops and wagons had built up before they sailed into port on 14 January. By then, Soult had caught up and was already dispersing his troops in the surrounding hills. Moore had no alternative but to turn his exhausted and bedraggled men and fight.

The British drew up immediately in line of battle. A massive 16,000 men under arms were hurried into position to meet the oncoming assault. On the right of the line was the division of General Sir David Baird, with Lord William Bentinck's brigade of the 4th, 42nd and 50th Regiments in pole position. Soult's corps began their full-frontal assault on the British line on 16 January. Battle commenced with a huge artillery onslaught by the French, followed by the advance on the British line by four columns, two of which moved directly towards Baird's position. Moore himself took command at the post occupied by Bentinck's brigade, directing every movement. Twice the French were driven back, and as he sent the Black Watch forward he bellowed,

'Highlanders, remember Egypt', which harked back to the last time he had personally sent the regiment into action. As the valley became a mass of fallen soldiers, Moore ordered up a battalion of the Guards to the left of the Highlanders who, believing that as their ammunition was running low the Guards were to relieve them, began to fall back. Moore realised what was happening and shouted, 'My brave 42nd, your ammunition is coming.' Thus inspired, the 42nd put in a typically ferocious charge ahead of their colleagues in the other regiments, and the French retreated at the point of Black Watch bayonets. That single charge turned the battle. The rout of the French was under way.

Moore would not witness the successful outcome. As the Black Watch charged again, he was struck by a cannonball and knocked to the ground, severely wounded. Bentinck would record: 'He raised himself and sat up with an unaltered countenance, looking intensely at the Highlanders, who were warmly engaged. His aide-de-camp Captain Hardinge threw himself from his horse and took him by the hand; then observing his anxiety, he told him the 42nd were advancing, upon which his countenance immediately brightened up.'

Refusing to be put on a wagon, Moore was placed on a blanket and carried away by six soldiers of the 42nd. As they went, he frequently made the soldiers stop and turn around so that he could see the battle, until the firing died and it became clear that the French were withdrawing. He died four hours later with the knowledge that the French had retreated and the battle was won. Sir David Baird had also been carried from the field after cannon fire shattered an arm, and command of the army passed to General Hope. In his subsequent report to Baird, he wote:

> The first effort of the enemy was met by the commander of the forces and by yourself, at the head of the 42nd Regiment, and the brigade under Lord William Bentinck. The village on your right became an object of obstinate contest. I lament to say, that, after the severe wound which deprived the army of your services, Lieutenant-General Sir John Moore, who had just directed

the most able disposition, fell by a cannon-shot. The troops, though not unacquainted with the irreparable loss they had sustained, were not dismayed, but, by the most determined bravery, not only repelled every attempt of the enemy to gain ground, but actually forced him to retire, although he had brought up fresh troops in support of those originally engaged. The enemy finding himself foiled in every attempt to force the right of the position, endeavoured by numbers to turn it . . . Before five in the evening, we had not only successfully repelled every attack made upon the position, but had gained ground, in almost all points, and occupied a more forward line than at the commencement of the action; whilst the enemy confined his operations to a cannonade, and the fire of his light troops, with a view to draw off his other corps. At six the firing ceased.

The loss to the British was 800 men killed and wounded, a toll borne heavily by the Black Watch, with 148 killed or wounded. The ferocity of the British attack against a vastly superior force in both numbers and equipment was demonstrated by the French losses of over 3,000 men. In general orders issued as the British began to board the transports on 18 January, General Hope applauded their courage and added: 'On no occasion has the undaunted valour of British troops been more manifest. The lieutenant-general has the greatest satisfaction in distinguishing such meritorious services as came within his observation [and especially] the brigade under his command consisting of the 4th, 42nd and 50th Regiments, which sustained the weight of the attack.'

The final act of this ill-fated expedition as the troops embarked was the burial of Sir John Moore on the city ramparts. But it was not the end of their troubles. At sea, the fleet of transports was scattered by gales, and it was indeed a bedraggled army that went ashore at Plymouth and Portsmouth. Their appearance caused widespread comment, and even alarm given that these forlorn-looking soldiers, many without shoes and with worn and tattered clothing, looked as if they had come from a terrible defeat. In fact, it was they who were the victors at Corunna, although *The Times* described the whole episode as a shameful disaster. The entire operation was indeed a dire chapter in the series of wars with Napoleon. Not least among the ammunition for the critics was the appalling behaviour and break-down of discipline recorded in some of the regiments on the march to the coast, a journey incidentally during which far more men became categorised as 'dead or missing in Spain' than were actually killed or wounded in battle. A further disaster along similar lines was about to emerge.

The Black Watch barely had time to repair the damage and make up their losses with new recruits (and this will become a familiar story) before the men were called on again to take a front-line posi-tion in what became one of the most notorious events in the war with France – not a battle but devastating sickness.

In July the regiment learned they were going straight back across the North Sea to participate in what would go down in history as one of the most disastrous of the expeditions of the Napoleonic Wars. The British landing in the Low Countries in the summer of 1809 was aimed at assisting the Austrians, who were under threat from the French. The plan was to cause a diversion by destroying the French fleet at Flushing (Vlissingen) on the fever-ridden island province of Walcheren at the mouth of river Scheldt (in present-day Holland). Almost 40,000 men began landing on Walcheren in the last week of July, but by the time the troops had been assembled the French had moved its fleet to Antwerp and the Austrians had been heavily defeated in the infamous Battle of Wagram, twelve miles north-east of Vienna. The battle had been fought by an aggregate of almost 300,000 men between the two sides, of whom 80,000 were left dead or wounded on the battlefield. With such disastrous losses, more or less equally divided between the two sides, Austria immediately opened peace talks, which were being finalised as the British captured Flushing on 15 August and fought on to take Walcheren.

The British military planners had overlooked the severe conse-quences of any lengthy stay in this notoriously dangerous place. The fever took hold almost immediately and, with British troops falling to malaria by the hundred, medical resources simply could not cope.

Within the first month, over 8,000 fever cases were reported, and the situation only grew worse before the operation was finally called off in early September. By the time the last troops had been evacuated, almost 4,000 had died from the sickness. Thousands more were seriously ill, and remained so for many months, and in some cases years. The scale of the disaster was revealed by a British army log on 1 February 1810, which showed that 11,513 officers and men were still sick and unavailable for duty.

The fate of the Black Watch in this military disaster was immense. Although the men were withdrawn to England on 11 September, 130 subsequently died and only 200 were fit for duty and, as an officer wrote to a colleague, 'those that are look as yellow as a kite's foot'. The regiment carried its sick to barracks at Canterbury, where they remained until March 1810, when the regiment moved by sea to Scotland, quartered at Musselburgh. The effects were long lasting and the men so weakened that Wellesley, as he began the campaigns leading to the Battle of Waterloo, requested that no soldiers who had been affected by the Walcheren sickness should form part of his army until they were fully recovered, although many were indeed still suffering when they were called.

The Peninsular campaigns had been revived in the intervening two years when the British army returned to the region to complete the task previously assigned to General Moore. Wellesley took an army of 20,000 and had his first victory at Talavera that same year, for which he was awarded the title Viscount Wellington. He had crossed the border from Portugal into Spain on 2 July 1809, eventually to join forces with the Spanish armies of General Cuesta and General Venegas in an attack on the French in Madrid under Joseph Bonaparte, a successful beginning to what became a difficult, intense and grinding four-year campaign. The Black Watch were represented in the early part of the campaign by members of the 2nd Battalion, who were subsequently joined by the 1st Battalion when they returned to the fray in the early summer of 1812 after their long period of convalescence.

At that point the two battalions merged in readiness for the major battles that lay ahead as Wellington's army increased to 58,000 British, Portuguese and Spanish troops, still well short of the estimated 168,000 available to the opposition. In the winter of 1811 and spring of 1812, the two great fortresses of Ciudad Rodrigo and Badajoz were captured. The latter, only four miles from the frontier with Portugal, was a key to the success of whichever force had acquired its shelter. The French had held it for many months, and then it was Wellington's turn. His assault in April 1812 went into history, and Napier's definitive *History of the Peninsular War (Vol. IV)* named it as one of the great feats of the British army.

Wellington laid siege to the fortress from 16 March to 6 April, when he launched a large-scale assault to breach the walls and storm the defences. The main assault failed, with the loss of 2,000 men, but one of two diversionary attacks succeeded in scaling the walls, and the following day the defenders surrendered. In all, Wellington's army suffered 5,000 casualties in attempting to break the siege, and in the aftermath there was some unfortunate revenge-taking and looting of the town by troops of the allied army. It took three days for officers to restore order and brought a bitter response from Wellington, describing the men as a 'rabble' whose ringleaders were punished.

Using the captured fortresses as bases, Wellington moved off to win a brilliant victory at Salamanca, in which the Black Watch had only a limited involvement. But it was the most important victory so far in the Peninsular campaign, clearing the way for an advance to Madrid, where the Spanish awarded him the keys of their city and the British awarded him a dukedom and £100,000. With the capital secure, Wellington left Madrid on 1 September, marching northwards with the enemy withdrawing as he advanced. At the city of Burgos, 220 miles from Madrid, a stubborn garrison of 3,500 men had been left in defence at an elevated ruined castle, blocking Wellington's path. The defenders had orders to keep him detained until a French army of around 80,000 arrived. The castle proved to be a tough nut to crack, and a scheme was devised to attack the fortress utilising Portuguese troops and the Black Watch, which, incidentally, had volunteered en masse to provide covering fire and erect the ladders to storm the walls. Subaltern Donald MacKenzie, who had almost died from fever and dysentery just a month earlier, had come back to join his unit and was among those who were to take part in the assault:

Orders were received that the 42nd, with the light companies and a brigade of Portuguese, were to attack and storm the horn-work at 8 o'clock in the evening. The whole moved up the hill at 7: one Captain, two Subalterns and 100 volunteers were the storming party for the right angle, the same for the left, with the remainder of the regiment to attack the centre supported by the Portuguese so as to withdraw the enemy's attention from the storming parties. I was one of the subalterns with the leading party for the right. The men carried seven ladders. The evening was clear, but our prospects were gloomy, for we were going to attack walls and ditches whose strength could not be ascertained. Yet the brave soldiers were as steady and composed as on parade, although they must have felt that few were ever likely to return. When the signal gun for the attack was fired, we advanced, and had tolerable shelter till within forty yards of the ditch. Here we halted for a minute, formed into proper line, and, with a cheer, rushed forward. The enemy, who had their walls thickly manned, fired, killing or wounding half the party; amongst the former was my companion Lieut. Gregerson. I had him by the hand when we cheered and the next moment I was bespattered with his blood, although I did not know he was killed until I looked back from the ladder I was mounting and saw him lying back. Four of the seven ladders were rendered useless by the first fire, and the others proved too short. I sprang into the ditch, the men following, and I directed them only to fire when they could see anyone above, for the defenders could not fire to purpose without showing their bodies over the wall, and in this way exposing themselves. Captain Menzies who was in command [of my party] had got his leg broken by a stray shot, just as we advanced. We got within the horn-work, but we could never have done so had not the attention of the besieged been partially withdrawn and occupied by the attack on the centre.

Unfortunately, that was as far as they got. Defending fire was so great that the troops were pulled back. The 42nd spent five weeks at the castle, digging trenches under heavy fire from the defenders and making five further attempts to scale the walls. Two of the three British heavy guns brought to the scene were put out of action, and ammunition was so scarce that nine pence were paid for each ball found and brought to the artillery. It was all to no avail. The main area of fortification remained impenetrable, and by the middle of October the French army of 80,000 under Marshal Soult – the same commander who chased General Moore to Corunna – was now just days away. Wellington had no alternative but to lift the siege and call a withdrawal to winter quarters. Losses sustained by the 42nd in the assault on the castle and subsequently around it were heavier than those in any other unit: three officers, two sergeants, and 44 rank and file killed, and six officers, 11 sergeants, one drummer and 230 rank and file wounded. Donald MacKenzie continued:

On leaving Burgos, which we did after dark on 21 October, without being observed, the greatest silence being enjoined, and having the Artillery wheels muffled with straw, we had twelve hours' start of our pursuers. But the French being strong in cavalry were bold and pushed our rearguard much, and there was hardly an hour without severe skirmishing. About the third day of our retreat, and after a march of eighteen hours, we crossed the river when pitch dark, at Torquemada, and bivouaced in the greatest confusion. To increase it, some soldiers had stumbled on the well-stocked wine vaults of the town, and we found them in the morning in such a disorderly and disorganised condition as cannot be described: it is said that 10,000 to 12,000 men were in a state of helpless inebriety.

We could not move till 4 o'clock next day and, even then, 400 had to be left behind incapable. Had the French known and attacked us, we could have made no stand. Some days afterwards a flag of truce was brought in [by the French] with some women who had got drunk and fallen behind. They were awful-looking wretches, some half drunk still. We continued retreating, fighting as we retired, and blowing up all bridges to retard our pursuers. On 15 November we crossed the Tormes, where the two armies were in full view of each other, but Wellington, calculating his opponents too strong for him, continued to fall back on Portugal. At this time the weather was dreadful. Rain fell in torrents; the roads were knee deep with mud; men, women, children and horses were lying about dead or powerless. For four days we had scarcely a bite of meat, or a place to rest in except the branch of a tree. During this time I lost three animals and all my baggage; the poor animals stuck in the mud from want of nourishment, and had to be left to their fate. When the enemy had pushed us a day's march of Ciudad Rodrigo, he halted, which gave us time to pass the river Aguada, and we bivouaced between Ciudad and Alamda.

Next day, we entered cantonments on the Coa. The hut I and the other officers got contained only one apartment, in which apparently the family formerly resident had occupied. But it contained now no trace of furniture. There was no bed, and the place was covered with dirt and smoke. Our previous privations, however, reconciled us even to this, and we felt thankful at the idea of having any shelter for the winter. But even this poor consolation was denied us, as, after but four days' occupation, we received a sudden order to march towards the centre of Portugal . . . [to] our winter quarters, by no means elegant or comfortable. Yet the spirit of contentment came to our aid, and we were glad that our toils were over for a time, although sad to think that the campaign, which some months before had begun so gloriously, should have ended so disastrously.

In six months the 42nd had been reduced from 1,200 to 300

fighting men, and had difficulty ever afterwards of mustering above 500. Fatigue and bad feeding caused fever and dysentery, carrying off the men by the score, these diseases being far more deadly than the most bloody encounters with the enemy. Our privations were on many occasions beyond description. I will give some idea of the mortality of the Army when I mention that the 1st Battalion of the Guards which joined from England in October, 1,200 strong, buried 700 men in their quarters during the winter and spring.

Over the winter, Wellington's army, which had now been in the field for four years, finally received some of the essentials the commander had been begging for, including stores, ammunition, hospitals and tents (of which there had been a particular shortage). Equipped and refreshed, the army prepared to re-enter the conflict and moved out of their winter quarters at the end of April 1813, marching in two columns, with the Black Watch leading the 6th Division towards the French positions, with Pamplona as their first target ahead of the Pyrenees and on into France.

Soult's army was taken completely by surprise as Wellington's pincer movement surrounded the enemy's position. It was the beginning of a rout that continued as the French retreated. Of an estimated 30,000 French troops who faced successive battles, more than 9,000 were killed or wounded and hundreds threw down their arms and fled. With little over half able to join the order to retire, Soult's army was, for the time being at least, a broken force, and Wellington had no difficulty in securing Pamplona, enabling him to begin the long trek across the Pyrenees and into France in pursuit of Soult. The French commander was heading for Toulouse, which was defended by an ancient wall, flanked with towers. It was a difficult city to attack, and Wellington knew it. Three sides were surrounded by the great canal of Languedoc and by the Garonne, while the remaining approach was flanked by hills that carried the main road into the city.

By the time Wellington arrived, Soult had received reinforcements and had erected a mass of defences linked by trenches. Bridges on approaches to the city had been destroyed, and the whole of Soult's army was spread behind these extensive fortifications as he prepared for what he knew would be a final stand. Given the natural impediments to taking the city, Wellington had no alternative but to make a frontal attack by stretching pontoons across the river over which his entire attacking divisions would cross. What followed on the morning of 10 April 1814, and the role of the Highlanders in the efforts to capture the city, can be no better summarised than these words by John Malcolm, of the 42nd, in his 1822 book *Reminiscences of a Campaign in the Pyrenees*:

Major-General Pack, who commanded our brigade, came up, and calling its officers and non-commissioned officers round him, addressed them to the following effect: 'We are this day to attack the enemy; your business will be to take possession of those fortified heights, which you see towards the front. I have only to warn you to be prepared to form close columns in case of a charge of cavalry, to restrain the impetuosity of the men, and to prevent them from wasting their ammunition.' The drums then beat to arms, and we received orders to move towards the enemy's position. Our division [the 6th] approached the foot of the ridge of heights on the enemy's right and moved in a direction parallel to them, until we reached the point of attack. We advanced under a heavy cannonade, and arrived in front of a redoubt, where we were formed in two lines. Darkening the whole hill, flanked by clouds of cavalry, and covered by the fire of their redoubt, the enemy came down upon us like a torrent. Their generals and field-officers riding in front, and waving their hats amidst shouts of the multitude, resembled the roar of an ocean. Our Highlanders, as if actuated by one instinctive impulse, took off their bonnets, and waving them in the air, returned their greeting with three cheers.

A death-like silence ensued for some moments, and we could observe a visible pause in the advance of the enemy. At that moment the light company of the 42nd Regiment, by

108

a well-directed fire, brought down some of the French officers of distinction, as they rode in front of their respective corps. The enemy immediately fired a volley into our lines, and advanced upon us amidst a deafening roar of musketry and artillery. Our troops answered their fire only once, and unappalled by their furious onset, advanced up the hill, and met them at the charge. Upon reaching the summit of the ridge of heights, the redoubt, which had covered their advance, fell into our possession, but they still retained four others, and into which they had retired.

Meantime, our troops were drawn up along a road, which passed over the hill, and which having a high bank at each side, protected us in some measure from the general fire of their last line of redoubts . . . Major-General Pack rode up in front of our brigade, and made the following announcement: 'I have just now been with General Clinton, and he has been pleased to grant my request, that in the charge which we are now to make upon the enemy's redoubts, the 42nd Regiment shall have the honour of leading on the attack.'

We immediately began to form for the charge upon the redoubts, which were about two or three hundred yards distant, and to which we had to pass over some ploughed fields. The grenadiers of the 42nd, followed by the other companies, led the way . . . but no sooner were the feathers of their bonnets seen rising over the embankment, than such a tremendous fire was opened from the redoubts and entrenchments, as in a very short time would have annihilated them. The right wing, therefore, hastily formed into line, and without waiting for the left wing of the regiment, which was ascending by companies from the road, rushed upon the batteries, which vomited forth a most furious and terrific storm of fire, grape-shot and musketry. The redoubts were erected along the side of a road, and defended by broad ditches filled with water. Just before our troops reached the obstruction, however, the enemy deserted them and fled in all directions, leaving their last line of strongholds in our possession, but they still possessed two fortified houses close by, from which they kept up a galling and destructive fire. Out of about 500 men that the 42nd brought into action, scarcely 90 reached the fatal redoubt from which the enemy had fled.

Forward we drove, in the face of apparent destruction. The field had been lately rough ploughed or under fallow, and when a man fell he tripped the one behind, thus the ranks were opening as we approached the point whence all this hostile vengeance proceeded . . . In a minute every obstacle was surmounted; the enemy fled as we leaped over the trenches and mounds like a pack of noisy hounds in pursuit, frightening them more by our wild hurrahs than actually hurting them by ball or bayonet. [By then] two officers [Captain Campbell and Lieutenant Young] and about 60 of inferior rank were all that now remained without a wound of the right wing of the regiment that entered the field in the morning. The flag was hanging in tatters stained with the blood of those who had fallen over it. The standard, cut in two, had been successively placed in the hands of three officers, who fell as we advanced; it was now borne by a sergeant, while the few remaining soldiers who rallied around it, defiled with mire . . . stood ready to oppose with the bayonet the advancing column, the front files of which were pouring in destructive showers of musketry. To have disputed the post with such over-whelming numbers would have been hazarding the loss of our colours, and could serve no general interest to our army, as we stood between the front of our advancing support and the enemy; we were therefore ordered to retire.

As soon as the smoke began to clear, the enemy made a last attempt to retake their redoubts, but they were repulsed a second time, leaving the battlefield littered with dead and wounded. Soult evacuated Toulouse the same evening, well aware that he had insufficient stores to sustain his army and the 60,000 inhabitants in a siege. Wellington allowed him to retire without further attacks. The losses of the 42nd in the battle of Toulouse amounted to four officers, three sergeants and 47 rank and file killed, and 21 officers, 14 sergeants, one drummer and 231 rank and file wounded. Wellington rode into Toulouse the following morning and was warmly welcomed by the residents, who were well aware that they had escaped the horrors of an artillery bombardment. That same day, news reached Toulouse of the abdication and exile of Napoleon and the restoration of Louis XVIII.

The hostilities ceased and the British troops prepared to return to Britain. The Black Watch were destined for Ireland, where the survivors of the 1st Battalion were joined by the remainder of the 2nd, which had been disbanded at Aberdeen in October 1814.

CHAPTER SEVEN

Praise from Wellington

Ireland provided only a brief respite from the wars in Continental Europe, and new orders barely gave the Black Watch the time to take delivery of new boots and clothes before they were called to arms once more. Napoleon was back in business. On 1 March 1815 he landed at Cannes with a detachment of his personal guard that had been assigned to him in exile and gathered a fresh army about him as he crossed the Alps. At Grenoble he was joined by soldiers sent to arrest him, and by 20 March he had reached Paris to snatch power again. The British immediately began shipping troops to Flanders yet again to meet the threat of renewed campaigning by the French, joined by the armies of other European nations, massing on the French border. Wellington, summoned to take the helm, assembled his troops at Brussels, where, in fact, the 42nd Regiment was already well known and recognised by residents. They were, according to one account:

> . . . on such terms of friendly intercourse with the inhabitants in whose houses they were quartered that it was no uncommon thing to see a Highland soldier taking care of the children, and even keeping the shop of his host, an instance of confidence

perhaps unexampled. The 42nd and 92nd Highland Regiments were first to muster . . . About four o'clock in the morning of 16 June [they] marched through the Place Royale and the Parc. One could not but admire their fine appearance; their firm, collected, steady, military demeanour, as they went rejoicing to battle, with their bagpipes playing before them, and the beams of the rising sun shining upon their glittering arms . . . The kind and generous inhabitants assembled in crowds to witness the departure of their gallant friends, and as the Highlanders marched onward with a steady and collected air, the people breathed many a fervent expression for their safety.

The safety of Brussels was one of Wellington's key objectives, i.e. to save the city, and his own army, from attack expected from a westerly direction through Mons. The second of his priorities was to support the Prussian army at Ligny, thirty miles in almost the opposite direction. In fact, Napoleon had carefully devised a plan to attack both centres at the same time, advancing not from Mons but through Charleroi, where the road forked left to Quatre Bras, Waterloo and Brussels and right to Ligny. When news of these movements came in, Wellington famously retorted, 'He's humbugged me!' Vital to the whole scheme of things, as it transpired, was control of the crossroads at Quatre Bras, where Wellington had placed only a guard of 7,000. There were now 20,000 French troops advancing towards that very spot, while another 80,000 men were marching to begin battle with the Prussians. The 42nd joined the 1st, 44th and 92nd Regiments in a brigade under Sir Denis Pack, who was unaware that the original intelligence on Napoleon's movements was faulty. The brigade was almost leisurely in their approach, marching through a forest towards the business of the day, passing through Waterloo, the bright fields of Wellington's later fame, and on towards Quatre Bras. The account of Sergeant James Anton reveals what happened next:

A luxuriant crop of grain hid from our view the contending skirmishers beyond, and presented a considerable obstacle to our advance. We were in the act of lying down by the side of the road, in our usual careless manner, as we were wont when enjoying a rest on the line of march, some throwing back their heads on their knapsacks, intending to take a sleep, when General Pack came galloping up, and chid the colonel for not having the bayonets fixed. This roused our attention. Our pieces were loaded, and perhaps never did a regiment in the field seem so short taken. We had the name of a crack corps, but certainly it was not then in that state of discipline which it could justly boast of a few years afterwards. Yet . . . none could be animated with a fitter feeling for the work before us than prevailed at that moment. We were all ready and in line. 'Forward!' was the word of command, and forward we hastened, though we saw no enemy in front. The stalks of the rye, like the reeds that grow on the margin of some swamp, opposed our advance; the tops were up to our bonnets, and we strode and groped our way through as fast as we could. By the time we reached a field of clover on the other side, we were very much straggled; however, we united in line as time and our speedy advance would permit. The Belgic skirmishers retired through our ranks, and in an instant we were on their victorious pursuers. Our sudden appearance seemed to paralyse their advance. The singular appearance of our dress, combined no doubt with our sudden debut, tended to stagger their resolution: we were on them, our pieces were loaded, and our bayonets glittered . . . Those who had so proudly driven the Belgians before them, turned now to fly, whilst our loud cheers made the fields echo to our wild hurrahs. France fled or fell before us, and we thought the field our own.

We had not yet lost a man . . . [and] we drove on so fast that we almost appeared like a mob following the rout of some defeated faction. Marshal Ney, who commanded the enemy, observed our wild unguarded zeal, and ordered a regiment of lancers to bear down upon us. We saw their approach at a distance, as they issued from a wood, and took them for Brunswickers coming to cut up the flying infantry . . . We stood with too much confidence, gazing towards them as if they had been our friends . . . making no preparative movement to receive them as enemies, further than the reloading of the muskets, until a German orderly dragoon galloped up, exclaiming, 'Franchee! Franchee!', and, wheeling about, galloped off. We instantly formed a rallying square. Every man's piece was loaded, and our enemies approached at full charge; the feet of their horses seemed to tear up the ground. Our skirmishers having been impressed with the same opinion, that these were Brunswick cavalry, fell beneath their lances, and few escaped death or wounds. Our brave colonel fell at this time, pierced through the chin until the point of the lance reached the brain. Captain Menzies fell, covered with wounds, and a momentary conflict took place over him. He was a powerful man, and, hand to hand, more than a match for six ordinary men. The grenadiers, whom he commanded, pressed round to save or avenge him, but fell beneath the enemy's lances.

Colonel Dick assumed the command on the fall of Sir Robert Macara, and was severely wounded. Brevet-Major Davidson succeeded, and was mortally wounded; to him succeeded Brevet-Major Campbell. Thus, in a few minutes we had been placed under four different commanding officers. An attempt was now made to form us in line; for we stood mixed in one irregular mass, grenadier, light and battalion companies, such is the inevitable consequence of a rapid succession of commanders. We now formed a line on the left of the grenadiers, while the [enemy] cavalry were cutting through the ranks of the 69th Regiment. Meantime the other regiments, to our right and left, suffered no less than we; the superiority of the enemy in cavalry afforded him a decided advantage on the open plain, for our British cavalry and artillery had not yet reached the field.

A line of French infantry now appeared ahead, waiting for the cavalry to complete the mission. General Pack ordered the men to form a square to oppose, the traditional manoeuvre under such circumstances, but this time with a difference. A number of the French were actually trapped inside it, although many were wounded and remained unmolested. Outside the square, the battle raged again and again. Anton went on:

A moment's pause ensued . . . the pause of death. General Pack was on the right angle of the front face of the square, and he lifted his hat towards the [opposing] French officer as he was wont to do when returning a salute . . . but when the general raised his hat, it served as a signal, though not a pre-concerted one, [and] a most destructive fire was opened. Riders [of the enemy cavalry] in heavy armour fell tumbling from their horses; the horses reared, plunged and fell on the dismounted riders; steel helmets and cuirasses rang against unsheathed sabres, as they fell to the ground; shrieks and groans of men, the neighing of horses and the discharge of musketry rent the air, as men and horses mixed together in one heap of indiscriminate slaughter. Those who were able to fly, fled towards a wood on our right, whence they had issued to the attack, and which seemed to afford an extensive cover to an immense reserve not yet brought into action. Once more clear of those formidable and daring assailants, we formed a line, examined our ammunition boxes and found them getting empty. Our officer commanding pointed towards the pouches of our dead and dying comrades, and from them a sufficient supply was obtained [to continue]. The enemy were at no great distance, and, I may add, firing very actively upon us. Our position being without any cover from the fire of the enemy, we were commanded to retire to the nearby farm, where we took up our bivouac on the field for the night.

Six privates fell into the enemy's hands; among these was a little lad [Smith Fyfe] about five feet high. The French general on seeing this diminutive-looking lad is said to have lifted him up by the collar or breech and exclaimed to the soldiers who were near him, 'Behold the sample of the men of whom you seem afraid!' This lad returned a few days afterwards, dressed

117

in the clothing of a French grenadier, and was saluted by the name of Napoleon, which he retained until he was discharged. The night passed off in silence. Round us lay the dying and the dead, the latter not yet interred, and many of the former, wishing to breathe their last where they fell, slept to death . . .

The losses sustained by the Highlanders that day included Lieutenant-Colonel Sir Robert Macara, two other officers, three sergeants and forty-eight rank and file. The wounded taken from the field numbered 243. Behind them, they left Ney's light cavalry decimated in this incredible feat in which so many had been trapped inside the Highlanders' square, as well as those who had fallen to the frontal assault. Sergeant Anton makes the point regularly that the 42nd was one element in the battle, and it is worth reminding ourselves again as we travel through this account that, while focusing on the activities of the Black Watch, they were always part of an overall force which prevailed. That said, although there were more than forty-six British army regiments engaged overall in the battles around Waterloo, only a small proportion were being used at any one time, until the climax. It can be seen, however, that the 42nd were now being used repeatedly in particular pre-battle missions, in the mode of modern-day Special Forces, and in the lead infantry role of so many of the most vital battles. As we have seen, this often entailed a fairly high casualty rate, given the Highlanders' preponderance for the cut and thrust of close-quarters battle.

The Battle of Waterloo, for which the Quatre Bras fight was a prelude, was certainly another case in point. Through their involvement in the heavy fighting for vital positions at the outset, which undoubtedly aided Wellington's overall position, they were kept back from the main battle, much to their own disgust, purely because of their reduced numbers. Eventually, their impatience for action was heard and they joined the fighting in the latter stages. Consequently, they had only five men killed and forty-five wounded at Waterloo itself. However, the Duke of Wellington in his public dispatches concerning Quatre Bras and Waterloo paid them the particular honour (for such it was in the circumstances) of a compliment: 'Among other regiments, I must particularly mention the 28th, 42nd, 79th and 92nd, and the battalion of Hanoverians.'

Sergeant Anton, still in the fight, provided a more colourful commentary from his own perspective, which became especially interesting with the arrival on the scene overnight of Napoleon himself, to go head to head with Wellington; thus it became a very personal affair. Anton wrote:

Napoleon's presence gave an éclat to their busy preparations . . . and now, on our right, [he] urged on his heavy columns, while a like movement was made against our left. The guns opened their war-breathing mouths in thundering peals, and all along the ridge of Mount St-Jean arose one dense cloud of smoke. France now pushed forward on the line of our Belgic allies, drove them from their post, and rolled them in one promiscuous mass of confusion through the ranks of our brigade, which instantly advanced to repel the pursuers. We might have forced ourselves through as the Belgians had done, but our bare thighs had no protection from the piercing thorns and, doubtless, those runaways had more wisdom in shunning death, though at the hazard of laceration, than we would have shown in rushing forward upon it in disorder, with self-inflicted torture. The foe beheld our front and paused; a sudden terror seized his flushed ranks. We were in the act of breaking through the hedge, when our general gave orders to open our ranks. In an instant our cavalry passed through, leaped both hedges, and plunged on the panic-stricken foe. 'Scotland for ever!' bursts from the mouth of each Highlander, as the Scots Greys pass through our ranks. What pen can describe the scene? Horses' hooves sinking in men's breasts, breaking bones, riders' swords streaming in blood, waving over their heads and descending in deadly vengeance. Stroke follows stroke, like the turning of a flail in the hands of a dexterous thresher . . . there the piercing shrieks and dying groans; here the loud cheering of an exulting army, animating the slayers to deeds of signal vengeance upon a daring foe. Such is the music of the field! The guns cease their thundering peals; the infantry gaze in silent wonder at the indiscriminate work of slaughter before them, till, flushed with victory and bathed in blood, the victors drive beyond the bounds of well-timed support, and their bravest lie stretched on those whom their swords have laid low. A thousand prisoners are driven in before our cavalry as they return over the corpse-strewn field. Meanwhile, our heavy dragoons bore down all opposition on the left . . . [and so] a never-ceasing combat rages throughout the day.

The defeat of Napoleon finally ended this long-drawn-out series of wars between France and the rest of Europe, in which the Black Watch can be seen to have played a consistently significant role at heavy cost. Figures entered into the regiment's history at the end of the Battle of Waterloo were, however, especially interesting in that they were shown to demonstrate that the Highlanders' courage and speed at going forward in battle actually had the effect of reducing rather than increasing the mortality rate of their troops, and considerably more died from sickness than battle wounds. The figures show that in the 76 years since its inception, 8,792 men had passed through the 1st Battalion of the 42nd Royal Highland Regiment, excluding those of the 2nd Battalion formed during the North American wars (1780), or the conscripted 2nd Battalion formed in 1803. The casualty roll was as follows: 36 officers and 816 other ranks were killed in action, and 133 officers and 2,413 other ranks were wounded in action. But the toll for deaths from wounds, sickness and various other causes is immensely higher: 3,410 deaths were recorded, and this excluded those who were discharged or volunteered into other regiments when the 42nd left America in 1787. A further 138 were unaccounted for, having been left sick or as prisoners in enemy countries.

After Waterloo, a very much under-strength 1st Battalion of 530 battle-ready men was withdrawn on 24 June 1815. At first glance the figures seem to demonstrate that the Highlanders' modus operandi was a high-risk strategy. Yet to put these figures into proper perspective, we must add in the fact that forty-five of the regiment's seventy-six years so far were spent in active warfare. Military analysts at the time of the production of these figures saw the number killed in action as 'trifling loss' compared with that in other regiments, and a figure that would also appear extraordinary to the enemy. As Cannon recorded, the smallness of that loss 'can only be accounted for by the determined bravery and firmness of the men, it being now the opinion that troops who act vigorously augur less than those who are slow and cautious in their operations'.

From Waterloo, the regiment moved with British forces to the outskirts of Paris until Napoleon's future had been decided and the European nations were satisfied that the threat of further French ambitions towards their neighbours was no longer viable. Then, in the second week of December 1815, they marched to Calais to embark for England, arriving at Ramsgate on 19 December. The regiment began a leisurely march north to Scotland, and en route discovered that the fame of their exploits was widespread. Although many years had passed since they had made a similar journey, they were received with enthusiasm and quite lavish hospitality.

At Cambridge, the bells welcomed the Highlanders as they approached, and at an official banquet the 'table smoked with savoury viands', every cellar contributing a liberal supply of liquid refreshment. The same occurred in many towns as they progressed north, and in some cases monetary collections had been made to provide donations to the men equal to two days' pay. By far the greatest welcome was at Edinburgh, where a military band and a guard of cavalry were waiting to lead them into the city amid thousands of cheering crowds, according to one contemporary report:

> . . . while over their heads, from a thousand windows, waved as many banners, plaided scarves, or other symbols of courtly greetings. The road from Musselburgh, a distance of six miles,

was filled with relations and friends, and so great was the crowd that it was after four o'clock before they arrived at the Castle Hill, although they passed through Portobello about two o'clock. It was almost impossible for these gallant men to go through the people, particularly in the city. All the bells were rung, and they were everywhere received with the loudest acclamations.

If a rest was in order, none was immediately forthcoming, although the duties for many years hence would certainly be far less life-threatening than in recent times. The regiment were subsequently posted back to Ireland and, according to one account of the time, engaged in 'the harassing duties to which the troops were exposed during the disturbed state of the country, and its conduct procured the unqualified approbation of the general officers under whom it served and the respect of the natives among whom they sojourned'. The island was in deep trouble, politically, socially and financially. In the aftermath of the Napoleonic Wars, an immediate and dramatic economic slump took hold and lasted for almost two decades. It was accompanied by a series of natural catastrophes. Bad weather destroyed grain and potato crops, and smallpox and typhus killed over 50,000 people. The potato crop failed again in Munster in 1821, and people starved to death in Cork and Clare. The regiment arrived as the first potato famine took hold, and the men clearly were among the few to show a measure of compassion while dispensing their duties under the British Crown.

Black Watch Sergeant John Wheatley (later to become lieutenant-colonel) left a fascinating insight into the regiment's operations as they travelled the country:

The 42nd, which were quartered at Rathkeale, were joined in these duties by the 79th and 93rd, the former quartered at Limerick, and the latter at Ennis, County Clare. All three regiments were highly and deservedly popular with the inhabitants. Detachments were posted all over the country in every village

The Black Watch at the Battle of Corunna, where exhausted troops were finally rallied to beat Napoleon's army. [Bridgeman Art Library]

The earliest photograph of the 42nd Highlanders, dating to 1852. The scene, captured in The Citadel, Halifax, Nova Scotia, shows Colour-Sergeant Alexander McGregor who has just handed orders for return to Scotland to Company Commander Captain Henry Drummond, of the regiment's Light Company.

Iraq 2004: The Black Watch on patrol during their deployment to Camp Dogwood in December 2004 to assist American forces in their campaign against insurgents and suicide bombers.

Three of the men judged to be ringleaders of the deserters who feared they were being sent to desolate, disease-ridden lands far away. *From left to right*: Private Farquhar Shaw, Corporal Malcolm MacPherson and Corporal Samuel MacPherson. All three were shot by firing squad on 18 July 1743.

After taking part in the suppression of the Indian Mutiny in which soldiers of the regiment won a total of eight Victoria Crosses, the regiment was based in the country from 1859 to 1897. This photograph demonstrates the various orders of dress applicable at the time.

A group of Black Watch heroes, photographed by command of Queen Victoria in 1856: Piper Muir, Privates Glen and Mackenzie, and Colour-Sergeant Gardner. The latter was among the recipients of the VC two years later during the Indian Mutiny.

Almost genteel, sergeants of the 2nd Battalion stop for tea on the Khyber Pass, 1906.

The formation of a square was a long-established practice to meet the oncoming assault of cavalry. In the Sudan, similar tactics were used to face the onslaught of the Mahdi's fanatical tribesmen, and the Black Watch wore pith helmets rather than the feather bonnets worn in this photograph.

The Black Watch battalions in the Boer War were well applauded but for the men it was a long, harsh campaign, endless marching over long distances seeking a fleet-footed enemy.

Living conditions for the 2nd Battalion in the Boer campaign were Spartan – nothing new in that for the older campaigners – here demonstrated by this detachment camp with makeshift cookhouse.

As far as the eye can see: a church parade of the 2nd Battalion, who were posted to Cherat, India, immediately on completion of the Boer campaign.

Typical attire of the men posted to France at the beginning of the First World War. Regimental Sergeant-Major J. C. 'Punch' Wilson, MC, 6th Battalion, in front of his dug-out at Fauquissart, 1915.

Dress standards were maintained as far as was possible in the horrors of the trenches, but this peaceful scene was barely representative of the appalling conditions and horrendous artillery onslaught.

New orders of dress to meet diverse conditions abroad, such as Palestine in the 1930s, brought variations of kilt and trews: a range which covered full dress, winter and summer for the Pipes and Drums; and Drill order for summer, winter (dry), winter trews and winter (wet).

New colours were presented to the 4/5th Battalions by the then Duchess of York at Glamis Castle, her childhood home, in 1935. Two years later she succeeded her late father-in-law King George V as Colonel-in-Chief of the regiment, a role she performed with enthusiasm until her death. She was succeeded as Colonel-in-Chief by Prince Charles.

War clouds again, and the Black Watch TA units are expanded – here the 6/7th Perthshire and Fife practise their drill of firing at low-flying aircraft. The regiment went on to fight in virtually every theatre.

Forced to retreat from Crete, the 2nd Battalion prepare for a stand-off with the Vichy French in Syria.

Tobruk, 20 November 1941. The 2nd Battalion, dug in to secure their position, took murderous machine-gun fire and all too few reached their objective.

Into an unwelcoming landscape for the Battle of El Alamein, men of the 1st, 5th and 7th Battalions arrive as part of the re-formed 51st Highland Division which had gone into captivity in France.

or hamlet, where a house could be hired to hold from twelve to thirty men. But little could be done towards putting the Whiteboys[2] down, as the only offence against the law was being caught in arms. But as soon as the Parliament met, the Insurrection Act was hurried through both houses and became law on the night of 28 February 1822. By the Act, transportation for seven years was the punishment awarded to anyone found out of his dwelling-place any time between one hour after sunset and sunrise. It was harassing duty patrolling over the country, sometimes all night, calling the rolls, and apprehending such as had been found absent on former occasions.

The law was carried out by what was called a Bench of Magistrates, two or more, with a Sergeant-at-Law as president. All field officers and captains were magistrates, and seven years' transportation was the only sentence the bench could give; the prisoner had either to be let off with an admonition or transported. When the prisoner was brought in, evidence was simply taken that he was found out of his dwelling-place at an unlawful hour, or that he was absent from his habitation on such a night when the roll was called. The local magistrates knew the character he bore, a few minutes' consultation was held, when sentence was given, and an escort being already at the courthouse door, the prisoner was handcuffed and put on a cart. The words were given 'with cartridge prime and load, quick march', and off to the Cove of Cork, where a ship was at anchor to receive them. This summary procedure soon put an end to the nightly depredations which had kept the country in terror and alarm for months previous.

---

[2] The Whiteboys, an illegal organisation, first came into being in about 1760. Its inception was due to the indignation caused by the action of landowners in enclosing common lands previously reserved for grazing by the country-people's animals. Its activities were mainly concentrated on razing the fences erected by the landowners. Through the years, the movement gradually lost its impetus until, by the nineteenth century, it was at least quiescent in most districts.

The convicted were at once sent off to Sydney Botany Bay at this time.

Here is one instance of how the Act was put in force. Every road leading out of Rathkeale had a guard or outpost to prevent a surprise, and near to the Askeaton-road guard lived a character known as 'the red-haired man', a noted Whiteboy who had taken care of himself from the passing of the Insurrection Act, although still a leader and director of their doings. His house was close to the guard, and there were special orders to watch him, and at uncertain hours to visit the house, to find him absent, if possible. On an evening in June, the sentry called to the sergeant of the guard that 'the red-haired man, half an hour back, had gone into a house where he was still'. The sergeant walked about, the retreat beat, and watch in hand he kept his lookout; one hour after sunset the red-haired man came out without his hat, and laughing heartily. He was taken prisoner, and next day was on his way to the Cove of Cork.

Wheatley reckoned that pages could be filled with anecdotes connected with the doings of the several portions of the regiment in their various quarters, and he related what was clearly one of his favourite stories while serving in Ireland:

The major commanding at Shanagolden, while standing on the street on a fair day, was thus accosted by a tall, gaunt, wiry man of some sixty years of age. 'Good morning to your honour . . . I've a favour to ask of you, major.'

'Well, Mr Sullivan, what can I do for you?'

'Well, your honour knows that I've been a loyal man, that during them disturbed times I always advised the boys to give up the foolish nightwork; that I've caused a great many arms to be given up to yourself, major, but . . . It's a long time, major, since the boys have had a fight, and all that I want is, that yourself and your men will just keep out of sight, and remain at this end of the town, till me and my boys go up to the fair, and stretch a few of the Whichgeralds [Fitzgeralds, the opposite faction]. We'll not be long about it, just to stretch a dozen or two of them Whichgeralds, and then go home quietly.'

Much to Mr Sullivan's disappointment, the major replied that he could not allow the peace to be broken, and, grievously crestfallen, Mr S went to report the failure of his request to the fine set of young Sullivans who were in sight, waiting the issue of the singular application, and ready to be let loose on the Fitzgeralds. A Mr V—, a local magistrate, who was standing with the major, said that it would tend much to break up the combination of Whiteboyism to let the factions fight among themselves, and that he could not do better than to wink at the Sullivans having a turn with their opponents. But the major would not entertain the idea of having, possibly, half a dozen murders to think of.

Other events related by Wheatley included the case of a young soldier who dropped out of ranks without leave as they marched out of the city of Limerick for Rathkeale. He had apparently stopped to say goodbye to some friends but was found unconscious on the road with a deep cut on the back of his head and his musket stolen. On reaching Rathkeale, he was tried by a court martial held in a square, formed there and then, before the regiment were dismissed. He was sentenced to 300 lashes and had to pay for his musket. About three months afterwards, an officer of the 79th was out shooting snipe near the scene of the young soldier's misfortune. A countryman entered into conversation with the officer, then knocked him over and took his gun. Two dragoons on dispatch duty, bound for Limerick from Rathkeale, saw it; one of them leaped wall after wall and caught the culprit, who was taken before a special commission sitting in Limerick. He was tried the next day and hanged two days later. On the scaffold he confessed that it was he who had knocked over the Highlander and told the priest where the gun was to be found. When it was recovered it was found cut down to make it a 'handy gun'.

The Black Watch left Munster in June 1825 with a letter of

commendation from Lieutenant-General Sir John Lambert on the discipline and conduct of the men during their time there. After three months in Dublin, the regiment were divided into four depot companies, which moved to Scotland, and six service companies, which were bound for garrison duties in Gibraltar, where they remained for some years. The regiment again suffered severely during their time there from an outbreak of fever, and a large number of men fell sick. An officer, six sergeants and fifty-three rank and file subsequently died. For the next six years the regiment were employed on routine garrison work, and John Wheatley's log again provides a brief commentary on the changes that were not necessarily welcomed among the officers and men. For instance, the bugle to replace the drum for barrack duty was introduced in 1828 for a trial. Wheatley reported that 'officers were averse to the newfangled innovations' and in some instances complained that they could not understand the bugle, even for the men's breakfast or dinner, and wished to return to the drum.

However, the innovations, with numerous others, were supported by the commanding officers, and in due course the 42nd fell into line and accepted the changes. While at Gibraltar, in 1830, a regimental library was started, and Wheatley himself was one of the co-founders. It flourished for many years and was a remarkable achievement, given that at the time such institutions were virtually unknown in the army. In fact, such things were discouraged. It began as a hobby by a sergeant-major who collected volumes at book sales. From that, he formed a circulating library, lending books at a certain rate per month. When the arrangement came to the notice of one of the senior officers, it was suggested that a more substantial library should be formed. The men were canvassed to find out how many would be prepared to subscribe six days' pay, to be levied in three monthly instalments, and after the third month to pay a subscription of sixpence a month.

The result was that 224 men voted to subscribe, and within a month the library was formed and a large order for books was placed with a London bookseller. By this purchase, plus donations of books from the officers, the library accumulated 3,000 volumes within a few years, and subscriptions were soon reduced to four pence a month.

The library remained in operation for more than twenty years and was packed up and travelled with the regiment, except on longer journeys. However, just before being ordered to Turkey in 1854, the regimental library was closed and the books were disposed of, on the grounds that government reading rooms and libraries had become widespread. It had also grown to such an extent that packing and carrying a library of such size became a somewhat onerous task.

   As the peace stretched to twenty-five years, the regiment continued their travels to distant parts, and as well as garrison duties in Gibraltar they spent time in Malta, Ireland, Corfu, Bermuda, Cape Breton and Halifax. Indeed, the regiment were devoid of hostilities until the early 1850s, and in almost every place they visited they left with high commendation for their behaviour, as with this example on their departure from Corfu from the high commissioner, Major-General Sir Howard Douglas:

> I assure you that the conduct of the 42nd has given me the highest degree of satisfaction during the time it has been under my orders, and I wish to express to you the deep regret I feel at the departure of this gallant and distinguished corps from the station under my command. The highest professional obligation of a regiment is to act so as to render itself dreaded as well as respected by enemies. This the 42nd has hitherto nobly and effectually done . . . The good terms which so happily subsist between the protector and the protected here have not only been undisturbed, but cemented by your good conduct; and it affords me the greatest pleasure to have heard it declared by the highest authorities here that you take with you the regard, respect and good wishes of this population.

Through this period the Black Watch saw a considerable change in the make-up and type of recruits being taken in as the older Highlanders came to the end of their service. In fact, it was not entirely accurate during this period to class them collectively as Highlanders. With the Highland Clearances heading for their peak of evacuations and emigration, there was equally a like-for-like drop in the percentage of Highlanders coming forward to volunteer for life (although, effectively, that meant fifteen to twenty years' service). Whereas once the regiment was a hundred per cent Highlander in origin, this had fallen to sixty per cent by the turn of the 1800s, and to a mere fifteen per cent by 1850, the lowest ever. This reduction was doubtless due to a combination of events, ranging from the general situation in the Highlands through to the appalling recent losses through illness and general nervousness among potential recruits about the unhealthy nature of being a soldier in the British army. For the time being – and it proved to be a temporary phase – the character and make-up of the regiment had altered immeasurably. Whereas originally recruits came from well-to-do families in an area specifically outlined on the first page of the first chapter of this work, in the late eighteenth century and through the nineteenth there was a quite diverse intake of men from trade and industry backgrounds, from servant to shipwright, cobbler to weaver, the last thrown out of work as machines began to take their place.

There was also a higher percentage of Lowlanders moving in to what was once the sole preserve of the Highlanders, and the originators of the regiment's proud traditions were doubtless turning in their graves. Not least among the complaints would have been the use of the terms 'Jocks', a nickname that came with the Lowlanders and which eventually became the commonplace name for the description of the Black Watch soldiers, and the one that exists in the twenty-first century. The original nickname for the Highlanders had been 'Rories', which undoubtedly had a more forceful ring to it.

One further aspect that helped to dissipate the overall Highland influence on the regiment was that, for first time, country of birth was no longer an issue. Recruits were now taken from England, Wales and Ireland. There were still some Gaelic speakers among them, and the criteria of being strong, fit and taller than average remained the aim of the recruiting sergeants. That was soon to become evident from their performance in the upcoming war when, back in Scotland in April 1853, the regiment were mobilised to proceed at once to

England, eventually reaching Chobham, Surrey, there to join a massive encampment of soldiers from at least a dozen other regiments. The span of thirty-eight years with barely a shot fired in anger was coming to its end.

CHAPTER EIGHT

Crimea, India and Eight VCs

Given the period of inactivity described above, for all but the most senior officers the experience of battle was entirely new. The mobilisation now under way resulted from a threatening situation that would result, ultimately, in the Crimean War. The conflict arose initially from a quarrel between Russian Orthodox monks and French Catholics over precedence at the holy places in Jerusalem and Nazareth. Tsar Nicholas I of Russia demanded the right to protect the Christian shrines in the Holy Land and made his move towards Turkey by crossing the borders of what is today Romania. The Tsar's Black Sea fleet then sank a Turkish flotilla off Sinope, and war became a certainty when Britain, fearful of the Russian domination of Constantinople, announced support for Turkey. The Emperor of France, Napoleon III, eager to show some of the military prowess displayed by his uncle, Napoleon I, made clear his intention to defend French monks in Jerusalem and joined in on the side of the British and Turks. It was an altogether murky background to a very nasty conflict that formally began in March 1854. By the end of the summer the Franco-British expeditionary forces had driven the Russian troops out of the territory they had invaded, and in theory the fighting should have ended there. But the British weren't satisfied.

The Russian naval base at Sebastopol was seen as a direct threat to the future security of the region, and the British began to assemble an allied force to take the port and close off the Russian route into these sensitive territories. The conflict was already progressing through the early stages when the Black Watch were brought to Portsmouth, to sail out on 20 May 1854. The regiment were to provide ten service companies, which embarked in the hired screw ship the *Hydaspes*, consisting of thirty-two officers, forty-five sergeants, twenty drummers and pipers, and 850 rank and file. They travelled first to Malta, where they joined two other regiments, the 79th (Camerons) and 93rd (Sutherland), to form a Highland brigade under the command of Sir Colin Campbell. This brigade, in turn, was to combine with the Brigade of Guards to become the 1st Division of the British Army under the command of Lord Raglan.

The British force consisted of 27,000 men of all arms, while the French fielded around 30,000 and the Turks contributed 7,000 to the total of 63,000 men, with 128 guns. The allied armies landed unopposed at Kalameta Bay, about thirty miles north of Sebastopol, on 14 September 1854. The controversial historian A. W. Kinglake had travelled with the British army at the suggestion of Raglan and subsequently produced eight volumes of his *History of the Crimean War*. He was clearly taken by the arrival of the Highlanders, and wrote somewhat insultingly of the Black Watch:

> The seamen knew that it concerned the health and comfort of the soldiers to be landed dry, so they lifted or handed the men ashore with an almost tender care: yet not without mirth, nay, not without laughter far heard, when, as though they were giant maidens, the tall Highlanders of the 42nd placed their hands in the hands of the sailor, and sprang, by his aid, to the shore, their kilts floating out wide while they leapt.

From their landing beaches the allies marched southwards to invest Sebastopol, and one of Campbell's young staff officers, Captain Sir Arthur Halkett, was none too pleased with the company he was forced to keep. 'Never, if you can help it,' he wrote, 'be brigaded with the Guards.' He complained that, by their seniority, all others had to follow in the wake of the Guards and into the dust clouds they kicked up. It was also apparent that the Guards were not among the healthiest of regiments, based as they were in Kensington, and began to suffer a horrendous daily sickness rate, through dysentery, typhus and cholera. A further difficulty for all soldiers on this march was the fact that all the mules and baggage wagons had been left behind and, quite apart from the discomfort of having to carry their own bags, food and decent water were in short supply. When the 42nd set off for their first objective, they had enough food for only three days, slung on their backs with other necessary items. In an officer's case, the load consisted of nine pounds of salt pork and biscuits, cocoa and sugar, brushes, shell jacket, towel, blanket, greatcoat, claymore, dirk and revolver.

On the way towards Sebastopol, the Highlanders fought their first major battle and collected honours. At the River Alma, the Russians were entrenched in what looked a formidable position. Over the hills along the south side of the river, they had amassed a force of 40,000 men and 100 guns, while the various slopes of the undulating area were guarded by columns. The French and Turks, who formed the right of the allied army, were appointed to attack the left of the Russian position, while the British had to bear the brunt of the attack and take on the enemy at its most powerful points, thus to meet the full force of a murderous response. That section of the Russian force comprised 3,400 cavalry, 24 battalions of infantry and seven batteries of field artillery besides 14 heavy guns, a total of 23,400 men and 86 guns. Kinglake provides a colourful précis of the period of confrontation immediately before the guns opened up and the cavalry charged:

That 20th of September on the Alma was like some remembered day of June in England, for the sun was unclouded, and the soft breeze of the morning had lulled to a breath at noontide, and was creeping faintly along the hills. It was then that in the allied armies there occurred a singular pause of sound – a pause so

133

general as to have been observed and remembered by many in remote parts of the ground, and so marked that its interruption by the mere neighing of an angry horse seized the attention of thousands; and although this strange silence was the mere result of weariness and chance, it seemed to carry a meaning; for it was now that, after near forty years of peace, the great nations of Europe were once more meeting for battle. Even after the sailing of the expedition, the troops had been followed by reports that the war, after all, would be stayed; and the long frequent halts, and the quiet of the armies on the sunny slope, seemed to harmonise with the idea of disbelief in the coming of the long-promised fight. But in the midst of this repose Sir Colin Campbell said to one of his officers, 'This will be a good time for the men to get loose half their cartridges,' and when the command travelled on along the ranks of the Highlanders, it lit up the faces of the men one after another, assuring them that now at length, and after long expectance, they indeed would go into action. They began obeying the order, and with beaming joy, for they came of a warlike race; yet not without emotion of a graver kind – they were young soldiers, new to battle.

Battle commenced at about 1.30 p.m. and lasted a little over two hours. The French attack on the left was, according to Kinglake, a 'comparative failure', and their losses small. The British commanders began their assault with their Light and 2nd Divisions, while other units were crossing the Alma, and after the initial skirmishing the Highlanders and the Guards of the 1st Division began their advance:

This magnificent division, the flower of the British army . . . formed up after crossing the Alma, and although they incurred considerable loss in so doing, they nevertheless moved in most beautiful order, as if on parade. I shall never forget that sight, one felt so proud of them. Lord Raglan had been looking on all this time from some high ground . . . [and] said, 'Look how well the Guards and Highlanders advance!' The three battalions of the

134

Highland Brigade were extended. But the 42nd had found less difficulty than the 93rd in getting through the thick ground and the river, and again the 93rd had found less difficulty than the 79th so, as each regiment had been formed and moved forward with all the speed it could command, the brigade fell naturally into direct echelon of regiments, the 42nd in front. And although this order was occasioned by the nature of the ground traversed and not by design, it was so well suited to the work in hand that Sir Colin Campbell did not for a moment seek to change it. [As] the other battalions of the Highland Brigade were approaching ... the 42nd had already come up. It was ranged in line. The ancient glory of the corps was a treasure now committed to the charge of young soldiers new to battle but Campbell knew them, was sure of their excellence and was sure, too, of Colonel Duncan Cameron, their commanding officer. Before the action had begun, and while his men were still in column, Campbell had spoken to his brigade a few words – words simple and, for the most part, workmanlike, yet touched with the fire of warlike sentiment. 'Now, men, you are going into action. Remember this: whoever is wounded – I don't care what his rank is – whoever is wounded must lie where he falls till the bandsmen come to attend to him. No soldiers must go carrying off wounded men. If any soldier does such a thing, his name shall be stuck up in his parish church. Don't be in a hurry about firing. Your officers will tell you when it is time to open fire. Be steady. Keep silence. Fire low. The army will watch us; make me proud of the Highland Brigade!'

Campbell chose to lead from the front of the Black Watch, but before he had ridden far he could virtually stare the enemy in the face as they reached the crest of the hill where the redcoat soldiers of the Light Division were already taking a hammering. The Highlanders 'seemed to glide up the hill', according to Kinglake, and in a few instants 'their plumes were on the crest'.

Captain Halkett with the 42nd takes up the commentary:

The Light Division we saw in front of us, also in line and advancing slowly, but losing an enormous lot of men. We could see great gaps suddenly in their ranks, which again closed in but leaving little heaps of red-coated men on the ground. The noise of the artillery with the whine of round-shot and grape, the harsh scream of the jagged fragments of shell rushing through the air, made our inaction very tedious. We could see the guns being pointed and aimed at us. Two of them especially the men christened 'Maggie' and 'Jessie'. *Look out for a shot from Jessie. Now Maggie's coming.* The Highland Brigade was immediately formed in 'fours' also and passed through the Light Division. As we passed through, I heard one of them say, 'Let the Scotchmen go on; they don't know what they're going to get.' Again forming a line, we advanced and found ourselves the leading division of the army on the left flank . . . confronted by five columns of Russian infantry. At this moment the 42nd was alone, and closest to us were two columns on the further side of the hollow; the Sousdal and Kazan column; one battalion wore helmets, the others were in forage caps.

We were now advancing firing, and approaching nearer and nearer the great solid mass of Russian infantry who poured in a hot fire, their front rank kneeling. The Russian columns were beginning to waver, and we could see their officers waving their swords and pushing the men into their places. [Russian support columns] were now caught on their right flank by the 93rd coming up [and with] the 79th appearing, the columns faced about and began to retire. Seeing the time had come, Sir Colin lifted his hat; in an instant each man seemed to grasp the situation, fixed bayonets and charged after the retreating Russians. Such a cheer went up from the throats of the three Highland Regiments as never was heard. On arriving at the summit of the ridge, the brigade was halted and formed once more into line. We could see the masses of Russian infantry retreating along the whole line; they several times halted but we kept firing into them.

Kinglake recorded the final minutes of the battle:

Campbell's charger, twice wounded already, but hitherto not much hurt, was now struck by a shot in the heart. Without a stumble or a plunge the horse sank down gently to the earth, and was dead. Campbell took his aide-de-camp's charger but he had not been long in Shadwell's saddle when up came Sir Colin's groom with his second horse. The man, perhaps under some former master, had been used to be charged with the 'second horse' in the hunting field. At all events, here he was; and if Sir Colin was angered by the apparition, he could not deny that it was opportune. When the 93rd had recovered the perfectness of its array, it again moved forward, but at the steady pace imposed upon it by the chief. The 42nd had already resumed its forward movement; it still advanced firing. The turning moment of a fight is a moment of trial for the soul, and not for the body; and it is, therefore, that such courage as men are able to gather from being gross in numbers can be easily outweighed by the warlike virtue of a few. To the stately Black Watch and the hot 93rd with Campbell leading them on, there was vouch-safed that stronger heart for which the brave pious Muscovites had prayed.

Over the souls of the men in the columns there was spread, first the gloom, then the swarm of vain delusions, and at last the sheer horror which might be the work of the Angel of Darkness. The two lines marched straight on. The three columns shook. They were not yet subdued. They were stubborn but every moment the two advancing battalions grew nearer and nearer, and although – dimly masking the scant numbers of the Highlanders – there was still the white curtain of smoke which always rolled on before them, yet, fitfully, and from moment to moment, the signs of them could be traced on the right hand and on the left in a long, shadowy line, and their coming was ceaseless. But moreover, the Highlanders being men of great stature, and in strange garb, their plumes being tall, and the view of them being broken and distorted by the wreaths of the smoke, and there being, too, an ominous silence in their ranks, there were men among the Russians who began to conceive a vague terror – the terror of things unearthly, and some, they say, imagined that they were charged by horsemen strange, silent, monstrous, bestriding giant chargers. Unless help should come from elsewhere, the three columns would have to give way; but help came. From the high ground on our left another heavy column – the column composed of the two right Sousdal battalions – was seen coming down. It moved straight at the flank of the 93rd. This was met by the 79th.

Without a halt . . . it sprang at the flank of the right Sousdal column, and . . . wrapped in the fire thus poured upon its flank, the hapless column could not march, could not live. It broke, and began to fall back in great confusion; and the left Sousdal column being almost at the same time overthrown by the 93rd and the two columns which had engaged the Black Watch being now in full retreat, the spurs of the hill and the winding dale beyond became thronged with the enemy's disordered masses. Then again, they say, there was heard the sorrowful wail that bursts from the heart of the brave Russian infantry when they have to suffer defeat; but this time the wail was the wail of eight battalions and the warlike grief of the soldiery could no longer kindle the fierce intent which, only a little before, had spurred forward the Vladimir column. Hope had fled . . .

There was to be a reminder of the cost. The Black Watch's Captain Halkett mentioned in his memorandum the heaps of redcoats, and after the battle he went into the field to search for a fellow officer who had fallen. With darkness closing in, he spotted a light from a marquee which he assumed was the medical station. In fact, it was the scene of one of the realities of battle: the amputation tent. Looking inside, he saw rows of long trestle tables 'covered crossways with wounded men; the doctors in their shirts with sleeves rolled up above their elbows. Although there was no chloroform, only a few suppressed groans could be heard, and as fast as the legs and arms could be amputated, they were placed outside the tent. There was a heap of these.'

Even so, the losses were not as high as many had anticipated. The achievement of the British 1st Division of Guards and Highlanders in their dispersal of the 12,000 Russian infantry had been so swift that the six battalions suffered remarkably light casualties. The British losses were 8 officers and 19 sergeants killed, and 81 officers and 102 sergeants wounded, 318 rank and file killed, and 1,438 wounded, with 19 missing, a total loss of 1,985. The French, who were not deeply involved, had fewer than 60 killed and 500 wounded, while Russian casualties were over 6,000. The Black Watch, which had so often been in the lead, suffered just one killed and 37 wounded, a total, as will be seen, which was terribly and hugely dwarfed later on by sickness.

Victory in the Battle of Alma should, in theory, have given Raglan's army the opportunity of moving quickly towards Sebastopol which, according to some, could have been taken with an immediate attack. But supplies to the British army were in a parlous state, and Sebastopol was left untouched for the time being in favour of taking unopposed possession of two natural harbours south of the city. One, at Balaklava, served as a base for landing supplies, and it was here that the famous battle of the same name occurred when the Russian army struck on the British right flank. They were forced back by a charge of the heavy cavalry and then with even greater loss and near annihilation of the British light cavalry. The 93rd took up positions guarding the harbour, while the 42nd and 79th had been assigned the laborious work of digging and guarding trenches on the heights overlooking Sebastopol. And here the siege of that city began, dragging on for months in the stalemate shambles of the Crimea that brought much criticism, both at home and among senior officers of the British army *in situ*.

As Lieutenant-Colonel Anthony Sterling, assistant adjutant-general of the Highland Brigade, wrote on 10 August 1855, 'There was a conference of generals yesterday. I am sure I hope they have a plan;

any plan, even a bad one, is better than none. We are losing our men daily in the trenches and their lives seem to go for nothing.' On 8 September the Highlanders marched to Sebastopol where they took part in the assault and capture. But apart from these activities, the Highland Brigade were kept in reserve, and Colonel Sterling complained bitterly in his published letters about the inactivity of the brigade and the misuse of the three regiments, whose time had been more devoted to labouring and service tasks, more suited to what the colonel described as 'totally inexperienced' men who were barely fit to carry arms.

Thus, when a report in *The Times* on 4 October 1855 suggested that Sir Colin Campbell 'had been laid up in lavender' with his Highlanders, Sterling quickly put pen to paper to correct this calumny and to express his amazement that such a report should have been printed at all. His response to the report also provides a commentary on the situation in which the Highlanders found themselves:

As I was also in lavender with them, I have better reason than the writer of this article to know what the fact was as to our comforts. The three regiments, the 42nd, the 79th and the 93rd, were united in front of Balaklava on the day after the so-called action of Balaklava. Their business was aided by the Brigade of Royal Marines, consisting of some 1,200 men, and several thousands of the poor Turks, who were driven out of the redoubts on the day of Balaklava, and who nearly all died during the winter of the cold and hardship, which the sturdy Scotchmen endured without a murmur, under the cheerful, noble, generous leading of Sir Colin Campbell; their business, I say, was to finish the works on the heights, and to construct trenches, in mud, and frost, and snow, and, when made, to guard them. The guarding consisted in the whole of the soldiers being fully accoutred all night and every night. One half of them lay every night in the trenches, and the other half in the muddy tents, from the 25 October to the 6 December, when the Russians retired across the Chernaya. During this period, and for many weeks afterwards, they were never dry. Immediately on the enemy's retreat, the fatigue-parties to the front began; on which subject I beg to introduce an extract of a letter written by Sir Colin Campbell to Major-General Airey, dated 25 January 1855: 'During the last eight weeks the European troops under my command have been employed on fatigue to a very great extent. When I understood from the Artillery Officers here that the progress of the siege would be assisted by my doing so, I employed, of my own accord, and without any order, all the available soldiers [6,826] in carrying to the park . . . ordnance, stores, besides a quantity of shot and shell. Besides which, these men have carried to Lord Raglan's house nearly 4,000 bags of biscuit, being above 13 days' consumption for 25,000 men. Frequently, 1,300 European and from 300 to 500 Turks have been thus employed. At the same time, the troops had to carry up from Balaklava the whole of their rations, their regimental transport having been taken from them . . . and their public animals by the Commissary, the latter for the purpose of carrying the rations of the 1st Brigade of the 1st Division. During these fatigues there frequently remained to protect the position merely the ordinary day guards and the cooks: these fatigues usually lasted from seven to eight hours daily, during which time the men were mid-leg in mud.'

Until the 6 December, the small British force in the lines of Balaklava had 18 battalions of Russian Infantry, and 24 guns in position, close overhanging them, and threatening an attack at any moment. The vigilance, the energy, and judgement displayed all this time by Sir Colin Campbell will be long remembered by those who witnessed the exhibition. That officer, during the winter, exposed himself to more cold and hardship than all the other generals in the army and all their staff-officers put together; always on parade, with all his officers and men, in rain and mud, before daylight, he slept in his clothes regularly for eight months, and *this is the lavender you write about.*

141

As Sterling well knew, criticism would have been more correctly directed at the British hierarchy and especially the total mismanagement of the war effort itself, with an inefficient supply line, shortage of equipment, dire medical facilities and a commissary organisation whose lack of provision ensured that large numbers of the men were in rags, and broken footwear, and were cold, hungry and, again, as Sterling pointed out, 'short of everything'. As one commentator noted, a solitary bright light in this débâcle was that of Florence Nightingale and the medical teams who undoubtedly curtailed what would have been even greater mortality rates for the British sick and wounded at the hospital in Scutari. The figures were bad enough, and especially through the ravages of ill health, resulting from the sheer torture of the hellish living conditions, which brought so many men down. During the Crimean campaign, the 42nd Regiment lost thirty-nine men (including just one officer) killed in action and one hundred and forty with wounds serious enough for them to be repatriated. Deaths from other causes, however, amounted to 227. Throughout the British army as a whole the figures were much greater: in all, 19,600 dead, of whom more than 13,000 died through disease.

Another winter still lay ahead when, on the first anniversary of the Battle of Alma on 20 September 1855, the first distribution of Crimean medals was made. It was an occasion on which Sir Colin Campbell had planned to make the presentation and had prepared a stirring speech. But he had been promoted to take a leading role in the final push, so, instead, he sent a copy to be read to his men, in which he said:

> The fatigues and hardships of the last year are well known, and have greatly thinned our ranks since we scaled the Alma heights together, but happy am I to see so many faces around me, who, on that day, by their courage, steadiness and discipline, so materially assisted in routing the Russian hordes from their vaunted impregnable position. To that day Scotchmen can look with pride (and Scotchmen are everywhere). For your deeds upon that day you received the marked encomiums of Lord Raglan,

the thanks of your Queen, and admiration of all. Scotchmen are proud of you!

The Crimean War was still to be won, and the Black Watch played their part in the final push for Sebastopol, which was subsequently abandoned by the Russians, although peace terms were not formally signed until April 1856, and much of the army remained *in situ* until then. In fact, it was 15 June before the Black Watch embarked for England, landing at Portsmouth on 24 July. Now with the luxury of rail travel, the men were ferried direct to Aldershot and were honoured by a review by Queen Victoria.

Elsewhere, trouble was brewing that would soon demand their attention and reunite the regiment with Sir Colin Campbell. The so-called Indian Mutiny was stirring, and, still in a state of recovery from the Crimean campaign, first Sir Colin Campbell was sent to India, then, at his request, the Black Watch would soon follow as part of the reinforcements needed to re-establish control. The mutiny is usually blamed on the order by the British that in future Bengali soldiers were liable to service overseas, fighting for the imperial nation. In truth, the reason was a much more domestic matter, and one that in the modern age is far more likely to be understood as a definite grievance.

The army began supplying its native soldiers with cartridges for their new Enfield rifles greased with the fat of pigs and cows, one an unclean and the other a sacred animal. Nor did it help that Western ideas were being introduced and native customs suppressed, causing real feelings of disaffection. The army chose to respond in typically heavy-handed fashion, rather than attempting to meet the grievances head on. After some months of sporadic outbreaks of violence, the mutiny proper flared at Meerut on 10 May 1857 when native regiments murdered their officers and their women and children, marched to Delhi, forty miles away, and restored the old Mogul Empire in the person of Bahadur Shah. Other centres of revolt were Kanpur and Lucknow, and at both places the British garrisons, aided by some loyal sepoys, were besieged. On 27 June Kanpur surrendered and, in spite of a safe conduct agreement, all men, women and children were murdered. Sir Henry Havelock, leading a British force, fought several battles on his way to Kanpur, which he entered too late to save the garrison. From there he marched to Lucknow, where the British residency managed to hold their own until his arrival on 23 September, albeit with a much reduced strength. He could only join the besiegers and wait with them for further aid.

besieged

Sir Colin Campbell had arrived with reinforcements from Britain. He reached Kanpur, and with 8,000 men relieved the garrison at Lucknow. The Black Watch were mobilised at the end of August and, dispatched in six ships for the east, arrived in Calcutta in late October and early November 1857. The Highlanders included many young new soldiers recruited in the aftermath of the Crimean campaign and who as yet had not witnessed live action. They arrived as Sir Colin Campbell was preparing to attack the rebels in Kanpur, and the Highlanders were ordered to make a forced march to join him. In company with a wing of the 38th Regiment, a wing of the 3rd Battalion, Rifle Brigade, a party of sappers and artillery with two eight-inch howitzers and four field-pieces, they completed the eighty-mile journey in under three days, arriving on 4 December.

They went into battle immediately, placed in the lead of a column pursuing sepoys for twelve miles and capturing fifteen guns. A month of heavy fighting continued, and although the rebels were put to flight the 42nd suffered few casualties. At the end of December the regiment joined a slow, lumbering siege train as Sir Colin's army began the sweep through the area of Oudh, with 25,000 troops, 15,000 attendants, 16,000 camels and 12,000 oxen, mules, horses and elephants. The force worked its way through the region, bringing calm to the population and putting the rebels to flight, and headed north to Lucknow, where an estimated 60,000 rebel soldiers were now holding the city, with the British garrison bottled up. The tangled maze of streets had been barricaded, and the population, perhaps as many as 80,000, were armed and dangerous.

The siege train arrived at the outskirts of Lucknow to begin the attack, with the infantry moving in from the south while the cavalry and artillery bombarded from the north. The Black Watch was brought forward to attack one of the key strongholds, called La Martinière. Sir Colin Campbell personally gave the instruction: 'The 42nd will lead the attack and the men employed will use nothing but the bayonet.' They had a distance of 1,000 yards to cover, and the Highlanders went steadily on until within 200 yards of the place, when, giving three cheers, they rushed on in double time as the pipers played 'The Campbells Are Coming'.

At that, the rebels' first line turned and ran, but there remained two guns that could have caused the Highlanders great damage. At that point, and at great risk to himself, twenty-year-old Lieutenant Francis Edward Farquharson led a section of men into attack on the two guns; although he was himself shot and wounded as they went, they put the guns out of action. Farquharson was awarded the first Victoria Cross to be gained by a member of the 42nd Regiment. The award, initiated in the name of Queen Victoria in 1856, was and still is the highest honour achievable for valour. The citation read:

> For conspicuous bravery, when engaged before Lucknow on 9 March 1858, in having led a portion of his company, stormed a bastion mounting two guns, and spiked the guns, by which the advanced position held during the night of 9 March was rendered secure from the fire of artillery. Lieutenant Farquharson was severely wounded while holding the advanced position on the morning of 10 March.

The young officer recovered from his wounds and later achieved the rank of major. His Victoria Cross is today displayed at the Black Watch Museum, Perth. Even *The Times* correspondent reporting on this action at Lucknow was moved to observe: 'Most of the regiments were in a highly efficient state, but the Highlanders were most conspicuous, not only for their costume, but for their steady and martial air, on parade and in the field.'

The result was that the first stage of the assault on the city was won without a single loss. Another ten days of fighting saw Lucknow back under the control of the British, and Campbell and his advisers were certain that the mutiny would begin to subside. It might well have done but for an order issued by the British civilian administration that the estates of those who had supported the rebels would be confiscated, which meant that a number of the most influential princes decided to fight on. The tactics now to be employed included the formation of flying columns, to be sent to attack the forts and townships of the rebellious princes. The 42nd joined one of the first of these missions, under General Sir Robert Walpole, in company with the 79th and 93rd Highlanders, to challenge Nurpert Sing, a rebel chief who had barricaded himself and his army in Fort Ruhya.

The fort was surrounded by dense jungle, almost completely hidden from view. Four companies of the 42nd and the 4th Punjab Rifles that went in to reconnoitre came under heavy fire from soldiers in the tops of trees and, along with a number of casualties, were trapped for almost six hours until after dark, when they managed to withdraw under equally heavy fire. Brigadier Adrian Hope, Lieutenants Douglas and Bramley and a sergeant were wounded and six privates were killed during the expedition and numerous acts of bravery were recorded, four of which drew Victoria Cross awards.

The first went to Quartermaster John Simpson, aged thirty-two, who volunteered twice to dash under heavy fire to within forty yards of the parapet, first to rescue a lieutenant and a private, both of whom were badly wounded. Lance-Corporal Alexander Thompson, thirty-four, and Private Edward Spence, twenty, also volunteered to help bring in the wounded. Spence's citation recorded that he 'deliberately placed himself in an exposed position so as to cover the party bearing away the body of a lieutenant'. In doing so, Spence was himself hit and died from his wounds two days later, the VC thus being awarded posthumously. The fourth decoration won during this incident went to Private James Davis, twenty-three, who helped carry back the body of the lieutenant.

Sir Colin Campbell himself took command and brought up reinforcements as they continued on through the region of Rohilkand, arriving in early May at the state capital of Bareilly. The reason for Campbell's own involvement was immediately evident. This vast and sprawling city, with teeming suburbs, was impossible to capture simply by launching a siege. Instead, the commander brought all his guns to the fore, with a second line of three regiments of infantry and a third line of infantry and engineers. The 42nd were placed as skirmishers alongside the artillery in two lines and immediately found themselves under attack from rebel horsemen. Sergeant James Cooper described the attack in his diary:

> Uttering loud cries . . . about 150 of these fanatics, sword in hand with small circular bucklers on the left arm, and green cummerbund on, rushed out. With bodies bent and heads low, waving their tulwars [swords] with a circular motion, they came on with astonishing rapidity. Fortunately Sir Colin, close at hand, cried out, 'Close your ranks, bayonet them as they come.' Some of them got in rear of the right wing. Three dashed at Colonel Cameron, pulled him off his horse, and would have hacked him in pieces, but for Colour-Sergeant Gardner.

And so another Victoria Cross was won. The citation on the award to Colour-Sergeant William Gardner, aged thirty-seven, read:

> For his conspicuous and gallant conduct on the morning of 5 May, in having saved the life of Lieutenant-Colonel Cameron, his commanding officer, who, during the action of Bareilly, on that day had been knocked from his horse, when three fanatics rushed upon him. Colour-Sergeant Gardner ran out, and in a moment bayoneted two of them and was in the act of attacking the third, when he was shot down by another soldier of the regiment.

Bareilly was back in British hands, and the region entered an era of calm, although close surveillance work on the rebel strongholds was necessary and was maintained by the regiments for the next two years.

This in turn involved a good deal of exposure to the sun, particularly during the hot season. In fact, the climate took a greater toll on the men than their work. Eight men died from heatstroke during active patrols, and a system was introduced whereby the companies alternated their patrols to give the men a break from the excessive heat.

Further action arose when 2,000 rebels crossed the river into the deep jungle in Maylem Ghat, and troops moved speedily to head them off. Black Watch Ensign Coleridge was detached in command of forty men and forty levies, all raw recruits, to move into the thick jungle, but they were sidestepped and cut off by the rebels, who now met head on the remaining thirty-seven men under the command of Captain Lawson. The company put up a terrific fight against so many, and during the action Captain Lawson received a leg wound from which he later died. Colour-Sergeant Landles was also shot and badly mutilated by the enemy; two corporals, Ritchie and Thompson, were also killed, and there were several other casualties. Now without either officers or NCOs, Privates Walter Cook and Duncan Millar immediately went to the front and took a prominent part in directing the company as the soldiers fought on and held their ground, cheered constantly by older soldiers in the group. They managed to keep the enemy at bay for the entire day until they could make their escape. Cook and Millar were each awarded a Victoria Cross for 'displaying courage, coolness and discipline which was the admiration of all who witnessed it'. Later, a pipe tune, 'Lawson's Men', commemorated this action, and the survivors were paraded before Sir Hugh Rose, who had succeeded Campbell as commander-in-chief, when he presented new colours to the regiment.

Similar skirmishes went on regularly during the coming months, but once again sickness took over as the major enemy when in July the men were confined to camp following an outbreak of cholera which resulted in the deaths of one officer and forty other ranks. The whole regiment returned to barracks the following month, laid low by malaria, which at one point rendered more than 400 men unfit for duty. There was a further outbreak of cholera, endemic in the Ganges valley, in March 1861. Forty-six men died in a month, and at its worst nearly 500 men were in hospital or convalescing. When it was over, Dr Murray, the surgeon-general, presented a set of pipes to the regiment to commemorate 'the calm heroism of the 42nd' in the manner in which they dealt with this scourge. Sadly, it was not the last round of severe sickness to hit the regiment while in India. Later, sixty-six men, two women and four children died from a further outbreak, the toll increasing to more than 100 by an outbreak of severe dysentery when the regiment were moved to the hill station at Cherat. They were indeed glad to get out of that country when their posting ended in December, and a General Order was raised which praised their courage in the face of the 'trials which would have demoralised a less-disciplined regiment, undergone without a murmur'.

One piece of good news arrived from London during the regiment's time in India, in that as a 'mark of honour' Queen Victoria had authorised the 42nd Royal Highland Regiment to be distinguished, by adding the name by which it was first known, so to become: the 42nd Royal Highland Regiment (the Black Watch).

CHAPTER NINE

Mr Stanley, I Presume

Without doubt, the activities of the Black Watch continued to attract an enthusiastic following far and wide, of course with considerable pride in Scotland. Nor was this extraordinary public affection due in any way to the regular presence of the regiment within the home country. It is already evident from these chapters that, in fact, the 42nd Royal Highland Regiment were seldom in the Highlands, or indeed in Scotland. When the men came back from India, to be quartered as the garrison at Edinburgh Castle for a year, it was only the third time in sixty-five years that they had stayed in the Scottish capital and even then for a total of just fifteen months. The reception for Scotland's oldest Highland regiment on its arrival in Edinburgh in October 1868 was overwhelming and emotional, and a report in the *Scotsman* captured the mood exactly:

The train arrived at the station about ten minutes past 1 p.m. but long before that hour large and anxious crowds had collected on the Waverley Bridge, in Princes Street Garden, on the Mound, the Calton Hill, the Castle, and every other point from which a view of the passing regiment could be obtained. The crowd

151

collected on the Waverley Bridge must have numbered several thousands. The scene altogether was very imposing and animated. Immediately after the train entered the station, the bugle sounded, and the men were arranged in companies, under the command of their respective captains. The regiment was under the command of Lieutenant-Colonel J. C. M'Leod, assisted by Major Cluny M'Pherson, Major F. C. Scott, and Adjutant J. E. Christie, and was drawn up in eight companies. On emerging from the station the band struck up 'Scotland yet', and the appearance of the regiment was hailed with hearty cheers from the spectators. The crowd in Canal Street was so great that it was with some difficulty that the soldiers managed to keep their ranks. Their line of march lay along Princes Street, and every window and housetop from which a view of the gallant 42nd could be obtained was crowded with spectators. The regiment proceeded by the Mound, Bank Street and Lawnmarket, and was loudly cheered at every turn. On the Castle esplanade the crowd was, if possible, more dense than anywhere else. A large number of people had taken up their position on the top of the Reservoir, while every staircase from which a view could be obtained was thronged with anxious spectators. Large numbers had also gained admission to the Castle, and all the parapets and embrasures commanding a view of the route were crowded with people. It is now thirty-two years since the regiment was in Edinburgh, and certainly the reception which they received yesterday was a very enthusiastic one.

When they left a year later, the same scene was repeated, with the whole route to the port of embarkation for the ship carrying them to the south of England so crowded that the marching troops literally had to force a passage through the masses blocking the streets. During the march, twenty-one drummers and pipers played 'Scotland for Ever', 'Home, Sweet Home', Loudon's 'Bonnie Woods and Braes' and, as the Highlanders marched along the pier to their ship, 'Auld Lang Syne'. Before long, the 1st Battalion of the Black Watch were preparing to embark again, this time for active service in Africa, a continent that would require their particular skills for many a year hence.

The first port of call would be Ashanti, the West African state that occupied what is now southern Ghana. Extending from the Comoé River in the west to the Togo Mountains in the east, the Ashanti empire came to the fore in the eighteenth century when it supplied slaves to British and Dutch traders in return for arms, which its rulers used to slaughter local opposition and extend their boundaries. The threat to British interests came when Ashanti ruler Kofi Karikari attempted to preserve his empire's last trade outlet to the sea at the old coastal fort of Elmina, which came into British hands in 1869. In the early 1870s the Ashanti army began amassing tens of thousands of warriors in the region, apparently bent on restoring its possession of coastal regions. In doing so the Ashantis attacked a protectorate of the British and, having failed with a spot of gunboat diplomacy, the politicians in London decided that British influence must be restored forthwith.

They appointed Major-General Sir Garnet Wolseley, a veteran of many successful campaigns and an efficient commander admired by the public, as troubleshooter-in-chief for this region of the British Empire. English territory extended for 300 miles east and west of Cape Coast Castle, the seat of government. But at the time the local British commander had a mere 1,000 men, mainly West Indian troops, at his disposal. They managed with some difficulty to hold the fort until Wolseley arrived with his staff and 500 marines, although they were still in danger of being overrun.

The Black Watch, expanded by a large number of volunteers from the 79th, left Portsmouth on 4 December 1873, along with the 23rd Regiment, 2nd Battalion, Rifle Brigade, and detachments of Royal Artillery, Royal Engineers and Royal Marines. They arrived early in January to discover a landscape completely different from any they had previously experienced. The Ashanti kingdom was in the heart of a country of marshes and dense forests, forming impenetrable ambush situations for the opposing force, not to mention – once again – the threat of illness and disease. As one senior officer remarked: 'This will be an engineers' and doctors' war.' The engineers were needed to hack a route through the forests for roads, bridges and telegraphs, while the doctors would have their hands full with British soldiers new to the 'pestiferous climate'. And then, as they settled down to business, into this jungle of undergrowth to tell the world of their exploits stepped H. M. Stanley, the explorer and writer who, just twenty-seven months earlier, had uttered his world-famous quotation, 'Dr Livingstone, I presume', when he found the missionary and explorer living at Ujiji. Now, Stanley would be sending back graphic reports of Wolseley's efforts – and, as it turned out, those of the Black Watch – to the *New York Herald*, and this rather small war caught the imagination of readers in America and in Britain. His impression of the landscape where the fighting took place was recorded thus: 'The bush is so dense that one wonders how naked people can have the temerity to risk their bodies in what must necessarily punish their unprotected cuticles.'

Through it, Wolseley's men had to forge 70 miles of jungle roads by felling trees, bridging 276 river or water crossings and laying corduroy and logs over marshland. Along the road, thousands of porters carried four hundred tons of biscuits, rice and bully beef in tins, and a million rounds of ammunition. To make matters worse, the porters deserted in droves, and consequently the soldiers often found themselves humping their own supplies.

The *London News* also drew attention to the fact that a person might 'wander for hours [in the undergrowth] before he finds that he has mistaken his path. To cross the country from one narrow clearing to another, axes or knives must be used at every step. There is no looking over the hedge in this oppressive and bewildering maze. Such was the battlefield . . . the enemy's army was never seen, but its numbers are reported by Ashantees to have been 15,000 or 20,000. The Ashantees were armed with muskets, firing slugs, but some had rifles. As they were entirely concealed in the bush, while our countrymen stood in the lane or in the newly cut spaces, precision of aim was no advantage to our side.'

Five companies of the 42nd were in skirmishing order, and the musket slugs were dropping thick and fast from an unseen enemy. It was reported that had they been bullets, scarcely a man of the Black Watch would have lived to tell the tale. Even so, only few of the officers did not receive a scratch, and 104 of the men were wounded in their very first sortie into the undergrowth. The first major battle, at Amoaful, also found a spirited and daring enemy, and the action was such that H. M. Stanley, in an article for his newspaper, wrote a colourful description:

The conduct of the 42nd Highlanders on many fields has been considerably belauded, but mere laudation is not enough for the gallantry which has distinguished this regiment when in action. Its bearing has been beyond praise as a model regiment, exceedingly disciplined, and individually nothing could surpass the standing and gallantry which distinguished each member of the 42nd or the Black Watch. They proceeded along the well-ambushed road as if on parade, by twos. 'The 42nd will fire by companies, front rank to the right, rear rank to the left,' shouted Col M'Leod. 'A Company, front rank fire! Rear rank fire!' and so on; and thus vomiting out two score of bullets to the right and two score to the left, the companies volleyed and thundered as they marched past the ambuscades, the bagpipes playing, the cheers rising from the throats of the lusty Scots, until the forest rang again with discordant medley of musketry, bagpipe music and vocal sounds. It was the audacious spirit and true military bearing on the part of the Highlanders, as they moved down the road toward Coomassie [Kumasi], which challenged admiration this day. Very many were borne back frightfully disfigured and seriously wounded, but the regiment never halted nor wavered; on it went, until the Ashantees, perceiving it useless to fight against men who would advance heedless of ambuscades, rose from their coverts, and fled panic-stricken towards Coomassie, being perforated by balls whenever they showed themselves to the hawk-eyed Scots. Indeed, I only wish I had enough time

155

given me to frame in fit words the unqualified admiration which the conduct of the 42nd kindled in all who saw or heard of it. One man exhibited himself eminently brave among brave men. His name was Thomas Adams. It is said that he led the way to Coomassie, and kept himself about ten yards ahead of his regiment, the target for many hundred guns; but that, despite the annoying noise of iron and leaden slugs, the man bounded on the road like a well-trained hound on a hot scent. This example, together with the cool, calm commands of Col M'Leod, had a marvellous effect upon the Highland battalion.

From start to finish the campaign took less than six weeks before Wolseley brought it to a satisfactory conclusion, with the king of the Ashanti accepting 'unqualified submission'. The job done, the troops were hurriedly evacuated from the dangerous climate and were back in Portsmouth by 23 March. There it was learned that the queen had awarded the regiment's ninth Victoria Cross, to Lance-Sergeant Samuel McGaw who, on 21 January during the Battle of Amoaful, had 'led his section through the bush in a most excellent manner and continued to do so throughout the day, although badly wounded early in the engagement'. Although the decoration and the external plaudits, such as Stanley's, were very welcome, there were probably no better observations of performance and recognition of individual acts of bravery than those drawn from within the regiment itself. An archive document, which consisted of a Regimental Order dated 24 May 1875, announcing the distribution of the 'Ashantee Medal' to those who had participated, contains insights into the private feelings of the men and their officers. It is a brilliant memorandum, displaying something of the tribalism that has existed in the Black Watch since the beginning, but above all the loyalty to brother soldiers is clearly evident in this extract:

Sir John M'Leod believes the Ashantee War medal now received in full and issued to the regiment will be worn with satisfaction by the men. He thinks, though the expedition for which it is granted was only a little war, that the medal may take its place, not unworthily, beside the other decorations on the breast. Though little, the war had a magnitude and audacity about it to awaken the interest of the civilised world, and to exhibit in a marked degree those same qualities latent in you which sustained the corps of old in the Savannah, in Flanders, and in other unhealthy places . . . There is no page in your regiment's annals brighter than that which tells of your encounter with your savage foe in the murky bottoms at Amoaful; of the valour and discipline which carried you into the gaping chasm of the forest at Ordah-su; through the fetid Soubang swamp, headed by Colour-Sergeant Barton, who, though wounded at Amoaful, continued working hard, hardly missing a shot, never halting until you had set your foot in the market-place of Coomassie.

And on this day it is fitting to remember the distinguished conduct of Privates Alexander Hodge and John Arthur carrying Major Baird, more desperately wounded than themselves, to a place of safety, and the noble heroism of Private W. Thompson, one of the party, sacrificing himself rather than see his captain fall into the hands of the enemy, how Sergeant M'Gaw won the Victoria Cross; the sustained gallantry throughout of Privates Thomas Adams and George Ritchie; the cheerful disregard of personal danger of Sergeant-Instructor of Musketry Street, though badly wounded in the thigh; of Quartermaster-Sergeant Paterson running the gauntlet of fire upon the road for a hammock to carry the dangerously wounded sergeant-major to the rear, assisted by Paymaster-Sergeant Bateman; of Pioneer-Sergeant Gairns' look of scorn when, disabled in the right arm, he was advised to fall to the rear! How was the flame of battle to be fed if he were at the rear and not there to serve out the ammunition? How Sergeant Butters, shot through the leg at Amoaful, marched with his company till again struck down in the gloomy Pass of Ordah-su; of Sergeant Graham Gillies, and Privates Jones and John Grant of B Company, and Private W. Nichol, always to the front; how wounded Piper Weatherspoon, taking the rifle and place of dead Corporal Samuel, fought till overpowered with wounds, of Sergeant Milne and Private Hector White, and gallant Privates W. Bell, Imray, and M'Phail fighting with remarkable bravery.

But the space I would allow myself is more than filled and I have before me Sergeant John Simpson, Colour-Sergeant Farquharson, Privates Calderwood, W. Armstrong, J. Miller, Peter Jeffrey, Colour-Sergeant Cooper, and Piper Honeyman, 'tangled in the bush' and lost to his company; Surgeon-Major Clutterbuck, your old doctor, using few hammocks, how he marched all the way, his own recipe for surmounting all difficulties, defended successfully his helpless wounded on the roadside with his revolver; and Hospital Orderly M'Cudden – the hammock men hesitating to follow the regiment into the dread Pass of Ordah-su – encouragingly he threw aside his sword and revolver, placed himself at their head, led thus into Coomassie; and Quartermaster Forbes – unsurpassed – how, in the hottest of the fray, you had your ammunition always handy; your ration – sometimes more – ready. The first to swim the Ordah on your return, few will forget the hot tea he welcomed you with to your bivouac on that wet dreary night. Private Johnston, the last to pass over, how he lost his clothes in the dark and was sandwiched by the doctor between two hammocks, faring not so badly; and others unmentioned, generous men, and remembered. Scattered as you are at present over Cottonera, I regret I have been unable with my own hand, and the fever on me, to give to each of you his well-earned medal. But I address you, on this the Queen's birthday, that you may be sure your good conduct is not forgotten. Wear the medal, with its ribbon yellow and black, significant colours to you. If any man ever makes away with it for unworthy ends, it will be a double disgrace to him.

In 1876 Queen Victoria directed the word 'Ashantee' to be added to the honorary distinctions on the colours of the regiment. By then, the regiment had already left the country, this time bound for Malta, taking up residence in Isola barracks, to which they were no strangers. It was the beginning of a build-up of troops over the next two years on Malta and Gozo as a result of strained relations between Britain and Russia. They were later joined by an expeditionary force from India, the whole to secure Britain's Mediterranean interests, again under the command of Major-General Sir Garnet Wolseley. The operation was extended to the east, and now the Black Watch moved to take over as the occupying force of Cyprus. They were based at Larnaca, where they received news of the sudden death of Sergeant McGaw, VC, who had accompanied an advance detachment on the previous day. In fact, it soon became clear that the camp was in a particularly unhealthy part of the island, and the regiment was moved again within a matter of days, some to Kyrenia and others to Paphos.

This was viewed as especially important, given that the men were expecting to remain there for several months. Those destined for Kyrenia had to build their own huts, because the old fort there was currently housing 300 Turkish convicts, but no sooner was the work complete than they were ordered to prepare to move again, this time to Gibraltar, another place where maintaining a healthy regiment was always fraught with problems. In fact, it was because of this threat that they were moved again six months later, this time heading for home service. They were subsequently brought back to Cowes in June before moving to Aldershot for summer drills with the Grenadier Guards and Scots Guards. The stay in Britain, which continued until 1881, included a return to Edinburgh specifically for a recruiting drive.

Other developments that year included another name change and reorganisation. All regiments were to lose their numerical titles under the Cardwell Reforms of 1881. The 42nd now became the 1st Battalion, The Black Watch (The Royal Highlanders). The 73rd, which had been formed from the 2nd Battalion of the 42nd in 1786, now became the 2nd Battalion of the Regiment.

The call of foreign parts was never far away, nor indeed in this instance was that of Major-General Wolseley whose latest task was to rescue British interests in Egypt, notably the Suez Canal, which was opened in 1869. Britain had gained a controlling interest in the canal by buying the shares of the Khedive of Egypt, thus ensuring continuing access to this vital seaway to the east, and with it the troubles that came with maintaining a force capable of repelling those who, down the decades, had ideas of ejecting the British from the scene. The first serious attempt came in May 1882, when a group of Egyptian military officers led a revolt against foreign interference in Egypt's affairs. By August that year, Wolseley was assembling a force of 35,000 men from Britain, India and the Mediterranean to secure the canal. He landed his forces at Alexandria to feign an attack on the forts at Aboukir but then rapidly altered his area of operations, using the canal itself to sail to Ismailia, halfway down the waterway. From there, Wolseley would lead his men in a dramatic night-time march to launch a surprise attack on the Egyptian lines at Tel-el-Kebir, where around 20,000 opposition forces were preparing for battle.

The Black Watch were part of the 3,000-strong Highland Brigade, which formed the left-hand portion of the attacking force, positioned 1,000 yards ahead of the right-hand line. The force was guided under cover of darkness in its march west by Royal Naval Lieutenant Wyatt Rawson, who kept his course by the stars. At daybreak on 13 September, the battle lines were reached and the sound of a bugle in front warned of the dark shape rising above the sand-hills ahead. At once the cry went up: 'Fix bayonets!' Even as the shout went up, the whole line of trenches was ablaze with rifle fire . . . and 'Charge!' – the order was bellowed, and the brigade began the 150-yard dash towards the glow of the firing line, under orders not to fire themselves but to attack with bayonets.

In that short run, 204 men of the Highland Brigade were felled. The rest charged on, as ever, running up the sand-hills and into the trenches, calling for surrender but in the end having to resort to bayoneting the defenders. 'The infantry did not stand long,' one of the Black Watch reported, 'but honour where honour is due . . . the artillerymen stood to their guns like men, and we had to bayonet them. As soon as that job was done, I saw two regiments of cavalry forming up on the right. "Prepare for cavalry" was given, and we formed in a square and were waiting for them; but when they saw this they wheeled to the right-about and off. They would not face a square of Scottish steel.'

The fighting was over in twenty minutes, and the Highlanders and the force went on to capture the Egyptian army's stores – and several thousand camels – along with a railway station. It was a remarkable timetable of events, which began at five minutes to five and ended when the men were called to order sixty-five minutes later. The Khedive of Egypt was restored, but the British remained to secure control of the Suez Canal and its fast link to India.

The trouble, however, was not over yet. Within the area of the Khedive's rule was Egyptian Sudan, which was in renewed turmoil following the uprising in Egypt itself. The history was this: the Khedive, having met the renowned British General 'Chinese' Gordon – so called for his role in command of Chinese forces during the Taiping Rebellion in the 1860s – specifically requested that he should be appointed Governor of the Egyptian Sudan to establish a military presence capable of securing British interests and to organise some form of local government structure. Gordon remained on the scene until 1880, when he returned to Britain, partly through illness. But now, in the face of a Dervish rebellion that broke out after he had left, he was sent back by the British government to organise the evacuation of Egyptian civilians and troops from Khartoum, where they were under attack by rebels led by the Muslim mystic Muhammad Ahmad al-Mahdi.

Gordon reached Khartoum on 18 February 1884 and quickly succeeded in evacuating 2,000 women, children and the sick and wounded before al-Mahdi's forces closed in on the city. Gordon sent an urgent request to the British government for immediate assistance by way of troops, because the situation was becoming desperate. London ignored the request, deciding that the clearance of opposition to the British presence in Egypt was more vital. Five days earlier, a British force under the command of Major-General Sir Gerald

Graham, which included the Black Watch, had already begun moving towards northern Sudan to relieve a number of Egyptian garrisons under siege from tribes that had rebelled against the Egyptian government. These operations continued for many weeks, with a number of hard-fought battles, costing the Black Watch alone over 100 men killed or wounded, and requiring these places to be filled by additional troops sent over from Cyprus.

In August the regiment were back in their former camp outside Cairo, but that respite did not last long. On 16 September the men turned out in best order for an inspection by Major-General Wolseley himself, and rumour had it that this was a prelude to something rather special. But the general gave no clues when he addressed the men:

Black Watch . . . I am very glad of this chance of again meeting you. I have often been with you before, in Ashantee, in Cyprus, and in the Egyptian campaign, and I am proud and glad to be once more associated with you. During the late campaign in the eastern Sudan you were opposed to a most brave and determined enemy. You will believe me when I tell you that the people at home, and not only your own countrymen, were proud of the gallant way in which you upheld the honour of your splendid and historic regiment and there was no one in all England, I can assure you, thought more of you than I did . . . I am proud of the highly efficient state in which you have turned out this morning. It reflects the highest credit on all of you. In the coming campaign I do not think there will be much fighting, but there will be very hard work, and I shall want you to show that you can work hard as well as fight. If there is any fighting to be done, I know that I have only to call on the Black Watch, and you will behave as you have always done.

So what was the 'coming campaign', and what did the 'hard work' entail? There were no clues then, but all would soon become clear. Their destination was to be Khartoum, standing at the junction of the Blue and the White Nile, 1,356 miles from Cairo. The city had been under siege, surrounded by al-Mahdi's army, since 13 March. From that day, it was to continue its bloody course for almost a year against the backdrop of mounting fascination in Britain and the rest of the world until, in the face of desperate pleas from Gordon and increasing pressure of public opinion, the Gladstone government belatedly – and too late, as it turned out – agreed to send a relief force under General Wolseley.

Still unaware of what lay ahead, the Black Watch and other regiments involved were being assembled at Aswan. The first part of their journey was relatively straightforward, travelling by rail to Assiout, there to embark on two steamers and four barges heading down the Nile to Aswan, historic site of the Nilometer, where the Pharaoh's officials measured the annual flood and set that year's tax level. They arrived on 5 October, but after an outbreak of smallpox among the men they had to march two miles down the river to encamp in a palm grove on the bank of the Nile, where the regiment remained in quarantine until 12 November.

At that point, it became clear what lay ahead: one of the most exhausting and dramatic journeys undertaken by the Black Watch in recent times. The men were to travel south, part-rowing and part-sailing in whalers along this most difficult of rivers in a race against time to rescue General Gordon in Khartoum. And there, on the east bank of the Nile, in November 1884, this army, looking wholly out of place in the desert with its soldiers dressed in red-serge uniforms and Highlanders in their standard attire, prepared to enter new arenas. The regiments were embarking on a journey that involved the long-distance traversal of deserts and the hazardous negotiation of the Nile that required specialist Canadian pilots to guide them. It had been done before, of course, but not quite in this manner. Furthermore, on reaching certain points on the journey, the force would divide into two, a Desert Column and a River Column, with the Black Watch in the latter.

The 84 boats allotted to the Black Watch – out of the 274 for the entire expedition – were 30 feet long, with a 7-foot beam and with a draught of 2.5 feet – and even that proved to be too deep for some shallow stretches of the river. Each boat was designed to be self-supporting, in case any were lost, so they carried men, food, medical supplies, ammunition and ordnance for the fourteen men and a crew of eight for a hundred days, a load weighing in excess of four tons. These supplies were not to be touched until the first stage of the journey had been completed. Immediate needs were to be carried additionally and topped up en route at commissariat stations that were at that moment being set up at appropriate points along the river bank for a distance of 600 miles. Thereafter, the supplies carried on board would have to suffice. However, with the massive weight in each boat, the craft rode low in the water, and on numerous occasions it was necessary to stop, unload the stores and literally carry the 1,000-pound boat beyond the shallows or over the cataracts. The hazards of such a journey by these heavily laden craft can be imagined, and all the unfortunate events that might be expected did indeed occur, such as boats hitting unseen rocks and having to be hauled ashore for repair. This happened often. The men developed bad sores on their hands, and their clothes – the uniforms packed away for safety – became nothing less than rags.

In the first week of January 1885 the leading companies of the Black Watch arrived at Korti, 250 miles north of Khartoum, and by 20 January the whole of the regiment had arrived to form into the River Column with the South Staffordshire, the 2nd Battalion of the Duke of Cornwall's Light Infantry, the 1st Battalion of the Gordon Highlanders, one squadron of the 19th Hussars, an Egyptian battery of six seven-pound guns, an Egyptian Camel Corps and a section of Engineers and Bluejackets. They now intended to advance on Khartoum through Berber, continuing on via the river, which if anything began to get worse, especially the Edermih Cataract, which was the most difficult obstacle they encountered on the entire journey. At the end of the first week of February, the Black Watch and the 1st South Staffordshire had reached the advance position of Dulka Island, only to discover that an enemy force was 2,000 yards ahead of them, occupying a high rocky ridge near the river. A battle was clearly imminent, and the troops quickly unpacked their red serges and kilts, which were to be the fighting dress of the River Column regardless of the circumstances. At first light on 10 February, six companies of the South Staffordshire, six companies of the Black Watch, the squadron of the 19th Hussars and the native Camel Corps marched out of camp, leaving behind an adequate force to guard the boats.

The Battle of Kirbekan began soon after 9 a.m., and a heavy fire-fight ensued for almost an hour before sections of the Sudanese force began fleeing across the river. Troops on higher ground firing down on the British refused to budge, and Major-General Earle gave orders for the Black Watch to take the position with the bayonet. The pipers began their battle music, followed by a great cheer as the Black Watch dashed ahead to be met by a hail of fire. Enough of the Highlanders managed to scale the rocks to drive out the opposition at the point of their bayonets. The South Staffordshire stormed the second line and the battle was won. General Earle was among the casualties, and the Black Watch lost Lieutenant-Colonel Coveny and five men killed and twenty-two men wounded. Major-General H. Brackenbury took command, and on the morning of 11 February the advance was resumed with the troops now facing rapids close to Dulka Island for seven miles, dodging huge rocks straddling the river. The general recalled one incident in his diary:

As my boat shot down we passed the adjutant of the Gordons with his boat stuck fast in the very centre of the boiling rapid, a useful beacon to the following boats. His was not the only boat that struck; four others of the same battalion were on the rocks. Three were repaired, but two of the five sank and were abandoned. The quartermaster was thrown into the water and lost all his kit. The adjutant had a narrow escape for his life. Thrown into the water, as his boat sank, his head had struck a sharp rock, and he was severely cut. The Black Watch had also to abandon a boat that struck on a rock near Kaboor . . . and [later] at the fourth cataract three boats [were] wrecked, alas with the first fatal accident in all our downward journey. One boat of the South Staffordshire, having safely shot the weir, struck a rock and upset. Unfortunately she had in her two wounded men, both of whom with a sergeant were drowned.

The swiftness of the current meant that 215 boats of the force completed a dozen miles of water in double-quick time, reaching their mooring towards their next stopping point at El Kab by early afternoon on 23 February before going on to Huella. In fact, this was as far as they would go. Early the next morning a message from Wolseley was read to the troops: 'Please express to the troops Lord Wolseley's high appreciation of their gallant conduct in action, and of the military spirit they have displayed in overcoming the great difficulties presented by the river . . . [but] it is not intended to undertake any further military action.'

The men could hardly believe their ears. After all they had been through, the whole operation was cancelled. But what about General Gordon? The truth was withheld at that point: that the Mahdi's rebels had finally broken the heroic defence of Khartoum after 312 days, and the defenders had been butchered to a man, General Gordon among them. Having sacked the city, the Mahdists retreated downriver, abandoning Khartoum, and set up base in Omdurman. The British newspapers acclaimed 'Gordon of Khartoum' as warrior-saint and blamed the government for his death in their failure to send a relief force earlier. Even so, having seen the retreat of the Mahdists, the British force promptly retired to Egyptian territory, much to the delight of the Mahdi, whose army immediately began receiving hundreds of new recruits in the mistaken belief that the British had been defeated. The British public was stunned, Gladstone was publicly booed, and Queen Victoria bitterly described Gordon's death as a 'stain left upon England'. The Mahdi would not live long enough to enjoy his victory. Five months later, he died of typhus. The River Column and, indeed, the Desert Column of Wolseley's expeditionary forces could do no more than turn round and head back the way they came – and by the same route, a journey that proved even more hazardous than the first.

The Sudanese campaign continued intermittently under the command of General Herbert Kitchener, who was appointed commander of the Egyptian army in 1892, and for the next seven years led a continuous series of campaigns, resulting in the rout of the Mahdists at the Battle of Omdurman in 1899. It was in this era that he was joined by a young second-lieutenant in the 21st Lancers, Winston Churchill. For now, though, the Highlanders and indeed many of the elements who were engaged in this costly and totally unproductive operation were exhausted, and they took no further part in the Sudanese campaign after their arrival back at Cairo.

The Black Watch remained overseas, first with a tour of duty in the Mediterranean, and then they were split, with half the companies heading for Cape Town and the rest to Mauritius before being reunited for service in India in 1896, where the 1st Battalion remained on relatively peaceful duties until December 1901, when they moved to South Africa for the latter stages of the Boer War.

Their colleagues from the 2nd Battalion of the Black Watch had, by then, been through the mill, having been in at the start of the Boer War and suffering terrible losses in the process. The British were at the height of their imperial power and prestige and had ambitions to add the gold mines of the Dutch Boer republics of the Transvaal and the Orange Free State to the colonisation of Africa. In October 1899, however, the Boers invaded Natal and Cape Province and quickly invested three towns, Ladysmith, Mafeking and Kimberley. Britain retaliated with a massive force against the Boers, who could call on fewer than 60,000 men against Britain's vastly superior numbers. But far from bringing the promised swift conclusion – famously stated as 'it will be over by Christmas' – the British army, whose opposition for the past forty years had been native soldiers, found themselves totally outfoxed by the commando-style tactics of the Boers. Early misfortunes had already been experienced when the Black Watch, under the command of General Andrew Wauchope, arrived from England to join the Highland Brigade as part of Lord Methuen's force, and they set to work almost immediately as part of what proved to be a desperate enterprise. Arthur Conan Doyle, creator of Sherlock Holmes, in his book *The Great Boer War* captured the drama of the murderous situation that now confronted them:

> Lord Methuen's force had fought three actions in the space of a single week, losing in killed and wounded about a thousand men, or rather more than one-tenth of its total numbers . . . reinforcements were now reaching the Modder River force, which made it more formidable than when it had started . . . The magnificent regiments which formed the Highland Brigade [2nd Battalion Black Watch, 1st Battalion Argyll and Sutherlands, 2nd Battalion Seaforths, and 1st Highland Light Infantry] had arrived under the gallant and ill-fated Wauchope. Four five-inch howitzers had also come to strengthen the artillery . . . On the morning of Saturday, December 9th, the British general made an attempt to find out what lay in front of him amid that semicircle of forbidding hills. To this end he sent out a reconnaissance in the early morning, which included G Battery Horse Artillery, the 9th Lancers and the ponderous 4.7 naval gun, which, preceded by the majestic march of thirty-two bullocks and attended by eighty seamen gunners, creaked forwards over the plain. What was there to shoot at in those sunlit boulder-strewn hills in front? They lay silent and untenanted in the glare of the African day. In vain the great gun exploded its huge shell with its fifty pounds of lyddite over the ridges, in vain the smaller pieces searched every cleft and hollow with their shrapnel. No answer came from the far-stretching hills. Not a flash or twinkle betrayed the fierce bands who lurked among the boulders. The force returned to camp no wiser than when it left.
>
> About three in the afternoon of Sunday, December 10th, the [Highland Brigade] which was to clear a path for the army through the lines of Magersfontein moved out upon what proved to be its desperate enterprise. Besides the infantry, the 9th Lancers, the mounted infantry and all the artillery moved to the front. It was raining hard, and the men with one blanket between

two soldiers bivouacked upon the cold damp ground, about three miles from the enemy's position. At one o'clock, without food, and drenched, they moved forwards through the drizzle and the darkness to attack those terrible lines. Clouds drifted low in the heavens, and the falling rain made the darkness more impenetrable. The Highland Brigade was formed into a column – the Black Watch in front, then the Seaforths, and the other two behind. With many a trip and stumble the ill-fated detachment wandered on, uncertain where they were going and what it was that they were meant to do. Not only among the rank and file, but among the principal officers also, there was the same absolute ignorance. Brigadier Wauchope knew, no doubt, but his voice was soon to be stilled in death. The others were aware, of course, that they were advancing either to turn the enemy's trenches or to attack them, but they may well have argued from their own formation that they could not be near the riflemen yet. Why they should be still advancing in that dense clump we do not now know, nor can we surmise what thoughts were passing through the mind of the gallant and experienced chieftain who walked beside them. There are some who claim on the night before to have seen upon his strangely ascetic face that shadow of doom which is summed up in the one word 'fey'. The hand of coming death may already have lain cold upon his soul. Out there, close beside him, stretched the long trench, fringed with its line of fierce, staring, eager faces, and its bristle of gun-barrels. They knew he was coming. They were ready. They were waiting. But still, with the dull murmur of many feet, the dense column, nearly four thousand strong, wandered onwards through the rain and the darkness, death and mutilation crouching upon their path.

It matters not what gave the signal, whether it was the flashing of a lantern by a Boer scout, or the tripping of a soldier over wire, or the firing of a gun in the ranks. It may have been any, or it may have been none, of these things. As a matter of fact I have been assured by a Boer who was present that it was the sound of the tins attached to the alarm wires which disturbed them. However this may be, in an instant there crashed out of the darkness into their faces and ears a roar of point-blank fire, and the night was slashed across with the throbbing flame of the rifles. At the moment before this outflame some doubt as to their whereabouts seems to have flashed across the mind of their leaders. The order to extend had just been given, but the men had not had time to act upon it. The storm of lead burst upon the head and right flank of the column, which broke to pieces under the murderous volley. Wauchope was shot, struggled up, and fell once more for ever. Rumour has placed words of reproach upon his dying lips, but his nature, both gentle and soldierly, forbids the supposition. 'What a pity!' was the only utterance which a brother Highlander ascribes to him. Men went down in swaths, and a howl of rage and agony, heard afar over the veldt, swelled up from the frantic and struggling crowd. By the hundred they dropped – some dead, some wounded, some knocked down by the rush and sway of the broken ranks. It was a horrible business. At such a range and in such a formation a single Mauser bullet may well pass through many men. A few dashed forwards, and were found dead at the very edges of the trench. The few survivors of Companies A, B and C of the Black Watch appear to have never actually retired, but to have clung on to the immediate front of the Boer trenches, while the remains of the other five companies tried to turn the Boer flank.

Of the former body only six got away unhurt in the evening after lying all day within two hundred yards of the enemy. The rest of the brigade broke and, disentangling themselves with difficulty from the dead and the dying, fled back out of that accursed place. Some, the most unfortunate of all, became caught in the darkness in the wire defences, and were found in the morning hung up 'like crows', as one spectator describes it, and riddled with bullets. Who shall blame the Highlanders for retiring when they did? Viewed, not by desperate and surprised men, but in all calmness and sanity, it may well seem to have been the very best thing which they could do. Dashed into chaos, separated from their officers, with no one who knew what was to be done, the first necessity was to gain shelter from this deadly fire, which had already stretched six hundred of their number upon the ground. The danger was that men so shaken would be stricken with panic, scatter in the darkness over the face of the country, and cease to exist as a military unit. But the Highlanders were true to their character and their traditions. There was shouting in the darkness, hoarse voices calling for the Seaforths, for the Argylls, for Company C, for Company H, and everywhere in the gloom there came the answer of the clansmen. Within half an hour with the break of day the Highland regiments had re-formed, and, shattered and weakened, but undaunted, prepared to renew the contest. Some attempt at an advance was made upon the right, ebbing and flowing, one little band even reaching the trenches and coming back with prisoners and reddened bayonets. For the most part the men lay upon their faces, and fired when they could at the enemy . . .

The Highland Brigade had suffered over 900 casualties, and the Black Watch took a higher proportion than most. It was the worst single casualty toll in battle for almost 100 years. It was news of them, and indeed the Highland Brigade, that shocked Scotland to the core – and for Britain the whole enterprise was being severely challenged and criticised. In fact, Magersfontein was only one of the three disasters in what became known as the 'black week'. Other heavy losses were suffered at Stormberg and Colenso. Wolseley arranged the immediate dispatch of a second army corps, raising the number of troops to 440,000.

As the British gradually began to re-establish their hold, the Black Watch found themselves with the role of the 'pacification' of the Orange Free State, where guerrilla tactics were rife. They feared that if the war went on to an extended period, they might spend years wandering the Free State 'till', as one of their number put it, 'we become a phantom brigade, nothing to be seen, but at night the wailing of pipes and loud curses will be heard, to the terror of the inhabitants'. By the end of 1900, they had covered more than 2,000 miles on foot, a journey in which they were constantly sniped at, ambushed and generally aggravated by the commando operations of the Boers (on which Winston Churchill modelled the formation of British army commando units at the onset of the Second World War). In December 1901 they were joined by regiments including the 1st Battalion Black Watch that had come out from India, and in the next four months joined operations that finally brought about the Boers' capitulation on 31 May 1902. The news was greeted with considerable applause by the *Scotsman*, which also noted that the support for all the Highland units had been such that record numbers of young men were volunteering for service.

CHAPTER TEN

Brothers in Arms

The outbreak of the First World War saw an instant and massive expansion of the Black Watch as the clamour to volunteer stretched across the British Isles and dominions. At the time, there were seven Black Watch battalions. In addition to the 1st and 2nd Battalions, whose activities we have followed so far, a 3rd (Special Reserve) Battalion was formed in 1905, and in 1908 Territorial battalions with long links to the Black Watch became part of the regiment. These included the 4th (City of Dundee) Battalion, the 5th (Angus and Dundee) Battalion, the 6th (Perthshire) Battalion and the 7th (Fife) Battalion. The wartime organisation of the Territorials also involved the formation of second- and third-line battalions to provide trained reinforcements for front-line units. The original unit was referred to as the 1/4th, the second-line unit the 2/4th, the third-line unit the 3/4th and so on. Additionally, at the start of the war four additional service battalions were filled by the regiment, and at its height the Black Watch raised no fewer than twenty-five battalions for service on all fronts and most major battles during the First World War. According to Bernard Fergusson's calculations, more than 50,000 men would pass through the regiment during the four years of the war, of whom 28,000 were killed or wounded. The regiment were awarded sixty-eight battle honours, and another four Victoria Crosses were won.

They were joined by the 42nd Royal Highland Regiment (the Black Watch) of Canada, which sent three battalions, through which passed 11,954 officers and enlisted men, winning 26 battle honours. Among the Canadians who served, 2,163 were killed and 6,014 were wounded. Six of the decorated members were awarded the Victoria Cross. The Canadians officially became affiliated to the parent regiment in 1905, thus recognising a heritage that dated from formation in 1862 (see Appendix II).

At the onset of the Great War, the 1st Battalion of the Black Watch were already in Aldershot on a ready-to-move order and were fully mobilised on 8 August, landing at Le Havre on 14 August as part of the 1st (Guards) Brigade in the British 1st Division. The Royal Highlanders were therefore, once again, in the very forefront of British activity as the brigade went straight into action, taking part in the retreat from Mons before turning on the Germans at the River Marne and the subsequent advance to the Aisne. The 2nd Battalion were serving in India but arrived in France in October 1914 with the Bareilly Indian Brigade from the Meerut Division with which they were to serve throughout the war. In February 1915 the 1/4th (Dundee) went to France, and thereafter the remaining battalions that were to see service in France were progressively drawn in.

The 2nd, 4th and 5th Battalions were at the major battle at Neuve-Chapelle in March, and a total of six battalions fought at Festubert in May. In September came the initially successful but hugely costly Battle of Loos. What was remarkable, however, was the performance of the Territorials, the so-called weekend soldiers of the city and county battalions across the United Kingdom. While a detailed examination of the progress of the wartime battalions is clearly beyond the scope of this work, the author has chosen to focus this chapter on the progress of the 4th Battalion (Dundee) as seen through the letters home of two brothers who, like thousands of others, found themselves swept from an orderly civilian life into the horror of the trenches.

Through the letters, religiously saved by their parents and subsequently copied for inclusion in the Imperial War Museum documentary collection, an incredibly frank, moving and ultimately tragic account emerges of virtually every aspect, from life to death, of the young men so eager to 'do our duty' in what was supposed to have been the 'war to end all wars'. What also emerges is the great sense of comradeship among the Territorial battalions, which were generally recruited locally among young men who had largely grown up together, had gone to the same schools, played sports, and in many cases had married local girls. There is also outstandingly evident pride that the men had in serving under the Black Watch banner, and indeed in recognising the activities of other Scottish regiments.

So let us pick up the story focusing on the two brothers, the first of whom was with the 4th Battalion from Dundee when half of the unit went into the line for the first time while others remained at Richebourg and supplied working parties and carrying parties. The front line in this sector was opposite Neuve-Chapelle, which until then had been a pretty little village with a street of whitewashed cottages, a château and a church. At the beginning of the war it had been taken by the Germans, then retaken by the British in early October 1914; it again fell into German hands on 25 October.

Sidney Steven, aged twenty-four, was the second son of Robert Steven, a solicitor of Dundee. He was educated at the High School of Dundee, had qualified as a chartered accountant and had just arranged to become a partner in an old-established business in Dundee, when he surrendered all to serve his king and country in the 1/4th Battalion of the Black Watch. He obtained his commission as second lieutenant in April 1914. Later that year, his brother Harvey, twenty-seven, who was a lawyer, joined the same battalion. Extracts from an edited selection of their letters from a history of the Scottish family by Rollo Steven, lodged at the Imperial War Museum, now follows, beginning in March 1915, just before the infamous Battle of Neuve-Chapelle:

175

In the trenches, 3/3/15: One of my pals, Ian Law, was going out with a working party after dark so I went with him to keep him company. We started off and arrived at the spot where we were to meet another party, but they were an hour late, having been held up by a battery of artillery going into action. It was raining cats and dogs and exceedingly cold, but it was interesting to watch the battery going into action. It was all done without a word, and the guns were placed in position in a twinkle. Then the ammunition wagons came up, and the shells were piled beside the guns . . . within four hundred yards of the front line. One thing that struck me around that area was the maze of telephone wires. They were simply wound from tree to tree and are quite low. In fact, going back with the sergeant in the dark, his rifle, which he had slung on his shoulder, caught one of them. The telephone does a power of good out here. When I got back I nestled down in my straw and went sound asleep, got up in the morning and had breakfast, then inspected rifles, feet, ammunition and emergency rations of my platoon. Afterwards I took out a party of grenade throwers for practice, but it was so bitterly cold and snowing, so we did not stay out any longer than was necessary. Orders came in this afternoon to prepare my platoon for the trenches at 6.33 p.m. for our twenty-four hours of duty. I had to see that each man had 200 rounds of ammunition on him and had had a good meal, and then we started out. In this trench we are about 400 yards from the German trenches. The dugouts are quite comfortable and not as bad as I expected. I am at present sitting in an armchair, which is a thing I have not seen since I left Dundee. I hardly expected to find one in the front line of trenches. This trench is at the foot of a U [shaped] trench and is known as the Crescent. The firing line bends round in the snaps of a U, and we are practically under fire from two sides, which is, to say the least of it, an anxious position to be in. But no firing goes on in this trench until the pickets fall back. Two other officers came to relieve us for dinner, which consisted of soup, stewed meat and potatoes and fried sardines on toast, and fruit. We then slept for two hours, then went out on duty again.

From the descriptions in the letter, no-man's-land between the two armies was a wasteland, pockmarked with craters, with broken trees and stunted willows marking the course of innumerable swollen brooks. The craters were usually full of water, and the whole area was a mass of broken rusty wire. The communication trenches were usually full of water, in places two to three feet deep. The bottom edge of the soldiers' kilts used to float out on top of the water as the men made their way through them. Sidney was lucky with his dugout. They were mostly in a deplorable condition. They were merely holes cut out of the back of the trench and roofed with a piece of corrugated iron and sandbagged on top. The shelling and sniping were spasmodic, and sometimes at night it was quite quiet for long periods on end. The voices of the enemy could be heard, even the click of sentries' feet. Another subaltern wrote: 'I could hear a Boche playing Schubert on an old piano. It was 'The Trout', but before he got to the twiddly bit at the end someone put up a flare and the whole of no-man's-land went a pale green. Then a nervous sentry fired a short machine-gun burst and immediately firing started up all along the line.'

Sidney continued:

In the trenches, 11 a.m. 9/3/15: It's a beautiful morning. The sun is shining brightly and it is still frosty. You should have seen Germans run just now! Two shells in succession landed right in their trenches and broke down the parapet. Sometimes our shells fall short, and then it is we who have to duck. As I came out to relieve one of the other officers for breakfast, I saw a horrid sight. There are a number of wires across the road around here, and as an officer was training a party he stooped to hold up the wire for the man behind him and that man got shot right through the brain. He fell and never spoke a word. He was buried at once. *5 p.m.:* Must stop now. There is going

177

to be a show tonight or early morning. I do hope they do not send anyone to relieve me.

The Battle of Neuve-Chapelle was under way as the British lines tried to force the enemy back from the village and off the high ground, which was commanding the town of Lille, an important German supply base. At 7 a.m. British guns opened fire on German positions. The bombardment was not only to shake the morale and thin the numbers of the enemy but also to break down their formidable wire defences. Half an hour later, the guns changed their range and put their shells into Neuve-Chapelle itself. The infantry advanced, and after much isolated hand-to-hand fighting Neuve-Chapelle was taken at 11 a.m. Then companies of the 4th Black Watch were ordered to support the battalions holding the captured positions. No. 1 Platoon of A Company under Lieutenant Steven and No. 2 under Lieutenant G. B. Sherriff arrived first in the German trenches. No. 1 Platoon moved along the captured trench until they arrived at a point still retained by the enemy. There they delivered a bombing attack. The Germans, who were strongly dug in around a fortified house, opened heavy fire on the two Black Watch platoons. Then the British guns put down an intense artillery fire on the position. The gunners knew that the place was still in enemy hands, but owing to the telephone lines being cut by shellfire they were unaware of the presence of the A Company men. Under this fire the two platoons withdrew, but after the bombardment they advanced again and carried the position with the bayonet. No. 1 Platoon were then ordered to advance to another ruined house. The next letter gave details of the battle.

13/3/15: My God! What a show! I won't forget it in a hurry. Before the attack I had to clear out of this trench as someone came out to relieve me at 7 p.m.. I got safely back to billets at Richebourg about 8.30 and had just had a meal when all officers were ordered to go to HQ at 10 p.m.. We sat in conference until about midnight. Then we got our instructions to be ready for a fight in the morning. We had to get up at 2 a.m. and took up a position along a line of trenches. We were told what to expect . . . a terrific artillery bombardment. *[Later:]* We lay there from 2 in the morning to about 7.30. Then promptly at that time the bombardment started. The general has told us it is known to have been the biggest bombardment ever used. It was simply terrible. We were in the centre of everything . . . it lasted an hour and 45 minutes and after it ended we simply marched over to the German trenches . . . I shall never forget the sights I saw on that walk towards the battlefield nor on the field after the battle. The German trenches were in a terrible state, so great was the havoc wrought by our bombardment. Barbed wire entanglements, thought by the Germans to be impregnable, had been torn to pieces. The trenches in places had been totally obliterated and dugouts and shelters were smashed to pieces. The sight of those German trenches still haunts me. Standing on dead bodies all covered with blood . . . When we arrived here we looked like a regiment of tramps! But respectable tramps would have turned up their noses at us – we were dirty and unkempt, we had ten days of beard on our chins. Some of the boys had lost their puttees and they limped along barelegged and nearly every kilt had been caught and torn on the barbed wire entanglements. We had to scrape the mud off ourselves. Our jackets were stained yellow and green with fumes of lyddite. We stayed there after we had taken it until we were told to retire, which we did without further loss. Then we went under cover to let some regular battalions pass through to get into action. The battalion then marched back in single file to the redoubt to put up for the night, but just as we were settling down we got word to push forward again. Our company reported to HQ, and we were ordered into billets in a ruined farm close to the firing line. We drew our rations and got settled down about 2 a.m.. We had had twenty-four hours of it on end, and all we had to eat was just a bit of bread and bully beef at seven o'clock yesterday morning. I was, like the rest, dead beat. I lay down in the straw in the farm and fell sound asleep. We had to start again at 5 a.m. (11th), so we got up still

179

feeling tired. We carried ammunition and rations all day and finished again about 1 a.m. next day. There was one continual roar and flash from our guns. I saw the Seaforths, 1st Battalion, lining up for a charge; it was a grand sight; what a fine body of men they looked. I believe they lost a lot of officers and men in the action, but it's all in the game. All along the road there was a constant stream of wounded walking out of action and some poor fellows on stretchers. We branched off the road and . . . halted a few minutes while we looked at the ground ahead that we had to cross to get to the position that we had to take up. The British were then well in front of the German trenches and had swung round the German right flank. Being in command of No. 1 Platoon I had to advance first. I took my platoon over the British trenches and over into the captured German trenches. At this point they were a hundred yards apart. When I arrived there, a sergeant of another regiment came to me in a great state asking for assistance to clear about fifty Germans out of part of the trench that had not been taken. I sent word to the officer of the other regiment that I would bring a party round by the German trench and meet up with him. I tried to do this, and we battered them with hand grenades, but we could not get them. They had barricaded themselves well in and had got into a fortified house. All of a sudden our artillery started shelling the place. They had got word that this section of the German trench, which was in the centre of the line of attack, had not been taken. We had to double out of that trench as quick as we could! The colonel then sent for me and told me to advance on a ruined house. I got up over the back of the trench and got my men extended out and we made a rush for it. Three of my chaps were bowled over. One was killed and the other two wounded. One of the wounded was by my side, and I grabbed him as he fell and tried to drag him along, but he was a dead weight and could not help himself in any way, so I left him under cover of a ditch and pushed on to the house.

Lieutenant Steven gained the Military Cross for conspicuous gallantry on 10 March 1915 at Neuve-Chapelle, when he commanded the leading platoon of the battalion in the attack and gained his objective notwithstanding the heavy enfilading to which the men were exposed. The Battle of Neuve-Chapelle was an important success for the British, and was one of the only three clean breakthroughs in the German line throughout the whole war in the west (the others being the first day at Loos in September 1915 and the first day of the tank offensive at Cambrai, 20 November 1917). The Battle of Neuve-Chapelle ended with a gain of 1,200 yards.

Sidney continued his commentary by letter:

16/3/15: We have now been relieved from the firing line. We got ready on the 13th, but it was 2 a.m. on the 14th before we left. I lost one of my men by shrapnel fire, which went on pretty steadily all day. It is marvellous how so many escape being hit. Just before we were relieved, a message came in while I was on duty to say that the Germans were lining up for another attack on our front, but nothing came of it. I moved out with a guide right in front of our trenches, but all was quiet. A star shell showed us the country all around. I was in the trenches with Captain Inglis of the 2nd Black Watch. He had lost all his sub-lieutenants in the last two days. Sergeant Gilroy, with whom I was last on duty, was wounded and has since died . . . [he] was shot while bringing in prisoners. He was out with a corporal and six men against a strong party of Germans who had dug themselves in on our right flank. The rain has been pouring down for twenty-four hours. The company paraded in the darkness and after a long tramp we reached an open field, where we bivouacked until dawn. It was a quagmire, and we lay in about six inches of water. The colonel passed among us and said: 'You'll just have to make the best of it, boys.' So we did. Then we moved on with the brigade to a fairly comfortable billet.

17/3/15, Lacoutre: We left our billet this morning and had a march of about six miles to where we are now. We are away from the firing line and comfortably settled down. I received your letter and Mother's parcel. The arrival of the mail is a great boon. I have been told that the division who relieved us have been attacked and they have lost a lot of ground and a lot of men and we may be pushed forward again to help. The Germans have brought up large reinforcements. I'm afraid I can't tell you the number, but if what I hear is true we are in for a bad time of it. We have honestly had a terrible time out here since we arrived. The sights in those trenches will haunt me to my dying day. I think we have lost about one hundred and forty men but keep this quiet. [Among them was] Private T. Scott [whose] mother lives in Clepington Road. He was an excellent fellow and was beside me the whole time and a great help . . . He was shot dead just in front of me and fell without a murmur. I lifted him up and tried to carry him, but he was too heavy, and I just had to lay him down under cover and push on with the rest of the fellows to our objective . . . In this billet the men are sleeping in a cattle pen that we have covered with straw. They can sleep anywhere now and never grumble. All the water we drink must be boiled before it is drunk.

[Later, same day:] We had an inspection by the general commanding our division [Lieutenant-General C. A. Anderson]. You should have heard his flattering remarks about the battalion. He said something to this effect: 'Officers, non-commissioned officers and men of the Black Watch, you have not been out here very long, but in that short time you have adorned your-selves with lasting honour. You were pushed straight into the firing line, which must have been very trying for you, but you did magnificent work. In fact, I should say excellent work in the great battle fought by our division.'

[Same place, later (a message to his father):] Just a short note to ask you if you would kindly visit John Howie, 50 Ferry Road.

He is the father of one of my chaps killed in action on the 10th. He went missing and I got a note tonight to say that he was found dead by the 1st Seaforths when they were clearing up their field of battle and he was buried by them on the 11th. Howie was an excellent fellow and one whom I always respected and looked to for an example of a good soldier. He never caused any trouble and was always on parades . . . [Also] I'll tell you what one of your societies might do . . . send out to me, if at all possible, about forty shirts, socks, towels and any other things you think might be useful to a soldier in the field. The reason why I ask for these things is that while we were advancing to our position before we charged on the 10th, my platoon took off their packs as they could not fight with them on. We piled them up, left them to be reclaimed later, but another advancing regiment coming after us thought they were just a heap of dead men's kits lying about and flung them into a ditch to use as stepping stones. So my poor devils have absolutely nothing but what they stand up in. Some do not even have anything to eat with or from. I can't buy them anything out here, and it does not look as though we are going to get anything from the government. I am very sorry for them. Will you do what you can and send them out?

In the trenches, 25/3/15: Since I last wrote we have done quite a lot. We left our rest camp on 23rd and had a long march towards the front line . . . We came up to the entrance to it but found that we were up to our knees in water. We sent word back to brigade HQ to that effect, but we were told that we had to go in. I went in first with a sergeant and two men to try to find a way down it, and I can tell you that it was no picnic. I went along about three hundred yards and all the way I was in water and mud up to my calves. At times my kilt spread out on top of the water. There were some big holes made by shrapnel, and I had to step very carefully. At last I reached a place where there were some dugouts and the trench was reasonably dry. I retraced my steps and led the rest up. I am very sorry for the men and for myself! We were soaked to the skin and did not get into the comparatively dry dugouts until 2 a.m. on the morning of the 24th. Every man was dead beat. After posting sentries the rest lay down and went to sleep in the mud.

Same place, 26/3/15: Things are extraordinarily quiet here today. Very little firing on either side by either infantry or artillery. I suppose the bad weather is making everyone lie low. There are still some dead bodies lying about in front of us. I can see one British chap and two Germans, but there are many more. I am sending out a party after dark to bury the poor devils. They must have lain there since the 10th. The British chap lies only twenty yards in front of our trenches. The Germans are only about forty yards in front of our first line here, and we can hear them talking and singing.

28/3/15: We left the firing line at 5 p.m. last night. We marched about five miles to Vieille-Chapelle or rather just past it. It was a glorious evening with a beautiful sunset. We marched cheerily along, singing all the well-known songs. I enjoyed the walk. The billets here are quite good. There was even a roof on the house, and we found some straw to put down in the corners. The CO, Major Tosh, and the adjutant were in the same billet, but they had beds. I felt in great form for singing, so we had a concert, but after about an hour some of them began to feel sleepy and wanted to turn in. I sang on lustily for a while, then everyone else seemed to get a bit annoyed and let fly at me with bits of candles and anything else that they could lay their hands on.

In the trenches, 10/5/15: At 5 a.m. after a very cold sleep in an open trench without any dugouts, the artillery bombardment started. It was not quite as bad as it had been at Neuve-Chapelle but bad enough. From where we were you could see shells landing among the German barbed wire and tearing up all the ground around it. Then the attack started. The 1st Seaforths made a magnificent charge, the finest I have ever seen. They had a good bit of ground to cover before reaching the German lines, about one hundred to two hundred yards of open country, and the poor Seaforths were mowed down by machine fire, killing and wounding many of them. They could not move, so they had to lie out there all, and it was not until night fell at about 8.30 that those who could do so crept in under cover of the darkness. It was fine to see them scrambling over the parapet, as cheery as you like but numbed and stiff with lying out all day. Well, the attack did not succeed, as you will have seen in the papers by the time you get this, owing to a great extent to the number of enemy machine guns.

Word came through to us in the afternoon to move forward to the crescent trench of old fame which is now just fifty yards behind our front line. When we got there at 2.25 p.m. we were told that A Company (my company) would attack to support the 58th Rifles in the third line of advance. So we moved into the firing line. You could hardy hear yourself speak. The noise was so awful. Men were being knocked out right and left . . . I can't describe it, it was too terrible. No one can have any conception of what it is like unless they have been through it. We got into the fire trench with the 58th Rifles after a struggle (the 58th are an Indian regiment). My platoon was to support on the left. Everything was in confusion, and when anyone tried to get out of the trench a hail of bullets met them over the parapet. Podger McIntyre was ordered to put over his two platoons on the right, so he and Ian Law got out and over and all the men followed. They only got about twenty yards when they had to fall flat for cover. They had a miraculous escape. One officer was killed and any number of our fellows. Lieutenant Weinburg was killed as, holding his platoon flag, he gallantly waved his men forward. When he fell, the flag was picked up by Donald Pyott, son of Sergeant-Major Pyott, but he too was killed almost at once. The flag was then picked up by Private J. Ross, who ran forward through the deadly stream of lead, and he also was killed. Then I saw the 2nd Black Watch going over on our right, and they shared the same fate.

Everyone saw that it was madness to try to advance, and I am glad to say that Captain Walker, who remained as cool and collected as he always does under any circumstance, refused to let anyone else go out. So we started to get the trench manned for another attack. It was in a terrible state, with pools of blood and dead and dying bodies. Men seemed to fall all around me. It is a perfect marvel how I escaped. One minute I passed a machine gun manned by four men, the moment I looked again and the whole thing was a mass of debris. The post was blotted out. One man had his head blown off, and another was screaming for help. It is all too terrible to describe . . . I can't even try. All I can tell you is that our own company lost between sixty and seventy men (don't let this be known until it comes out in the papers). I have no sergeants now. My other one was shot through the head when he was standing just beside me. After regaining the trench our company was taken out of the firing line, and rightly too, and we were placed in a trench about 500 yards from the line. After my platoon was comfortably settled down, I went back again to get the wounded brought down. That was an awful job. However, we succeeded in getting them all down before we moved back to our old trench for the night. The last man I brought down was McIntosh of my platoon. I don't know whether I have spoken to you about him or not. I am almost sure that he is the son of that man McIntosh with the wooden legs. He had been hit in the shoulder; it was a job getting him down the communication trench. Poor chap, he was suffering a good deal of pain. We moved back after dark to where we were this morning and we are still there. Shelling has gone on incessantly since Saturday night, and it is a sight to see the red-hot shells sweeping over our head. We should be out of the trenches and into billets, but just now there are so many troops behind us that there can be no billets left for us. I don't think, although you never can tell what is going to happen the next minute, that we will be put in to attack again until we have had a rest. Our brigade has lost 1,030 men . . . cheery, brave, excellent fellows.

In the field, 9/6/15: We are in the front line again now. It is a rotten trench and the Germans are fairly active in front of us. We took over from the Indians last night. It was an awful job. We had to take over listening posts and pickets from whom we could not understand a word they said. While we were doing it our patrol bumped into a German patrol but they lay quiet. The Germans are firing only thirty yards in front of our listening post fellows, who are lying in grass. After lunch today, which was disturbed by shellfire, we had a concert in Patrick's dugout. He has a big gramophone. The shells were flying all around and one went through A Company sergeant-major's dugout . . . but the concert went on.

On 15 June the offensive in the action of Rue d'Ouvert, the northern end of the line, was held by the Highland Division with the 7th Division at the southern end. Its objective was to capture certain German advance posts from which trenches could be dug to connect with the British front. After its capture, the men took a well-earned breather.

24/6/15: This is Thursday now and I started this letter on Tuesday and all I have to report is that I am feeling very stiff. The 2nd Battalion [Black Watch] is quite close to us just now, and there is a great rivalry with regard to sport. Last night they dubbed us at football. A trial game was played on Monday and a Battalion Eleven was chosen afterwards. Jimmy Philip and I were among the chosen few, so last night when we strolled on to the field we found a huge crowd of Black Watch men there to watch. The whole touchline was three deep with them. It was just like a cup tie at home . . . In fact it was one general shout from beginning to end. The officers sat in chairs in a sort of grandstand. Everyone was there, including the CO. The game ended 2–2 and at the end I was done in.

[Later, as the men returned to action:] I have just seen something that, in ordinary circumstance, would have sickened me. A man near me was shot in the head. His brains were all over the place, but he was hanging on for dear life. Have I ever told you what happens to a man after he has been hit? I'll do so now. This man, for example, had been firing over the parapet at a German loophole, and the shot hit through his balmoral and right through the top of his head. He fell like a log, and the men near him got out a field dressing and laid it on the wound and called for the stretcher-bearers. They bandaged him and then carried him through a winding maze of trenches to Dr Rogers, who was waiting to mend the poor beggar. I was there when the man arrived. The stretcher-bearers just lay down their burden and go back at once to the trench. The doctor started with his scissors and cut away the hair all around the wound. The man was choking and quite unconscious. When all the hair was away, he started to cut off the bits of brain lying loose on the head. The wound was then revealed. It was about two inches long and about an inch deep. Not a word was spoken. He dressed it with a bandage and wound it round his head. I ventured with the words, 'Can I help?' He said, 'Yes, carry him down into the dugout.' I did so with the help of a corporal, and we turned him on his left to let the blood run into the heart. I left him in the charge of the corporal and went and had some dinner. I am now going down see how he is. *[Later:]* He is dead, poor chap.

Sidney remained at the front through July and on into August, when he was granted two weeks' home leave. His letters home resumed on 2 September 1915:

Depot on the La Bassée road: I must thank you for giving me such a good time while I was at home. I don't think I could have enjoyed myself better. I saw you looking for me as the train left, but you were not far enough down the platform and I could not catch your eye. I sat opposite an artillery colonel and we chatted sixteen to the dozen until we arrived at Folkestone. I collared a deck chair and I sat and watched the troops embarking. It was rather a fine sight.

Port du Hem 9/9/15: I am back with the battalion again, and I have been posted to C Company to take Ian's place. Now, suddenly, everything is very quiet here. We have been in reserve for about a week, but our brigade goes up tonight. All movements are being kept very quiet, and we dare not talk of impending operations. So don't you dare mention to a soul that I have told you that there is going to be another 'show' on here.

13/9/15: Two companies are still in the trenches, and I am still one of the two in reserve [but] you may expect news soon in the papers from our part of the line. To tell you the truth I think we are going to be in for a very hot time of it very shortly. The battalion is to be in an attack on the German front line one day very soon, and I think there is going to be some very severe fighting. I must say I am looking forward to it. I sound a bloodthirsty sort of a fiend. I only hope I come out of it without getting 'pipped'. If I am hit . . . well, I have done my best and that is all I can do. Above all, you are not to worry. I would not have told you anything about what I do if I had thought that you would. Letters may be stopped for a few days shortly . . .

In fact, for Sidney Steven they never did resume. On 23 September, just prior to the Battle of Loos, the 2nd, 4th and 5th Black Watch Battalions gathered for a sports day in a field near the Lys Canal at Estaires. It was a brilliant, sunny day, and the sports were enjoyed by the men of the three battalions. On 25 September battle commenced. The advance was to be on a five-mile front and every portion of it was already covered by a massive line of enemy machine guns. The assault began at 6 a.m.. A piece of red cloth had been sewn on to the back of every man's jacket so that officers, observing them from the rear, could distinguish them from the enemy. Gas was to be released against the Germans and all British soldiers wore masks. However, the wind changed quickly, and the gas, when released from the canisters, did as much harm to British troops as to the enemy. Major Tarleton, the adjutant of the 4th Battalion, led the attack and fell almost at once. Colonel Walker, Major Tosh and Sergeant-Major Charles crossed into no-man's-land, and Major Tosh was wounded at once and then hit a second time and killed. Two battalion machine guns were on the right flank manned by Lieutenant A. J. Stewart, Sergeant Craig, Corporal Proctor and fourteen men. Lieutenant Stewart was wounded and was later awarded the MC and the Croix de Guerre. Later in the action there was a breakdown of communications owing to the shelling of the telephone lines, and as Colonel Walker attempted to reach the brigade HQ he was fatally wounded. Twenty officers and four hundred and twenty men of 4th Black Watch took part in the battle, and nineteen officers and two hundred and fifty men were killed or wounded. Lieutenant Cunningham was the only officer who went through the action unscathed, only to be subsequently killed in 1916.

Just as this most tragic of battles for the 4th Battalion was ending, Sidney Steven's elder brother Harvey arrived in France and subsequently received a commission in the same battalion as his brother. He arrived at the front the day after the 4th Battalion had been decimated in the battle and discovered immediately that his brother Sidney was among those reported missing in action. Harvey's letters to his parents now take up the story, although at the time of the first one the Battle of Loos had not taken place:

23/9/15: After writing to you from Southampton we went and bought revolvers and other necessaries. We then booked seats at a theatre and after dinner went to see 'The Dollar Princess'.

We treated ourselves to the most prominent box and had a jolly evening . . .

24/9/15: We are now in camp outside Rouen, and we have no word yet of going into the firing line. It may be a day or two.

25/9/15: We leave this afternoon for the trenches. We have not come across anyone from the battalion yet but should do so tomorrow morning. Severe cannonading has been going on all along this front. It sounds as though something is going on, but we don't know what it is. This morning I was put in charge of about one hundred and fifty men of all regiments, and we were put to do a piece of work. We had dinner last night in Rouen. The best meal I have had in this country so far. When we go up this afternoon we are to carry a day's rations with us. It's a great life, and I am enjoying it so far.

Merville, 26/9/15: Mother . . . Sid has been killed. That is the news given to me on my arrival here. I was stopped by one of his men, who told me that Sid was killed in the second line of German trenches. I managed to get on to a hospital train and there I met Pat Duncan, who is wounded in the leg . . . It is all very sad reading for you, but they died nobly, so please, Mother, bear up and trust in providence. That advice from me also applies to Father and all the rest of the family. What is left of the battalion will likely get a rest, and I shall join them. I am in Ken Miller's room here, as we had to report to his office. I have nothing more to say except that I am in good health and you can depend upon it that I will do my duty.

In reserve, 27/9/15: Now I can give you more news. Sid was last seen, mortally wounded, in the second line of German trenches, firing the last rounds of his revolver and killing six Boche. That is authentic . . . He will be reported officially missing but there can be no doubt that he has gone. What a death . . . The colonel has just died after lingering for two days. Major Tosh's body has been recovered. We are in great demand and very busy. We shall soon be moving to another part of the line, but we may be held back here to recover. We are in no danger here.

[Later, same day:] We are to bury the colonel and Tosh tomorrow morning together. I am put in command of C Company [his brother's last posting]. They led the charge on Saturday morning and what is left of them is a pitiful sight. Mother, again I pray you to 'stick it'. Let me have a full account of how things are going at home. Ask Father, please, to tell Young to send the same amount of cigarettes and tobacco that they used to send to Sid and to stop my order. We have taken a lot of German prisoners and a vile lot they are. An ominous silence prevails tonight. Star shells are going up and a few bombs. Rest assured I shall take care of myself consistent with my duty for the sake of all of you at home. I am a little surprised at myself. I feel so cool and collected and I feel very sure of myself, which is a great feeling.

In reserve, 28/9/15: We are probably going back for a rest tomorrow. The 5th Battalion were in support on the 25th and got off lightly. We have two Seaforth officers with us in this barn where we are at present. They have just come out of the trenches in front of here and now they are going in on attack on Aubers Ridge, poor devils . . . they are in for a hot time. The battle is not finished yet, and although it is raining heavily and is pitch dark the trenches are lit up with star shells every few minutes. I went through Sid's things this afternoon, and I am sending very few things back, except one or two souvenirs. His clothing I am distributing among his company, of which I am now in command. I am sleeping in the barn with the doctor. Poor chap, he is terribly cut up. He has come through more than anyone except Cunningham. In our present state we cannot possibly go back into the trenches, so you can rest assured about my safety. They are trying to attach us to the 2nd Black Watch, but we must try to still keep the name of the 4th. God bless you all at home.

[Later, same day:] I have just met a man who was with Sid when he was hit. He has told me all about it. Sid, with his company following him, was attacking the second line of German trenches when he came upon seven Germans. The report I have is that he shot six of them with the six rounds in his revolver. The seventh shot him through the thigh. It was a ghastly wound. He applied a field dressing, but it would not go round, so he stuffed the whole bandage into the wound, and when he was being carried away he was hit again and killed. Today, in a quiet orchard, amid shot and shell we buried the colonel and Major Tosh together, side by side. It was awful, but not an officer flinched at their graveside. There were about a hundred there, from the general down. Dear Father and Mother, be brave. We are gaining a glorious victory. What is going to be done with us we still do not know, but we are not going to allow this famous battalion to be joined to any other. We would rather fight on alone. Sid's new tunic has arrived, but it is of no use to me.

30/9/15: We are in billets not far from the firing line and are under orders to move down to Givenchy, where there is going to be a 'show'. We are supposed to be taken there by motor bus as an early advance is contemplated. Gowans is going home for an operation, and I have been put in command of half the battalion. What with all the administration work and looking after the men, things hum some out here. Dear Mother, do not grieve but rather be proud to take so big a share in this great victory. I shall avenge the death of my pals but always with regard to my safety.

In the trenches, 2/10/15: A lot has happened since I wrote to you last. We left our billets at 6. a.m. yesterday morning and by forced marching got here in the evening. I was put on a horse, and after a halt Major Wauchope and I rode on in front up to the trenches. The general gave me our orders and directions as to which part of the country we were to cover . . . I have a certain part of the trench to look after, and when I first entered it in the dark it was very difficult to find one's way around. However, now it is light, and I have been able to have a good look round. Under Major Wauchope, who is a strong, firm man, we are forming part of the 2nd Black Watch for the moment. Things have been moving fast in my life these days. Twelve months ago I was a trooper in the Scottish Horse, now I command a double company of a famous regiment only seventy yards from the Prussian Guards. Yesterday they shouted across to us: 'It won't be long now till it's all over, Jock.' Last night I slept in a dugout with Bobbie Cunningham. I had no kit or coat, so he kindly asked me to share his blanket with him. We slept well but it is very cold now at nights out here.

[Later:] Since writing the above I have received Father's last letter to Sid and myself. You had evidently heard of the move by then but did not know what the cost was going to be. I have been out in front with my observer having a good look around. It is quite safe. The town in which we are in front of [La Bassée] is a terrible ruin but still provides ample accommodation for Bosche snipers. We are pouring shells in on them and in return they give us a dose of rapid rifle fire.

In the trenches, 3/10/15: We have been here for three days now and but for seven casualties on the first night in the 2nd Black Watch, nothing else has happened. A severe bombardment is going on over to our right. All day big guns, little guns, machine guns and rifles have been firing away, and yet I have been able to sleep. Last night two mines were exploded by us which shook all the ground around, yet I slept all through it! We look forward to letters like starving men long for food! Father said he was sending on an *Advertiser*. It has not arrived yet. I am anxious to read what they say in Dundee about their now famous battalion. I believe, if it were not all so sad, that you would laugh if you saw me now. I am covered from head to foot in mud. I am quite content with this life, and I shall not mind a bit as long as it does not get any worse. I can imagine the church bells ringing at home. It must be just about their time as I write. This letter appears to be very egotistical, but I feel you would want to know all about me.

In the trenches, 4/10/15: All goes well. I have received many letters, including yours. Here are some more details about the 25th. Sid was hit just before the second line of German trenches were reached, so his body could not be recovered when it was reoccupied. We had search parties out every night while we were there, but they only found the body of a private. The place is a few miles in front of Merville, which should be on the map. It is called Moulin de Piètre and it is not far from La Gorgue. The attack was made in a mist with the help of smoke . . . and gas put up by us. (For goodness' sake say nothing of this to anyone.) . . . There is one thing that I want to make quite clear. It is possible that when the casualties are reported officially, Sid may be reported as missing or wounded or something like that. You must take no notice of that because unless an officer is actually seen killed by another officer it cannot be officially reported. With so many officers gone from us, there is no brother officer here who saw him so the information rests with the men from whom I have had quite clear evidence as to how Sid died . . . Remember that Sid was not the only one killed that day and many were seriously wounded.

7/10/15: It is a lovely day and if only the sun could get through down into the trenches it would dry them up rapidly. They are much better already than when we first came in. Mother, you ask me to take care of myself. I shall do that, never fear, consistent, as I have said before, with my duty. I shall do it for your sake . . . and probably for my own . . . Tonight my boys are out repairing the parapet in front of our trench. Shells have been coming over pretty freely tonight, but it is time that I went along and visited them. Cheerio.

Lieutenant Harvey Steven went out and almost immediately was killed by a grenade. He had been on active service in France for only twelve days.

CHAPTER ELEVEN

Unremitting Sacrifice

The shocking devastation of troops in the Battle of Loos was a precursor to greater sacrifice in the months ahead. The battle resulted in more than 60,000 British casualties, of whom almost 8,000 were killed in the field, many others dying later. Further analysis showed a particularly high level of casualties among Scottish battalions, which were widely placed among the leading assault groups. In pursuing this narrative of events, we can in fairness mention only in general terms a few of the actions in which the Black Watch were involved in this terrible landscape of death and destruction.

It was evident that many new army units comprising virtually untrained volunteers and Territorials hurriedly assembled in France under the banner of the 51st Highland Division were quickly decimated, quite apart from the substantial casualties among regular, fully trained troops for whom there was a dire need. Similarly, such a significantly higher proportion of officers were lost – 2,000 killed or wounded at Loos – that it became a severe handicap as experienced men and their leaders fell in the field in horrific circumstances that in no way detracted from their courage and commitment.

Even as the final stages of the first Battle of Loos were being played out, another drama that transfixed the world was unfolding at the other end of the spectrum of British combat, in Mesopotamia (Iraq). In December 1915 the 2nd Battalion of the Black Watch, as part of the Indian Meerut Division, were withdrawn with other units from France and sent as reinforcements to Basra for the attempted relief of British forces besieged at Kut-el-Amara (see below). This necessity put even greater pressure on the British Expeditionary Force (BEF) in Europe, and during those winter months the emphasis was, by necessity, focused on swelling the number of new recruits to fill the gaps. This was easier said than done, now that the raw reality of life in the trenches was becoming painfully evident to all in the home country, and of great concern to mothers and wives across the land, as well as to the politicians. The 4th and 5th Black Watch were amalgamated in March 1916 to make up a full battalion after Loos because of the shortage of men, a matter that was seriously affecting many units and led to the introduction of conscription in January 1916.

Such a move became even more urgent when a month later the Germans began the notorious campaign of attrition against the French at Verdun, a battle that went down in world history as the longest-ever single arena of conflict. It ran for almost eleven months on a battlefield that was less than ten miles square. Both sides suffered horrendous losses, with almost a million men killed, wounded or missing in just this one huge onslaught of an intensity and horror never before witnessed, or perhaps even imagined, in warfare. The French, under tremendous pressure, appealed to the British for greater help, which resulted in drawing in men from other sectors, and this became a baptism of fire for the 51st Highland Division. In spite of a shaky start through lack of training and expertise, the men of the 51st, which included Black Watch Territorial battalions, went on to serve with considerable distinction on the Western Front throughout the war. The task that lay immediately ahead, however, was to move south to take over the French sector at Arras. The division took possession of a complicated labyrinth of trenches, which became the home ground of the 6th and 7th Battalions, on and off, over the next two years, although they, too, were intermittently switched to other sectors.

Meanwhile, the British military hierarchy, which had begun the war supposedly as the junior partner in the alliance, now had to increase their commitment substantially, much to the fear and dismay of the politicians in Westminster. The military commanders, and General Sir Douglas Haig in particular, chose to turn the Battle of the Somme into a full-scale battle that would also have a diversionary effect, forcing the Germans to switch troops from Verdun and give the French a better chance. The plan did not work, and resulted in the continuing wholesale slaughter on all fronts. Almost 60,000 British and Commonwealth casualties fell at the Somme, a third of them fatal, on the opening day of battle, 1 July 1916 – the worst day in the history of the British army. One account described the opening:

Before dawn there was a great silence. We spoke to each other in whispers, if we spoke. Then suddenly our guns opened out in a barrage of fire of colossal intensity. Never before, and I think never since . . . had so many guns been massed behind any battle front. It was a rolling thunder of shellfire, and the earth vomited flame, and the sky was alight with bursting shells. It seemed as though nothing could live, not an ant, under that stupendous artillery storm. But Germans in their deep dugouts lived, and when our waves of men went over they were met by deadly machine-gun and mortar fire. Our men got nowhere on the first day. They had been mown down like grass by German machine-gunners who, after our barrage had lifted, rushed out to meet our men in the open. Many of the best battalions were almost annihilated.

Haig had believed he would achieve quick results from the opening bombardment, which exceeded all other previous such openings by the heavy-metal units by some considerable margin. In truth, although bad enough, it did not do the untold damage to the Germans that London had been promised, and soon more reinforcements would be required to sustain the fighting at the Somme as it ran into weeks and months, until winter prevailed. When Haig called a halt to the offensive in November, the British and Commonwealth troops had suffered 420,000 casualties. The French had lost nearly 200,000, and German casualties were estimated at half a million. The land gained by the Allied forces was a mere nine miles, and that at the deepest part of the incursion into German lines. The Black Watch battalions, as with most of the front-line infantry, took heavy losses. John Raws wrote in a letter to his brother just before he was killed in the Battle of the Somme on 12 August 1916:

The glories of the Great Push are great, but the horrors are greater. With all I'd heard by word of mouth, with all I had imagined in my mind, I yet never conceived that war could be so dreadful. The carnage in our little sector was as bad, or worse, than that of Verdun, and yet I never saw a body buried in ten days. And when I came on the scene, the whole place, trenches and all, was spread with dead. We had neither time nor space for burials, and the wounded could not be got away. They stayed with us and died, pitifully, with us, and then they rotted. The stench of the battlefield spread for miles around. And the sight of the limbs, the mangled bodies, and stray heads. We lived with all this for eleven days, ate and drank and fought amid it; but no, we did not sleep. Sometimes, we just fell down and became unconscious. You could not call it sleep . . . Had we more reinforcements up there, many brave men now dead, men who stuck it and stuck it and stuck it till they died, would be alive today . . . It is sad to think that one has to go back to it, and back to it, and back to it, until one is hit.

Five battalions of the Black Watch were also engaged in the next stage, at Longueval and Delville Wood, where they took heavy losses in fierce fighting, especially at Longueval, which changed hands several times before the British reclaimed it. When the 8th Battalion, for example, was withdrawn and relieved by the Durham Light Infantry from a position they had won and held against repeated attacks by a strong German force, there were just 141 men still standing. The battalion were applauded for their incredible fortitude in holding the position against seemingly overwhelming odds.

After the Somme, the remaining great and infamous battles of this brutal and murderous war took their place in history. Arras, the third Battle of Ypres, Cambrai and Marne came and went with all nations observing them with increasing wonder, anger and horror as their troops ploughed on with outstanding courage. The third Battle of Ypres, or Passchendaele, raged through the months of August to November 1917, claiming another 400,000 British and Commonwealth casualties. In London, Prime Minister Lloyd George even began to hold back reinforcements for fear that they were being 'wasted' on these huge battles that so often ended in stalemate. When a halt was called, the Allies had gained no more than five miles of ground at the deepest part of the salient, and the war still had a year to run. In the Battle of Cambrai, the Germans launched their spring offensive of 1918, now fortified by the release of divisions fighting on the Eastern Front after the Communist revolution took Russia out of the war. Conversely, the American armies were now adding to the Allies' strength.

The 1st Battalion of the Black Watch, battle weary and cut to ribbons on three occasions but still in business, now found themselves at Givenchy, near the northern bank of La Bassée Canascene. Here, in 1914, the Germans had demonstrated a new phenomenon: tunnelling under a considerable area with the intention of blowing up British positions. It was a task in which they became so proficient that the British made a mad dash to form their own companies of tunnellers. In fact, this was one of the most rapid deployments of the entire war, when men drawn from the ranks mixed with skilled miners recruited specifically for the task. Men who were working in British coal mines as civilians on 12 February found themselves underground at Givenchy less than a week later; the specialist miners were to lead the tunnelling teams. They set mines beneath defensive German positions in the tunnels, which stretched under no-man's-land and into enemy territory. After detonation, the infantry advanced towards the front line, hoping to find the enemy in a state of panic and confusion.

Various methods were devised by the troops to discover any tunnelling beneath their positions. One of the simplest was to place a stick into the ground and hold the other end between the teeth to test for underground vibrations. The miners also had to listen out for enemy tunnellers and not infrequently found themselves digging right into an enemy tunnel, leading to a fight under ground.

As the war progressed, techniques were improved, ammunition shortages were resolved and huge amounts of explosives were taken underground. The largest so far was at the opening of the Somme offensive, when the British detonated twenty-four tons. Another massive mine at Spanbroekmolen left a crater measuring 430 feet from rim to rim by 40 feet deep; it is now known as the Pool of Peace. By 1917 the British were even more proficient at tunnelling than the Germans, and in June 400 tons of explosive were placed under the German front line at Messines by the British, who burrowed their way through the earth at a depth up to 100 feet, and with the tunnels reaching 2,000 feet in length – in all, 7,000 yards of tunnels. At strategic points inside, they placed 19 mines, whose accumulated weight of explosives amounted to in excess of 500 tons. They were exploded simultaneously at 3.10 p.m. on 7 June, killing an estimated 10,000 soldiers. The explosion was so loud it was heard in London and Dublin. Two of the mines failed to explode, and papers relating to their location were subsequently mislaid. One exploded under a field during a thunderstorm in 1955, killing a cow; the other remains, at the time of writing, undiscovered.

In the wake of the explosion, nine British divisions advanced to seize their allotted areas. At Givenchy, the 1st Battalion found themselves in underground subways designed as shelters or for infantry to reach front lines with less risk of being bombed en route. These were utilised for an attack in which men of both armies met and a firefight opened up underground, where the gloom was lifted by the blaze of gunfire. On this occasion, the Highlanders took another bad hit when two companies became trapped. They were killed or captured when the Germans used flame-throwers and grenades. The platoon that came safely to the surface found themselves just forty yards from enemy positions and a second fierce battle developed, which the Black Watch held off aided by the Camerons and the Northamptonshire Regiment.

In a continuing conflict in which horror and human degradation had become the norm, there were occasional highlights of a job well done or some particularly heroic action where the participants, or at least some of them, survived to enjoy the glory. One such occasion involved the 6th Battalion, which had been assigned the task of capturing the hamlet of Chambrecy, on which they had made a rapid advance across 800 yards of open ground without hindrance. But as they closed towards the target area, a well-hidden German unit opened up with heavy shelling and machine-gun fire. As men began to fall rapidly, the order was given to close ranks and continue towards the village, there to stage a fightback to force the Germans out and on the run. When the battalion's nearest support, a French battalion, arrived, they were amazed to discover that the Black Watch, with just 140 men still active, had not only held the village but forced the Germans out so effectively that they did not stage a counter-attack. The French commanders reported what they considered to be an outstanding feat, and subsequently the battalion were awarded the Croix de Guerre for what the citation recognised as an important position taken by the Black Watch battalion after ten days of relentless fighting, ending on 30 July 1918.

By coincidence, on the same day French honours were being bestowed on the 4/5th Battalion for their action at Buzancy. Having joined the Seaforths and Camerons, they made a dramatic rush to the village, which was on high ground, and again found well-dug-in resistance. A battle raged for over four hours before the Highlanders were forced to retreat, suffering heavy losses. Later, when a French division arrived to take the village, they were amazed to discover the depth of the earlier attack and recommended there and then that a monument should be erected on the very spot where they found the body of the soldier of the Black Watch who had advanced the furthest. The memorial, which still stands, was inscribed 'Here to flower always, the glorious thistle of Scotland among the roses of France'.

The fighting for all the Black Watch battalions went on with the same intensity almost to the very day of the Armistice. Civilian celebrations were naturally filled with high spirits, but for the soldiers themselves it was at best sheer relief that the war was over. They all knew there were no winners in this war; the mile after mile of memorial gravestones that would soon be planted in the battlefields of France would bear testament to that. Three battalions of the Highland regiments – 1/6th Black Watch, 1/4th Seaforths and 1/4th Gordon Highlanders – moved to Germany as part of the Army of Occupation. There was also a rare irony that on Armistice Day, 11 November 1918, the 4th/5th Battalion of the Black Watch were to be found advancing across the very field of Fontenoy where the regiment had fought their first battle 173 years previously.

There were, of course, other components of the Black Watch whose stories are also filled with drama, courage and ultimately considerable suffering, and none more so that the 2nd Battalion. It will be recalled that in December 1915 the battalion joined a special force to be urgently dispatched to that other theatre of the war, the eastern Mediterranean. After the terrible saga of the Gallipoli campaign, in which the British, Anzac and Empire units suffered more than 250,000 casualties, the conflict moved to the deserts east of Suez, especially those in the ancient state of Mesopotamia (now Iraq). At the start of the war, the Turkish Ottoman Empire held Mesopotamia, which provided a vital link to the Gulf. Around it on either side were British and French colonial interest in Persia (Iran), Arabia and Syria, and Egypt and Suez. The Allies had two key objectives: to maintain control of Suez and to protect the Persian oilfields. In a region whose lands had been controlled by rival colonising forces for centuries, the war in Europe was of little consequence.

Turkey entered the war on the side of Germany, which provided senior military advisers and arms. Britain was forced to move a large body of troops into southern Mesopotamia, a region that was to become familiar to later generations of the Black Watch. General Sir John E. Nixon, who commanded the Anglo-Indian troops in the region, was under orders to annex what territories he felt necessary to give the British control of Mesopotamia. Major-General C. V. F. Townshend, a veteran of the Battle of Omdurman, was commanding operations in the field with the 6th Poona Division of British, Indian and Gurkha troops and had made creditable progress through Mesopotamia. After beating off two Turkish attacks, he began his advance up the Tigris in a flotilla of boats.

The summer heat beat on his men, and as they progressed they ran out of navigable water and the boats had to be pulled through swamps and finally manhandled over the desert. The troops dropped like the flies that surrounded them, from dysentery, malaria and heatstroke. Even so, they pressed on and fought several battles. In spite of almost a third of the troops being affected by illness at one time or another, the march through Mesopotamia went well. Much ground had been won with relatively few casualties, and General Townshend became aware that those above him had Baghdad in their sights. It would be a marvellous coup to take the capital, with its population of around 150,000, but Townshend was against the idea unless his army – a mere 14,000 troops, 1,000 cavalry, 38 guns and 7 aircraft – was substantially reinforced.

The issue was still being debated in London when he was ordered to advance on Kut-al-Amara, 200 miles from Baghdad, where the Turks had put down a force of around 10,000 men. Townshend had little difficulty with them and put the Turkish army to flight after capturing 1,300 prisoners and all their guns. The Turks drew back to Ctesiphon, the ruined former capital of Mesopotamia, and Townshend moved on in pursuit. He was ordered to advance to Ctesiphon, where the Turks were now spread out and dug in. Unknown to the British, reinforcements had been rushed in. Not only was Townshend outgunned, but he would face a combined force of regulars and Arab conscripts of close on 21,000 men. So began the countdown to one more great disaster. Townshend made several unsuccessful attacks on the Turks over the next eight days, and bitter fighting ensued, with the loss of 4,600 men of the British force. He was forced to withdraw his force back to Kut-el-Amara, a small town on the loop of the River Tigris, with the Turks in hot pursuit.

On 3 December 1915 the enemy pulled off a classic desert manoeuvre by throwing a cordon around the British encampment and called on Townshend to surrender. He refused, confident that a relief column would come to their aid and put the Turks to flight, just as Gordon had hoped to do in Khartoum. It was at that point that the Black Watch and other units were hastily recalled from France to be sent immediately to Basra, there to join a force that was to rescue Townshend, who had indicated he had only enough supplies and ammunition to hold out until 10 January.

The relief force did not arrive until ten days before that deadline, and with no training or preparation for the task at hand – and desert warfare was a breed apart – they began the journey forward. Worse still, because of the need for speed in transferring the men to the rescue area, some essential equipment was left behind. The relieving force consisted of a mixture of units, including the 7th Meerut Division, of which the 2nd Black Watch were part, two additional brigades, a brigade of cavalry and various engineers and other units. In total, there were just over 21,000 troops, under the command of General Sir Fenton Aylmer, who gave them the title of the Tigris Corps.

They set off in haste, but at Sheikh Sa'ad intelligence warned Aylmer of a Turkish encampment of about 8,000 men. What the British didn't know was that a much larger force was already on its way to join them, and in total they would face five Turkish divisions, amounting to 23,000 men, positioning themselves on either side of the river. As the British force approached on 7 January 1916, they were simply cut down by small-arms fire. The attacking infantry, led by the 2nd Black Watch and the 1st Seaforth Highlanders, were ordered forward only to be met by murderous crossfire, and by nightfall it became obvious that there would be no breakthrough. The relief column simply dug in for protracted fighting.

The brave attempt was a catastrophe for the infantry. Less than half of the Black Watch remained fit for duty from the 900-strong attacking force, with similar casualties among the Seaforth Highlanders and Indian battalions. What made the situation even

206

worse was that because of the light load being carried by the hurrying troop train, the Meerut Division had only the capacity to deal with 250 casualties but were faced with almost 4,000, a quarter of whom were still lying out in the open 11 days after the fighting. Of these, 100 were suffering from sickness and dysentery.

Elsewhere, the attempt to relieve Townshend's garrison continued, as more and more men were hurried into position only to be faced by increasing numbers of Turks. In a series of battles between January and March 1916, the relieving British troops suffered further heavy casualties and were still unable to break through to the beleaguered Poona Division. By April 1916 Townshend's position was critical. Men were now dying of starvation. The cavalry horses all had to be slaughtered and eaten, food that the Indian and Gurkha contingents would not touch on religious grounds, and the first-ever food drops by air were made. Light planes flying dangerously low over Turkish positions dropped 16,800 pounds of supplies over the relief force, which was bogged down just seventeen miles from the siege area. In London, there were rumours of an important announcement about the trapped British force, and on 29 April 1916 the War Office released a statement that shocked the nation:

> After a siege that has lasted for 143 days, Major-General Charles Townshend, commanding the 6th [Poona] Division, today surrendered unconditionally to the Turkish general Khalil Pasha at Kut-el-Amara in Mesopotamia. Resistance to the Turkish onslaught has been conducted with gallantry and fortitude but failed because of the shortage of supplies.

The news caused great dismay throughout the Empire, especially in India. For a British force of such magnitude to lay down their arms, *The Times* noted, was 'without precedent'. The surviving 2,600 British and 10,486 Indian and Gurkha troops surrendered into the custody of the Turks. Of those, 4,200 were never seen again, most having fallen and died by the wayside on a forced march across 500 miles of desert to Aleppo or were killed by acts of wanton cruelty and beatings by the Turks. More than 3,000 of those who surrendered at Kut were murdered in this way while in captivity. Those who survived were skeletal and many close to death when they were released two years later. Those casualties however, appalling though they were, and especially because of the treatment meted out by the Turks, paled against the casualties suffered by the forces which had come to relieve them in the four months of the campaign to reach Kut. The final number was 21,000 killed, wounded or who died through lack of medical treatment. The Black Watch and the Seaforth Highlanders were so badly mauled that they had to amalgamate, to form a Highland battalion consisting of just four companies.

The Black Watch were kept out of the action for several months while retraining, and repairs were carried out with a draft of new recruits. It was well into the New Year of 1917 before they saw action of any substance, and almost immediately secured the most coveted honour in the British military. The scene was still Mesopotamia, the enemy still the Turks, and the location was the ancient ruin of Istabulat on the west bank of the Tigris. The inexperienced men were in the firing line, along with other Highlanders, and the Turks continued to maintain a strong presence in every department of their attack. It was a tough battle, lasting a dozen days, so furious that it was sufficient to provide the scenario for two VCs to be won. The outstanding bravery for the first was demonstrated on 22 April, when Lieutenant Reginald Graham of the 9th Argyll and Sutherland Highlanders, attached to the 136 Company of the Machine Gun Corps, insisted on ferrying ammunition; although wounded twice, he continued in control of one gun, accurately firing on the enemy. When this gun was put out of action, he was forced to retire but before doing so disabled his gun and then brought a Lewis gun into action until he had used all the ammunition and had been wounded a fourth time. The lieutenant went on to become a lieutenant-colonel and later received a knighthood.

Next it was the turn of a Black Watch private to do his deed. Step forward a man considered to be an 'old' soldier at the age of thirty-one. He was Private Charles Melvin of Kirriemuir, whose moment came after a period of ferocious fighting at Istabulat. His company were waiting for reinforcements before attacking a front-line trench. While waiting, Melvin discovered that his bayonet was damaged and could not be attached to his rifle. In a moment of inspiration – or madness, depending on the outcome – he threw his rifle aside and, armed only with the bayonet, rushed into the attack on the Turkish position by himself, over ground swept by rifle and machine-gun fire. On reaching the trench, he immediately killed two of the enemy with the bayonet and then attacked the rest. Most of them fled, but not before Private Melvin had killed two more and disarmed nine others. He bandaged up one wounded man and took him and his other prisoners back to an officer before reporting back to his platoon sergeant. Melvin, who was awarded the Victoria Cross, may have had a hand in scaring off the Turks. The Turkish army, already flagging and unable to sustain its earlier successes, withdrew from Istabulat when reinforcements were now required to fight the advance through Palestine of General Edmund Allenby's army. In turn, the 2nd Black Watch were among those units sent to join Allenby and arrived just after he entered Jerusalem on 11 December 1917, entering the city officially at noon at the head of a parade of commanders of the French and Italian detachments, the heads of the political missions and the Military Attachés of France, Italy and America. A further Black Watch battalion were also formed, the 14th Fife and Forfar Yeomanry Battalion, but they were subsequently shipped off to the Western Front along with other battalions of Allenby's army because of the dire shortage of manpower in France. Allenby subsequently suspended his own operations until August 1918 because of these losses. But when the advance was resumed in August, the 2nd Battalion were among the key forces deployed in Allenby's most famous manoeuvre, which ended with the decimation of the Turks at the Battle of Megiddo in September. Damascus fell on 1 October, and four weeks later the 2nd Battalion were heading for Tripoli when news arrived that Turkey had capitulated and an armistice had been signed. Their final shots also signalled the end of hostilities for the Black Watch in the First World War. Throughout, the battalions, along with the affiliated units from the Canadian Black Watch, had shared in the battle honours and had also experienced the very worst of the action. Nothing in the regiment's history could compare with the decimation of its young men on the scale experienced since 1914, and no words could justify it either.

Chapter Twelve

And So to the Next One . . .

The brave weekend soldiers, many of the survivors of whom were mutilated or gassed, returned to the bosom of their families as the Territorials were stood down. The decimation of their battalions would take years to recover, and there were numerous amalgamations. The service battalions were also disbanded, and some of their manpower went towards the substantial rebuilding of the 1st and 2nd Battalions as they returned to the routine of alternating between home and foreign service. The 1st Battalion was destined for an eighteen-year posting to India after the due process of recovery from the war for an engagement that, little did they know it, would extend in time to the point where they were on the brink of the Second World War. They left Britain still not up to full strength because of the fall in post-war recruitment.

The 2nd Battalion, after almost twenty-one years overseas, in India, France and Mesopotamia, were placed on the home billet, although there was also a good deal of movement between the battalions now, to enable the bringing home of those who were due for leave and to give the experience of service abroad to newer young fellows during this eighteen-year turn and turn-about arrangement between the two battalions. A system whereby young officers could buy themselves out of foreign service was also in place. Lieutenant-Colonel David Rose, recalling the early days of his career with the Black Watch, explained in his autobiography:

> If you were posted to a battalion that was on foreign service, you could pay someone below you on the list to go in your place – probably for the price of a polo pony. I was warned for posting to the 1st Battalion in Meerut in Northern India. I didn't much want to go because of my mother's recent bereavement. [A colleague] said he would go in my place. His father had also died, so he wound up going out anyway . . . escorting his sister, who was to be married out there.

The 2nd Battalion had barely settled into life back in Scotland when the alert came for them to prepare for movement abroad – as it turned out, to Silesia, the tiny nation torn apart by centuries of the territorial disputes between Germany, Austria and Poland. After the war, the Treaty of Versailles called for a referendum to determine if Upper Silesia was to remain German or to pass to Poland. The result was favourable to Germany except in the easternmost part, where the Polish population predominated. After an armed uprising by the Poles, the League of Nations accepted a partition of the territory. The larger part of the industrial district, including Katowice, passed to Poland; the contested areas, including the city of Teschen, were partitioned between Poland and Czechoslovakia by the conference of ambassadors. But neither side was satisfied. As more unrest began, the Black Watch became one of the first regiments to operate as a military stabilising force under the mandate of the League of Nations, forerunner of so many similar operations under the United Nations later in the century. They were based there for two and a half years before returning to continue their home posting, which lasted until 1937. By then, the next flare-up was in the throes of creation – a development insightfully predicted by an officer of the Black Watch as they left Silesia. In the battalion's history, he wrote in 1924, 'Will the Poles benefit by their accession of territory? Many of us doubt it, and some even prophesy that within this generation the German flag will again fly from the Rathaus.'

The rest of the 1920s was as gloomy militarily as the economic scenario. Bankrupt Britain fell into the Depression, with unemployment, strikes and social unrest, and recruitment began to pick up as young men throughout the nation turned to the services for work. Even that prospect was not bright, given that soldiers' pay was cut and that the army was kept on a tight rein financially, with no money for modernisation. Consequently, horses were still much in use two years before the outbreak of the Second World War. Many regiments still found difficulty in bringing their numbers up to establishment, but the Black Watch historically attracted a good crop of budding young soldiers who were gradually filling the gaps.

There was a notable increase in the numbers coming forward from south of the border, an aspect of the era that did not especially please some of the diehard officers. But what was apparent from later recollections was that the men who did arrive were largely doing so by choice, and not under the direction of some recruiting sergeant handing round the whisky. John Frederick 'Fred' Baron was among those who went up to Perth from England, after specifically requesting a posting to the Black Watch. In his memoir for the Imperial War Museum Sound Archive he recalled:

I went to a recruiting office at the age of eighteen and was posted to Catterick. I did my basic training in the Corps of Signals, but as soon as that was over I put in for a transfer to the Black Watch. I had heard so much about them from a chap who lived in my village. When I transferred I had to buy my own kit, the kilt, tunics, boots and so on which I had to pay for out of wages. It was very expensive but it looked good once you had acclimatised to the draught.

The age-old question of the kilt was still present and invariably came up in conversations about the Highlanders. Those who covered themselves beneath it were called 'defaulters' by the old-timers, and that included most of the newer fellows. One of the many stories about this matter is told by Colonel Rose, relating to a company commander who possessed a complete lack of finesse when wearing the kilt. This man would sit behind his desk with knees wide apart, revealing what he described as the 'flesh and fur' to those entering his office. 'Sometimes,' Rose wrote, 'I would catch the eye of a young soldier on company orders looking aghast at this awesome spectacle. He knew that I knew what he was looking at with such rapt attention, and he would cast his eyes to the ceiling in a vain attempt to stop the giggles.'

But back to the account of Fred Baron:

The Black Watch was different altogether [from his posting to Catterick] in training and outlook. I'd already done weapons training and now proceeded to learn the Black Watch way. I got on very well with the chaps from the beginning. The language was a bit strange to me, difficult to understand at the beginning. I was treated very well. There was a decent intake of lads about my age. We did route marches of thirty miles once a month and plenty of PT to get us fit and hard. I was doing this for just six months before I joined a draft being sent to India, sailing from Southampton in the *Lancastria*, a huge troopship. She was a good ship, but very crowded. The journey took three weeks, and I worked in the troops' galley as a fatigue man during the trip.

We landed in Bombay and went from there to Meerut by train [800 miles as the crow flies]. The journey was long and diffi-cult. The windows were so dirty with sand and mud we couldn't see a thing. When we arrived, we saw all the sights as we marched through, including the church whose clock had stopped at the time of the Indian Mutiny and had been left untouched since. Once we settled in, we had a routine of guard duties around the garrison. There was a constant undercurrent of [nationalist] trouble, and we did regular thirty-mile marches to 'fly the flag', as the CO called it. We did have some social life off duty, and went into the local towns. Some of us even had girlfriends, from the local population, to which the army turned a blind eye. In the summer we went into the hills to Darjeeling for three months, which was very good, much cooler. There was a large British population there, of course, and there were dances every week, whist drives and so on, a very good social life.

Flying the flag was the way of showing the presence of a military prepared to enforce law and order if necessary in a country seething with nationalistic ambitions. There was seldom fighting as such; indeed, the battalion enjoyed a generally peaceful existence during their year in the country. Even so, service in India was no bed of roses. Although casualties from disease and sickness were nowhere near as high as in earlier years on foreign soil, there were other intolerable irritants, such as prickly heat, bad water, stinging insects, swarms of flies and the incredible dust kicked up by a route march that choked and blinded the soldiers. Such was the life for the 1st Battalion, year on year, through the 1920s and 1930s as Mahatma Gandhi and Jawaharlal Nehru led the independence movement towards greater public disobedience in their campaign for an India 'equal and free'.

Through these two decades, the Black Watch were part of the British military that continued to act as the buffer between the aspirations of a nation desperately seeking to control its own destiny and the intransigence of Westminster. In the 1930s, however, British attitudes towards India began to shift, partly as a result of Gandhi's protests, which saw him and his fellow nationalists in and out of prison along with tens of thousands of others. The economic importance of India to the British Empire began to wane, while the cost of maintaining a vast administrative staff and military rose. More and more concessions were made until in 1935 Parliament passed the Government of India Act and India was divided into self-ruling territories, which were to be a united federation along the same lines as Australia or Canada. Naturally, the Indian National Congress, headed by Nehru, wanted an end to British rule altogether, but the diehards of British politics, including Winston Churchill himself, were hugely against such a move. Even so, when the time came, India would send thousands of troops to fight for the British Empire.

The 1st Battalion completed their time overseas in 1936 and on the way home stopped off in the Sudan, and at Khartoum they were given a good briefing about General Gordon. It was no more than another flag-waving expedition, and after a year they were sailing back to the UK against a backdrop of growing anticipation in Europe of the Second World War.

By the time the 1st Battalion arrived home, the 2nd Battalion had already left for their overseas posting to the troubled region of Palestine, where widespread violence required additional British troops to reinforce an already large force. This was another leftover from the First World War, a region placed under British administration by the League of Nations, whose local advisers were convinced that Jew and Arab could peacefully coexist. This judgement was made before the Nazis began their purge of Jews in Germany, leading to mass arrivals of totally unexpected proportions. Thus, in April 1937 the partition of Palestine between Arabs and Jews was recommended by a Royal Commission and accepted by the British government as 'the best and most hopeful solution of the deadlock'.

The model was the partition of Ireland, and the results were a parallel of discontent for the rest of the century. It was proposed that, after a transitional period, sovereign independent states for the Palestinians and the Jews would be given strict borders. Jerusalem and Bethlehem, with a corridor to the sea, would form part of a small enclave to be reserved under a new British mandate. That was the plan, to which two former officers of the Black Watch, General Archibald Wavell and Sir Arthur Wauchope, had subscribed. At the time, they represented the military and civil authority, with the former as commander of British forces and the latter as High Commissioner.

According to his statements to the Royal Commission, Wauchope was convinced that the two races could live together in harmony. Unfortunately, it was a gross misjudgement and thus began decades

216

of bloodshed. The British began to attempt to enforce the peace and goodwill towards each other that, at the time of writing, had still not been achieved. The Black Watch were among those charged with attempting to keep the peace as a military police force, one of the first British units to attempt to maintain harmonious relations between the two sides. The Watch, in the mode of their ancestors in the years of the regiment's creation, assumed the role in Jerusalem in October 1937, and immediately two of their comrades were murdered on duty, shot in the back. The killers, and those who carried out subsequent shootings, were tracked to an Arab village, and in that region the Black Watch were the only battalion available to throw a cordon around the village.

The soldiers were fired up over the murders, and there was a briefly threatened mutiny when some men attempted to leave the barracks to go in search of the killers. They were quickly brought back in line. In his own recollections of this incident, General Wavell admitted that he was worried by the tense situation developing among his troops and that he spent an 'unhappy night, as I knew I had taken a certain risk. There were a great number of people, both in Palestine and at home, who were only too ready to accuse British troops of atrocities, and I did not want my old regiment involved in what might well be a serious incident.'

Whoever gave the troops their final briefing before deployment into the village the next day had the desired effect. They moved forward in a calm and efficient manner, and when shots were fired by their opposers only warning shots were returned. In fact, the soldiers later made friends with the locals, and, as Jerusalem itself also calmed down, the battalion moved on to continue this policing operation without further loss of life, aided by a draft of an additional 200 men dropped off by the 1st Battalion as they sailed from the Sudan.

The 1st Battalion arrived home in 1938 to a nation whose military commanders were in a state of great worry. In 1920 their best prophets had projected that there would be no war for at least twenty years.

217

By then, the nation would have recovered sufficiently to confront a modern enemy, should one arise, and so there was no great rush to re-arm. But, just like the tomorrow that never comes, substantial re-equipping of British forces was continually put off. By the mid-1930s, when not one but three enemies presented themselves with awe-inspiring potential, Britain was left desperately short of everything required to defend her corner. For almost two decades, military spending had focused on maintaining bases and garrisons around the world and putting on a bold front with a Royal Navy whose equipment, in truth, was also looking distinctly tired.

The building of new ships had stalled, and the development of military aircraft proceeded at a snail's pace (although fortunately private enterprise was making great strides). The army was still using First World War rifles, new artillery pieces were in short supply, total mechanisation was still a pipe dream and in some units guns were still pulled by horses. In 1935 the British Chiefs of Staff provided the government with a severe jolt, warning for the first time that the military would be in difficulties if confronted by the three-power enemy emerging. The British Cabinet chose not to accept the warning, in spite of the urging of Winston Churchill.

Mussolini took advantage of benign British policy and, with a nod of approval from the French, invaded Abyssinia. With virtually no opposition, he thus added Emperor Haile Selassie's realm, which he considered a jewel in the forging of the new Roman Empire, to the Italian colonies of Eritrea, Somaliland and Libya. Hitler, similarly inspired by the lack of any meaningful response by the League of Nations to Mussolini's warmongering, snatched back the demilitarised Rhineland in March 1936 and received not so much as a slap on the wrist. This was partly because he promised a new treaty guaranteeing twenty-five years of peace, which a large number of gullible British and American appeasers took as an 'assurance of Germany's pacific intentions', in spite of the already alarming attacks on Jews.

The Cabinet remained committed to a smooth relationship with both Hitler and Mussolini, but towards the end of 1937 the Chiefs of Staff renewed their warning of the three-power enemy when Italy joined Germany and Japan in a pact and then left the League of Nations. The plain fact was that Britain – even with the help of her Empire and dominion nations, such as India, Australia, New Zealand and Canada – was not ready to fight a war against even one enemy, let alone three. They were, for example, still at least four years away from putting effective bombers in the air, and on the ground the military hardware, such as tanks and guns, was certainly no match for that being manufactured in Germany. Prime Minister Chamberlain succeeded in stalling the issue only by flying to Germany for a meeting with Hitler, returning with a worthless piece of paper which he held aloft and said 'Peace in our time'.

Sensible military commanders were already doing their best to prepare for what now seemed to be the inevitable outcome, but there was a limit to what they could achieve. Hardware especially could not be conjured out of the air, and in 1938 the 1st Battalion began to take stock for future requirements. The tally was pathetic. Manpower was the greatest need, and never before in peacetime had the battalion been so undermanned. Nine officers and 200 men had been transferred to the 2nd Battalion in Palestine on the way home from the Sudan. Another 123 men had been detached to take part in a vocational training programme, which, of all things, was designed to teach them a trade before re-entering civilian life. That left barely 300 men available for duty in the 1st Battalion. Worse still was the state of their equipment, a sorry mess that was in fact witnessed by military attachés from Germany, Italy and Egypt, who were all present at manoeuvres in August. Bernard Fergusson tells us that the German attaché was also present at Sandhurst during the making of a film when the battalion possessed a mere twenty of the new Bren guns instead of the fifty they should have been awarded, anti-tank guns were represented by lengths of gas piping stuck into pieces of wood, and there were no mortars.

That representatives of potential enemies were present at all was a scandal, and they must have gladdened Hitler's heart with their reports of what they saw. Nor was this situation unusual across the whole spectrum of the British army, and it was worse still among the

Territorials. Across the country, the TA had been severely neglected in the intervening years, especially in equipment, and the Black Watch companies were no exception. The 4/5th and 6/7th Battalions, which had been conjoined after the last war, were separated, and recruiting began for additional battalions. Homecoming regulars who, like Fred Baron, had completed their term of service were placed on the reserve list and were liable to immediate call-up, as indeed was soon to happen. In the meantime the army was short of everything, and not long after that 1938 summer spectacle witnessed by the foreign attachés, when the reality of looming conflagration had finally been accepted by the politicians and the military planners, there was an almighty dash to re-equip, especially among the county and Highland regiments where the shortages had been most felt. That was easier said than done, and many would start the war on a make-do-and-mend basis.

During this period the 1st Battalion had been moved to Dover, where in the castle was a famous painting of their forebears, the 42nd, marching out of the gates heading for India at the time of the mutiny. As then, the present battalion was hastily injected with additional manpower and marched away again led by the pipes and drums. In September 1939 they headed ultimately to France, once again to become part of the British Expeditionary Force sent to fight with the French against the Germans, and incidentally with names among the officers and other ranks showing that some of the sons of the battalion's members were moving in the same direction as their fathers had done in 1914.

One aspect of the oil painting in Dover Castle and the 1939 battalion was drastically changed – that of the uniform. Only a few days before departure, the battalion were ordered to swap the kilt for trousers, thus ending a 200-year tradition of the Black Watch. The move brought great protests from the ranks, but the army was insistent on the grounds that the regiment, whose reputation among the enemy went before them, might be identified. But as Company Sergeant-Major MacGregor famously exclaimed: 'But damn it, we *want* to be identified.' Thus, the battalion were among the first troops to arrive in France to join French troops in the buffer zone against potential invasion by the Germans, but thankfully they had several months during the so-called phoney war to undergo much-needed training and welcome the arrival at last of some decent equipment. Among them was Piper John Grieve, who had enlisted in 1932 for seven years' colours and five years' reserve:

> I went straight into the pipe band at Colchester, and was due to go abroad . . . with the 2nd Battalion. In fact, I didn't go with the 2nd Battalion because I hadn't done two years' service. There were 100 of us who couldn't go, and so we were trans-ferred to the 1st Battalion at Dover. There was a wonderful atmosphere among the battalion, and especially the old soldiers. We may have thought war was coming but didn't give it a second thought. The battalion left Southampton in the second week of October, later to form part of the 51st Highland Division, and we sailed for France. By Christmas we were dug in at the Maginot Line. I was flabbergasted by the construction. We walked inside it and it was wonderful. We all thought that the Germans would never get through this. But, of course, they did, and we would be left fighting the retreat . . .

Winston Churchill, who visited the Maginot Line on 6 January 1940, immediately spotted its inherent weakness and, in a minute to the War Cabinet, pointed out that its fortifications ended at the Belgian border, leaving a gap of more than 150 miles between the northern end of the French defences and the North Sea. He suggested that this gap might become a less inviting target for the Germans if the Belgian government could be persuaded to invite British troops into Belgium. Neither was Churchill – nor the Black Watch, for that matter – impressed by the French preparations. As he later recalled:

> Throughout the winter there were many tasks that needed doing: training demanded continuous attention, defences were far from satisfactory or complete, even the Maginot Line lacked many

supplementary field works . . . Yet visitors to the French Front were often struck by the prevailing atmosphere of calm aloofness, by the seemingly poor quality of the work in hand, by the lack of visible activity of any kind. The emptiness of the roads behind the line was in great contrast to the continual coming and going which extended for miles behind the British sector . . . There can be no doubt that the quality of the French army was allowed to deteriorate during the winter.

Another of Churchill's observations would directly affect the position of the 1st Battalion of the Black Watch arriving in France that same month as the newly formed 51st Highland Division, which included the 4th and 6th TA Battalions of the Black Watch. The division, under the command of General Victor Fortune, included other famous regimental names of the Seaforth Highlanders, the Queen's Own Cameron Highlanders, the Gordon Highlanders and the Argyll and Sutherland Highlanders. Given Churchill's own fears about some of the French preparations, he worried that putting what was effectively a largely amateur army with little heavy support into the immediate fray was a risk. However courageous they might be, he believed that their part-time training was insufficient to prepare them for the anticipated onslaught, though he dare not say it, by one of the world's best-drilled armies. The following month, each brigade were ordered to strengthen their capability with a regular battalion, each replacing a Territorial. The 1st Battalion therefore came into the Highland Division in place of the 6th Battalion, which were transferred to Flanders, in fact close to Fontenoy. In doing so, the 1st Battalion became embroiled in one of the first catastrophes of the war, in which the Highland Division would be lost – some said sacrificed – as they continued fighting in France, while the rest of the British army escaped back across the Channel.

As the Nazi blitzkrieg allowed the Panzer divisions to pursue their relentless march across Western Europe, the British Expeditionary Force was being pushed ignominiously towards the sea, ahead of the invasion of France and possibly the British Isles. The Germans outmanoeuvred the British, French and Belgian armies and had surrounded 400,000 Allied soldiers, who were eventually cornered at the coast behind a defensive line at Dunkirk, still in Allied hands. It was literally their only way out, the alternative being the total humiliation of surrender and capture of the entire BEF.

On 26 May Lord Gort ordered British divisions, along with about a third of the French 1st Army, to abandon their forward positions on what was known as the Lille Pocket and to join the main body of troops forming a new front line around Dunkirk. The movement was carried out in the nick of time, for the very next day the Germans forced the surrender of Belgium. And so began the miracle of Dunkirk, in which 850 ships, boats and yachts of all kinds put to sea to bring the British army home. When Operation Dynamo ended on the afternoon of 4 June, 338,226 soldiers, including 123,095 French, had been evacuated. The remaining 60,000 were either killed or went into captivity. The BBC reported that the beaches of Dunkirk were littered with bodies and the debris of a shattered army that had retreated under the merciless hail of bombs and machine-gun fire and that in the surrounding roads and villages, all the way back to the original front line, thousands of vehicles and weapons had been discarded.

When they eventually pulled out, the BEF left behind a staggering inventory of weapons and equipment: 475 tanks, 38,000 vehicles, 12,000 motorcycles, 8,000 telephones, 1,855 wireless sets, 7,000 tons of ammunition, 90,000 rifles, 1,000 heavy guns, 2,000 tractors, 8,000 Bren guns and 400 anti-tank guns. On 6 June the War Cabinet was informed that there were fewer than 600,000 rifles and 12,000 Bren guns left in the whole of the United Kingdom, and the losses would take up to nine months to replenish. It was truly a desperate situation that was kept well away from public view.

The 51st Highland Division and the French 31st Division were still fighting, unaware of the extent of the catastrophe behind them and equally unaware that, if there was a sacrifice to be made, they would be making it. London, by then, must surely have known there was little hope of them escaping now. At that point the division were attempting to hold a twenty-five-mile front with only light tanks of the Lothian and Border Horse for support. General Erwin Rommel's Panzers were bearing down fast. On 5 June the Germans attacked along the whole front of the remainder of the line, and during courageous and costly battles the Highland Division were under constant attack. Notably, the men of the 1st Battalion held hills above Abbeville, over almost three miles of countryside, while the Argylls, to their left, were even more thinly dispersed, and their position was soon overrun. The 4th Battalion, in a similar position, were ordered to withdraw before they were cut to pieces. The men made their escape over a bridgehead and fell back to a position near Dieppe, where they were to team up with others to form a special force to prepare for the evacuation of troops through Le Havre under Operation Cycle.

More than 11,000 British and French troops were evacuated through the Channel port between 9 and 10 June, in spite of heavy enemy bombing. Twelve ships were sunk in the process. The 51st Division were not among those who reached the port. They remained inland to stand in the way of the oncoming Germans and to let those who could escape do so. German armoured troops had reached the outskirts of Rouen, and the following day General Fortune was driven back to the sea at St-Valery-en-Caux. Because of fog, evacuation was impossible that night and, although the French pleaded with him to surrender, he refused to do so while the 1st Battalion were still in position above the Somme. Under cover of darkness, the battalion drew back to the village of St-Pierre-le-Viger, six miles from St-Valery. The next day the battalion watched French soldiers retreating ahead of German infantry while the Highlanders were still fighting on. That night, as a further part of Operation Cycle, another 2,200 British and 1,100 French troops were evacuated. Time was running out for the 51st. The Germans were closing in from all directions, and finally General Fortune had no alternative but to surrender to General Erwin Rommel, and 9,000 troops went into captivity for the remainder of the war. Among them was John Grieve, the young recruit to the 1st Battalion whom we met earlier, who said:

We had been left fighting the retreat. It was terrible feeling, too, that we were going that way [forward to meet the enemy] and the French were going the other. We'd been going hammer and tongs, and fought one final battle after another . . . and then we were surrounded and captured. We couldn't believe it. We were marched through France, Belgium and Holland, where we were put aboard barges after a month on the road from the 12 June. We had very little food. We fed ourselves on the road, stealing food from gardens or being given a slice of bread by villagers.

Grieve and many of his comrades in the 1st Battalion spent the rest of the war in German prison camps, and in his case as slave labour working in German coal mines throughout. The fate of the 51st Division after such a tough battle has so often been overlooked by historians in the wake of the greater event, Dunkirk. There is little doubt, however, that General Fortune had been placed in a situation where he had no alternative but to fight on while the majority escaped, and then to surrender when the odds became impossible. The alternative would have been to watch his men being slaughtered, as they surely would have been, for nothing. The general was a hero, as were those alongside him. With no army left in France capable of raising a finger to the Germans, his cause was hopeless, and indeed had already been lost before it started. Surrounded by Rommel's troops and with all routes sealed, the 51st Highland Division were on their own. Some men escaped down the cliffs, and a few got away on the march to Germany. Fred Baron, who, it will be recalled, had been called up as a reservist after his time in India with the 2nd Battalion, was among the escapees:

I was one of the wounded, hit by shrapnel, and was taken to a German field clinic at the church hall. There, I managed to escape and dodged into an empty house in a village that had been evacuated. I rifled through it and found some clothes, changed and began walking to Paris, and after a short while I got a lift on a truck. In Paris, I went to the American hospital, where I was treated for my wounds, and I stayed there for three weeks, I had to get out when the census people came round. The Americans gave me 100 francs, took me out by ambulance and dropped me at Nevers to try to get back to the demarcation line. I had some help from a Frenchman who showed me the way to Chatereaux, which was pretty deserted, but the trains were still running and I bought a ticket to Marseilles, which, of course, was in unoccupied France. I was never challenged, but I did meet up with Reverend Donald Casksie, a Scottish minister who had evacuated from Paris and set up a seamen's mission in Marseilles. He gave me shelter for three weeks, and the American mission there gave me an identity card. I then took the train to the Spanish border and walked across the Pyrenees into Spain, where I gave myself up at the local police station. I was put into a local concentration camp. There were sixteen Brits in the camp, including a Black Watch private named Sangster, who had also made his way across France. We were taken to Madrid and from there transferred to Gibraltar, where I made contact with the 4th Battalion of the Black Watch [which had been transferred there from France and remained the duty garrison for the next three years]. They put me on a ship to Liverpool, then to a British embassy reception centre for a debriefing, and to check to make sure I wasn't a spy. I came back to the Queen's Barracks at Perth and was assigned to the depot, then on to Lanark to the recruit training centre, and I stayed there until 1945.

And so the Black Watch fought the last battles on the French mainland which, apart from commando actions, thereafter remained unassailable until the D-Day landings four years later, when again their troops joined the early landings. The 1st Battalion were done for, but a new battalion rose up in Perth, along with a re-founded 51st Highland Division, soon destined for greater glory in North Africa.

CHAPTER THIRTEEN

Classic but Costly

It was time now for the 2nd Battalion to join the war. For three years they had been chasing elusive, well-armed Arab groups through the rough terrain of Judaea and Samaria, escorting convoys and policing the townships of Palestine. For a battalion that had spent the previous four years in Glasgow, where demands on their physical fitness were few, the experience brought them to a high level of fitness and training. When news reached the 2nd Battalion of the disaster in France and the loss of the 51st, the companies of the only remaining regular Black Watch battalion were gathered up from their various posts along the Suez Canal by train, which began its journey at Port Said and delivered them to Suez for the Royal Navy to carry them on to Aden and then Somaliland. There, a joint French and British force was being assembled to rebuff Mussolini's expected invasion from Abyssinia to complete his East African ambitions to take French and British Somaliland.

Then, as France capitulated and signed an armistice with both the Germans and the Italians, French troops were withdrawn, and the British were in deep trouble. Somaliland was secured by a tiny native force, and consequently the 3rd Battalion, 15th Punjab Regiment, sailed from Aden to Berbera on 1 July 1940. They were followed over the next two weeks by the 1st Northern Rhodesia, 2nd Battalion, the Black Watch, 2nd Battalion, King's African Rifles, and 1st Battalion, 2nd Punjab Regiment, and 1st East African Light Battery of four 3.7-inch howitzers. By the first week in August, a strong Italian force was advancing in three columns from French Somaliland supported by a persistent air bombardment, with fighters strafing the ground. They crossed into the British colony on 3 August with an attacking force, which in total comprised around 30,000 native troops and 4,800 Italians. Clearly, the odds were somewhat onerous, and on 10 August Major-General A. R. Godwin-Austen arrived at Berbera to assume command of the British forces. He had been sent by General Sir Archibald Wavell, now commander-in-chief of British forces in the Middle East, just before his own departure for England to brief Churchill and the War Cabinet on his plans to withstand the antici-pated Italian invasion of the Western Desert. In addition, Wavell ordered a further 2,000 reinforcements to be sent immediately to British Somaliland. None of them were dispatched, because, by the time the mustering began, the cause was already lost.

The Italians hugely outnumbered the sparsely populated defensive positions established to block their movement, and, although the multi-national British fought a gallant action, the sheer weight of the opposition – rather than its skill – ensured the defence would fail. By 13 August Godwin-Austen ordered a retreat and then the evacu-ation of the British troops, with the Black Watch nominated to cover the retreat until the Royal Navy arrived to take them off. The battalion's position was ridiculously dispersed across a two-mile front, with companies placed on roadsides and hills. It was a near-hopeless task, although David Rose wrote breezily of the action: 'We had to hold the Barkasan Gap so as to give time for the withdrawal of troops in front of us. It was a poor prospect. For the next two days we were very busy digging our fighting trenches and cutting thorn bushes to camouflage them. We had no air support, no tanks, only one Bofors gun with a dozen shells . . . and no machine guns.'

He then recounted how, as the enemy came in force down the road, he had no alternative but to initiate a charge. What he didn't tell readers of his autobiography was that he was himself out in front of this charging horde waving a pistol while urging his men forward. Behind him the shouting and screeching troops, with bayonets out front, sent the Italians scurrying for cover. The halt gave the company a chance to withdraw safely back to a defensive position to hold out for a while longer. Rose himself was shot almost immediately, 'bowled arse over tip' by a bullet through his shoulder, and was eventually taken with the rest of the wounded to the military hospital in Bombay. The battle continued from the slit trenches on which the enemy pumped out a stream of metal from their ten guns. The battalion's solitary Bofors gun effectively commanded the road long enough to give the remaining troops time to reach the port for evacuation, and in the evening they began their own dash for the coast. This time the Italians chose not to pursue them. Even so, although they did not know it, at that moment there was a strong possibility that the 2nd Battalion, Black Watch, would also be lost into captivity. Royal Navy Commander Maurice Vernon was instructed by General Godwin-Austen to pull out. According to Vernon's own account, he protested that 'we haven't got the Black Watch down yet'.

Godwin-Austen replied: 'I'm afraid the Black Watch are a write-off. You won't see them again, Vernon. The last I heard of them they were doing a bayonet charge of one battalion against a division of Italians. The odds are pretty high.'

Vernon again protested: 'You can't write off a whole battalion just like that, General. The Black Watch can't be exterminated.'

But then the real reason for Godwin-Austen's reluctance to wait became apparent. He told the commander: 'No, but another tragedy is that the only bridge at La Peron was blown up by mistake by one of the sappers. We did, of course, have it mined, but I didn't give the signal. How they got it, I don't know, but the bridge was blown and they can't get back.'

In fact, the battalion were roaring down the road towards Berbera, and, although admitting that the premature demolitions on the road had caused them 'some difficulty', they rolled into the town in the early hours, even stopping for a quick drink at the deserted Berbera Club before going on to board their ships to sail away to Aden, and then on to Suez with the battered Bofors gun still intact. The severest of fighting for the battalion had lasted just a day and resulted in a casualty list of seven killed, sixteen wounded and four missing. In fact, one of those thought to have died was recovered alive a year later in Asmara, when the town was recaptured. With him, also alive and well, was Lieutenant A. C. T. Wilson of the Camel Corps, who had been awarded a 'posthumous' Victoria Cross for his bravery in the action. Somaliland was lost, not ignominiously but to the over-whelming numbers of the Italians, rather than that army's military prowess.

With East Africa secure, Mussolini then progressed to the next stage of his re-creation of the Roman Empire. In the east, his troops were heading for the Sudan, and in North Africa he ordered his forces to 'cross the wire', the boundary between Libya and Egypt, to begin their move towards Wavell's Western Desert force based at Mersa Matruh, the former watering hole of Antony and Cleopatra. The stage was set for the first in a series of scraps, racing up and down the North African coast, which was eventually to draw in Rommel and his Afrika Korps and Montgomery and the re-formed 51st Division, including the new 1st Battalion, Black Watch. The latter would not arrive for many months because the entire division had to be rebuilt, but in the immediate future the 2nd Battalion were already in line for more action and a starring role in the desert campaigns.

By late autumn 1940 the Italians had built a solid base around Sidi Barrani from which to begin their advance, supposedly to the Suez Canal. As the temperatures began to cool, they had 90,000 troops with 200 guns and 125 tanks ready to embark on the first stage of the journey, with more coming up behind, amounting to well over 200,000 men to take on a British force less than a quarter of the size. But as the two commanders, Wavell and Graziani, prepared for the Sidi Barrani showdown, events elsewhere threw a spanner in the works in a manner that neither commander had envisaged: at the end of October 1940 Mussolini decided to invade Greece.

Without waiting for a measure of whatever success his troops might achieve in the Western Desert, he sent five divisions through Albania into Greece, apparently believing that Wavell would be forced to send immediate assistance to the Greeks by way of troops and aircraft. In fact, Mussolini's intelligence services had failed him in two vital areas: their overestimate of Wavell's troop numbers in Egypt and in their belief that Greece had no stomach for a fight. Wavell, with Graziani just up the road, could afford to send only a few aircraft to help the Greeks, and even those had to be back on duty in the Western Desert in time for the anticipated head-to-head that was moving inexorably toward a 'go' situation. So in spite of Churchill's displeasure back in London, Wavell sent no British troops to Greece for the time being, although Churchill would insist on it in the New Year, when the Germans were forced to rescue the Italians from the surprisingly stout defence staged by the Greeks.

One aspect of the invasion of Greece that did require immediate attention was the strengthening of the garrison on the island of Crete, previously held by British commandos but whose position would be vital to the British if, as expected, the Germans themselves invaded the Balkans and Greece. In October 1940 the 2nd Battalion were dispatched to the island to take up positions at Suda Bay. There was speculation as to whether they would remain there or be shipped to bolster the Greek cause against the Italians. In fact, Wavell could not afford to lose either troops or Crete, so they stayed put while he continued preparations for the upcoming Battle of Sidi Barrani, which opened up on 6 December.

Against overwhelming odds and hugely outnumbered, the British force, led by the 7th Armoured Division, or Desert Rats as they famously became known, blasted the Italians aside and pressed on with incredible speed to Tobruk, and then Benghazi, taking 130,000 Italian prisoners en route and capturing 400 tanks, 1,800 assorted vehicles and 1,290 guns. But this was only the beginning of a long campaign along the Western Desert that would see fortunes swing violently as, in the New Year, Rommel landed his Afrika Korps of 25,000 men at Tripoli to get the Italians out of trouble.

At the same time, Hitler began moving more Panzers towards the Balkans and ultimately Greece to complete the job that Mussolini had botched. Churchill instructed Wavell to dispatch the maximum number of troops to Greece as soon as possible. Cutting his own force to the bone at the very time the Germans were landing and the Italians were closing in on the Sudan, Wavell could only muster four and a half divisions, many newly arrived and untried in battle, including the Anzac force of Australian and New Zealand infantry. This great diversion of activity allowed Rommel to assemble his counter-force in Tripoli, amounting to 25,000 men, and begin his charge down the North African coast in March.

In that same month the Black Watch moved from Suda Bay to Heraklion, in the centre of the north coast of Crete, to join a brigade with three other regiments. The battalion were concentrated on an airfield, built to support the campaign in Greece, and on a low range of hills running east from it roughly at right-angles to the runway. On 17 April Yugoslavia fell to a blitzkrieg of German armour striking from Hungary, Romania, Bulgaria and Germany itself. A week later this unstoppable Nazi machine moved into Greece supported by 1,250 aircraft, including Stukas and the deadly Messerschmitt 109s. The Greek army surrendered on 23 April, and Wavell ordered the immediate withdrawal of all British forces. There followed a mini-Dunkirk for the evacuation of Allied troops, of whom the Royal Navy rescued 43,000. Many others went into captivity, and large numbers of lorries, tracked vehicles, guns and ammunition were left behind along with 189 damaged but repairable aircraft.

Many of the troops were ferried to Crete, considered by the British military planners to be the 'must hold' island at the southern end of the Aegean. But Enigma decrypts from Bletchley Park revealed that the Germans were already planning a massive invasion of the strategically vital island, which at that particular moment had only fourteen Hurricanes and seven RN aircraft to defend against the enemy onslaught. Churchill, who was reading the decrypts daily, ordered Wavell to send reinforcements: more guns, more tanks, more everything. The commander wired back that he could spare only six tanks, sixteen light tanks and eighteen anti-aircraft guns, although the Allied manpower on the island was bolstered after the fall of Greece to around 30,000 Australian, New Zealand and British troops under the command of General Bernard Freyberg. Churchill, having viewed the Germans' precise order of battle, courtesy of the Enigma decrypts, still had grave concerns that they had insufficient firepower to hold on. His worst fears were realised on the morning of 20 May. Lieutenant J. C. Donaldson of the 2nd Battalion, Black Watch, takes up the story:

I had been into town [on 19 May] to get some supplies and was on the way back when a 'super-red' warning was sounded. This meant a big force of planes was on the way. We sped back as quickly as possible, and we were running alongside the aerodrome when a bomber dropped a stick [of bombs] down the main runway. The driver just about upset the truck, but no damage was done and we carried on. No other planes appeared [but] on 20 May bombers and fighters were overhead early and attacks were frequent during the morning. By noon fifty-four planes had been overhead and more came in the afternoon. Between three and four, the attacks really intensified. The sky was full of planes bombing and machine-gunning the aerodrome area. Everyone realised that this could only be the prelude to the expected attack. We had been told that the German planes would, after they had finished strafing us, continue to roar around to try to make us think they were still bombing us, to keep our heads down so that their parachutists could land unmolested.

And so I kept a steady watch on the skies. For an hour and a half this terrific attack was maintained. It seemed as if the Germans were trying to flatten the defences by weight of metal alone. One thing depressed me. There were a dozen Bofors sited around the drome. When the big attack began, they barked forth their defiance, but one by one they had fallen silent, and I believed they must have been put out of action. Then, around five-fifteen, the noise of the battle died down. The bombers had ceased to bomb, but enemy planes still swarmed above. Then from the north flew in two never-ending lines of Ju52s, and in a moment the air was full of parachutists blossoming forth. It was a beautiful, wonderful and thrilling sight.

In seconds . . . the aerodrome came to life. Bofors, light AA and Bren guns blazed skywards. Many parachutists were dead when they reached the ground. Others never left their planes alive, for some crashed in flames . . . The Germans had failed to spot many of our positions, and the first parachutists were wiped out completely. By dusk, the situation was well in hand. During the night there was an attempt to penetrate on to the aerodrome, but it failed. The attacks resumed at dawn: more bombing, and then the Ju52s came back with reinforcements and supplies. This became the regular procedure. They would come in out of range. It was very tantalising because a few fighters would have made mincemeat out of them. [Then they began to] fly wide and dropped hundreds of men both in the valley and on the apex. And so the Germans now controlled the two points, the range beyond the valley and the apex. With their long-range MGs, they could shoot up most of the drome, and movement by day became impossible, except for individuals. One of the worst moments I had during the battle occurred the morning I was over at Post C when seven bombers flying high came over in formation and dropped sticks simultaneously. This, I thought, will be a very close thing. When one sees seventy bombs coming down together, one feels that there is a good chance of one of them hitting you. So I put up a wee prayer and held my breath. There was a series of loud explosions and it was over, one short fifty yards and one over fifty yards. I looked towards the company HQ and my platoon HQ and saw them shrouded in dust . . .

And so it went on: wave after wave of stinging aircraft attacks and landings, including Ju52s towing huge DFS 230 gliders packed with troops, vehicles and guns, the greatest airborne invasion force ever mounted in the history of warfare. By late afternoon on the second day, almost 5,000 men had been dropped or landed on the island, and one of the most costly battles of the war to date was under way as more German paras and mountain troops were delivered to the island hour after hour, eventually totalling 22,040.

They met spirited Allied resistance whose strength had been hugely underestimated by German intelligence. Even so, it was a hopeless task for the Allies, even with the supporting bombardment from the Royal Navy. The Germans had, in fact, assembled a force of 650 combat aircraft, 700 transports and 80 gliders in Greece, many coming in on the west side of the island, where the Nazis had succeeded in capturing the airfield at Maleme, enabling them to fly in troops directly. For more than a week the Luftwaffe bombarded Crete and shot the few remaining British fighters out of the sky until, devoid of air cover, the British fleet was exposed to grave danger as it began the evacuation of Allied troops.

When night fell on 29 May 1941, the British troops headed for the harbour. The Black Watch battalion were, as usual, among the last to leave their post to cover the retreat, and even then their wounded and some soldiers who had been cut off by advancing Germans had to be left behind. The battalion were split into two groups to go aboard the cruisers HMS *Dido* and HMS *Orion*, and even as the evacuation was under way German aircraft swooped low and rendered a heavy punishment on the departing armada. Both cruisers carrying the Black Watch were hit. *Orion*, with 1,090 troops on board, took three bombs, killing over 260 troops, with 300 more wounded. *Dido* took two hits, the second of which exploded in the lower decks where most of the troops were jammed.

Many were killed instantly, and few of the injured survived, for fire broke out and the area had to be flooded. Many bodies disentangled from the wreckage were buried at sea. As the cruiser limped into Alexandria at dusk, a piper in a tattered kilt climbed up beside the bridge on HMS *Jackal*, which had not been hit, and began to play the battalion in. The navy picked him out with a searchlight and held it on him, while the ships steamed up the harbour, bringing back the defenders of Heraklion. Three cruisers and six destroyers were sunk, and an aircraft carrier, six cruisers and eight destroyers were hit, with varying degrees of damage, and many sailors were killed or drowned. The final toll showed the extent of the disaster: 4,600 Allied troops killed, 2,000 wounded and 11,000 taken prisoner.

Even as the Crete battle was being fought, activity elsewhere that would soon engage the services of the 2nd Battalion was already reaching a climax. But after their terrible experiences during and evacuating from Crete, the Jocks – as they were now universally known among their soldiering colleagues of other regiments – were given a brief respite to take in the sights and nightlife of Cairo. The city was still a relatively safe place and was well organised as a leave centre. Special arrangements were in place to ensure that troops coming in for furlough activity were well looked after. Most had pockets full of money, and they were pointed to decent hotels and given brochures telling them where they could and could not go.

Some even managed to get transport to Jerusalem to look up old friends and haunts. This didn't last long. By early August they were recalled for duty, this time in Syria. There they faced a curious situation in that troops of the Vichy French, well protected on a natural fortress-like hillside, were fighting a small British force and an even smaller Free French group near Damascus. The battle had been going on for days and the Allies had taken severe losses. The Black Watch were coming in as reinforcements, and the troops were already approaching the battle zone when they were drawn back. At the last minute, the Vichy forces in the region agreed to armistice terms and fighting ceased.

Another brief holiday of sorts ensued, with company concerts and a mountaineering challenge, led by Major Gerald Barry, over the Lebanon heights. It was also a time when reinforcements were arriving and those not so seriously wounded during the evacuation from Crete were returning, to provide the battalion with around three-quarters of its normal strength. Two other notable arrivals were Colonel G. A. Rusk, who had been seconded to command the King's African Rifles at the time of the Somaliland campaign, and Pipe-Major Roy, who was wounded and captured in Crete, taken to Greece, from where he escaped, and returned to the regiment via Turkey. The battalion now had several weeks to train for future operations, and in the event they would need to be at the peak of their abilities as a fighting force. They were destined to become major players in the famous event known as the Relief of Tobruk, a city ruined by incessant bombardment and for which a preamble is necessary.

After the second in the series of battles along the North African coast between Wavell's Western Desert Force, later to be re-formed as the 8th Army, Tobruk became surrounded by Rommel's Afrika Korps in April 1941. Legend has it that the 9th Australian Division (still short of two brigades, which had been sent to Greece) had become trapped inside the town. In fact, they dived in for the very purpose of taking up defensive positions. The division had artillery, anti-aircraft artillery and tanks, all of which would be needed to hold on to this valuable port through which British supplies were ferried and wounded taken away. At the height of the battle, Wavell flew to the scene from Cairo and in material first published in the author's earlier book, *Desert Rats*, General Sir (later Lord) John Harding recalled:

Wavell [arrived] with two of his staff officers. I had set up a blackboard on the first floor of the building, where we were headquartered, and I gave him my assessment of the situation at Tobruk. All he said was: 'Well, if you think you can hold it, you'd better hold it. What do you think?' I replied that provided the navy could maintain supplies and the Germans – Rommel – don't wheel up a mass of heavy tanks, we'd probably hold out. Wavell replied: 'Give me a millboard.' Everybody on the staff carried a millboard with some foolscap on it, and in his own hand in his big round writing he wrote a directive to hold Tobruk on one side of a sheet of foolscap and asked me to send a copy to his headquarters. Then off he went.

The order was given, and General Morshead's 9th Australians took their positions, unaware, of course, that they were about to initiate a defence of the city against a surrounding German force and taunted by Lord Haw-Haw as the Rats of Tobruk. Tobruk was not an easy place to defend. Protective devices built by the Italians were still there, including an anti-tank ditch, wire and trenches. But the Australian infantry dug into defensive posts covering the perimeter of the fortress and had a plan whereby every gun was ready for anti-tank action on receipt of the codeword. Harding, who was then with the nucleus of the Western Desert Force headquarters staff inside Tobruk, arranged the codeword, which varied according to the number of tanks that were reported to have broken into the defences so that they could be dealt with.

The result was that Rommel's forces were held at bay. In fact, those at the front were in dire straits, and German prisoners were easily picked up by the British because they had run out of drinking water and were going mad. While his ground forces regrouped to a safer distance, Rommel sent in the Stukas and Messerschmitts for violent raids, wave after wave strafing and bombing the Allied army positions inside and outside the confines of the city. Over the next three months more than 1,000 air raids were carried out in the area of Tobruk, with the 9th Australian Division and British artillery bearing the brunt. The Western Desert Force headquarters, or what remained of it, was withdrawn by sea in a frigate and was re-established further up the coast, where communications with Tobruk were maintained, and the Royal Navy continued to run the gauntlet of Stukas, ferrying supplies and carrying away the wounded for months.

An attempt was made to relieve Tobruk in the summer of 1941 during the launch of yet another round in the desert war to send the Germans back into Libya. Codenamed Operation Battleaxe, it failed badly. Wavell, whose army lost 1,000 men and half their tanks, took the blame, although in truth the continuing shortage of tanks and heavy metal and the lack of training for newly arrived men meant that he continued to struggle to put an effective force against the combined might of the Italian and German ensemble, by which he was totally outgunned and dangerously outnumbered. But that wasn't all. Wavell had been hugely stretched on all fronts, robbing Peter to pay Paul, and smart-talking generals from elsewhere could have done no better. Anyhow, he took the can and was replaced by General Claude Auchinleck, with whom he swapped jobs. Wavell went to India, from where he would control the fight against the Japanese in the Fast East, especially in Burma, which turned out to be an even bigger mess than the one he was leaving. Auchinleck, who refused to make any fresh attempts to unsettle Rommel until he was ready and reinforced, did no better and was himself replaced later.

When he inherited Tobruk, the city remained locked up by a German force extending across a wide perimeter, and this remained a centre of high tension and activity. In winning the day in Battleaxe, Rommel had quashed all hope of the Allied garrison breaking out, or so he thought. The siege was seemingly back on with a vengeance, with bombing stepped up, although the Germans lost 153 aircraft specifically to Allied gunners inside the besieged city. The whole perimeter facing towards the desert was bristling with German guns on the outside and plenty inside, too, lined up by the 9th Australian Division, along with their associates, which included elements of the 7th Royal Tank Regiment, the 3rd Royal Horse Artillery, the AA Brigade and the King's Dragoon Guards, who were all playing a blinder in defence. But inside that besieged city were 30,000 mouths to feed every day, and much-needed supplies of fuel, ammunition and all the other accoutrements of military activity required prompt replenishment. This was being achieved miraculously by sea under the auspices of the Royal Navy, with lighters and warships slinking up and down the coast, often under the cover of darkness, keeping up a constant, if barely sufficient, supply line under a hail of German bombs.

The greatest miracle of all came when Auchinleck approved an audacious plan to extricate General Morshead's 9th Austalian Division, which had been there so long that they were producing their own daily newspaper, *Tobruk Truth*, using BBC broadcast news, and staging bawdy concerts. For some time, however, the Australian government had been pressing for its 9th Division to be brought out and replaced by other troops. They had been at it hammer and tongs since they arrived in April, suffering many casualties after the failure of Battleaxe, so the decision was made to make a daring effort to bring the Australians out and replace them with the British 70th Division – including the 2nd Battalion, Black Watch, and two additional brigades, one Polish and one Czech.

The operation was conducted in three waves, beginning on 19 August and ending on 19 November 1941, during which time the Royal Navy took almost 16,000 men out through the port of Tobruk and brought in a similar number, in addition to more than 5,000 tons of stores. Most of the hardware and guns remained in place and were simply taken over by the incoming troops. This series of intricate and well-planned operations was overseen by Morshead, who had been an outstanding commander of the British fortress of Tobruk, withstanding enormous pressure and attack from the Germans while maintaining this vital outpost of Allied armoury deep inside enemy-held territory. Auchinleck made sure that the firepower inside the fortress was built up during the months of personnel replacement. During September and October, armoured units inside the Tobruk perimeter received eight separate shipments of Matilda tanks, bringing their total complement of fighting vehicles to in excess of a hundred and seventy.

The next stage of this incredible military saga in the Western Desert was the launch of a new attack on the German-Italian combination in late November 1941, the famous Operation Crusader, which turned into weeks of sheer attrition and ultimately without real conclusion when the two sides fell apart at the end of January when Rommel was running short of supplies. In the midst of this fighting was a secondary aspect to finally relieve Tobruk by way of diverting the attention of the Germans' surrounding force while those trapped inside the perimeter made the breakout, rather than trying the more dangerous way of trying to break *in*. This was to begin three days after the main assault, launched on 18 November. The 2nd Battalion's task was to reach a German position, codenamed Tiger, 4,500 yards from their position inside the Tobruk perimeter, while first attacking and silencing an opposing strongpoint, codenamed Jill. Colonel Rusk, one of only two First World War veterans in the battalion, who was in command at the time, prepared these afterthoughts for the IWM archive:

In my mobile HQ of four vehicles was Major P. R. Birkin of the 107th South Notts Hussars Regiment, RHA, attached to me as artillery liaison, and for the four hours following our crossing of the mile-long start line at 6.30 a.m. on that morning of 21 November I found I have never been so forcibly attached to anyone in my life as Birkin and the driver of his siege-battered carrier, Gunner Worley. A breakout from a besieged fortress has always been regarded as a desperate enterprise, and Tobruk was to be no exception. In the dark, the start line, 600 yards into no-man's-land, was secretly and successfully crossed. My forward companies, with a formidable array of tanks, armoured cars, artillery, Royal Engineers, carriers etc., advanced several hundred yards without incident, and then all hell broke loose. In the succeeding din, smoke, dust and flying ironmongery, [my thoughts] were suddenly diverted from our progress on hearing the chanter of Pipe-Major Roy [and Pipe-Sergeant McNicoll] penetrating [the noise of the battle]. I could even detect the tune he was playing, 'Lawson's Men', the tune that 'put the leap upon the lame'. So in the darkness I realised that I was in the forward C Company area, whose march it was. The penetrating power of the pipe chanter is well known.

The battalion had a rough time, as the colonel indicated. The troops made their dash from the trenches around Tobruk, having laid up through the night in minefields. The artillery bombardment should have been timed to coincide with the arrival of the tanks, but they were late, having run straight into a minefield themselves. The soldiers had to go on in towards the objectives anyhow, because of the timing of other units. They had crossed a mere 700 yards when German machine guns flared and rattled out of the gloom, and men were falling across the board as they reached the first objective, Jill, and more fell as they kept going towards Tiger. When the dust settled, a huge number of rifles were found sticking upside down in the sand – the signal for 'stretcher-bearer required' – before the battalion, cut to ribbons, reached their destination. Colonel Rusk, who had had two carriers blown from under him, was now standing atop the last one in the HQ group, that of Gunner Worley, a battered, rattling bone-shaker and the only one left with communications. Shouting and waving from the roof of the vehicle, he urged his men on, but the attack reached Tiger only to find that the enemy had departed. But in crossing those 4,500 yards of ground under horrendous fire, the Black Watch had once again excelled in courage – and suffered in losses. Of the 632 men who crossed the start line, only 168 made it through to consolidate Tiger, the objective, apart from, that is, the survivors of similar proportions of all members of the attacking force, who then went on to overcome other German and Italian positions.

Unfortunately, the action was to no immediate avail as far as Tobruk was concerned. The main battle raged with great ferocity, and in fact several units of the 8th Army actually took refuge *inside* Tobruk and were to remain there until mid-January, when Auchinleck's main body gradually pushed Rommel back beyond the furthest perimeter, which at last allowed the siege of Tobruk to be lifted. That also meant that the 2nd Battalion could be relieved from this godforsaken place, although their luck – as at Crete – had all but been expended on the battlefield. A hospital ship, the *Chakdina*, had brought reinforcements to the Black Watch, although the numbers – six officers and sixty men – were lamentably small when compared with their most recent losses.

Worse news was to follow. The *Chakdina* used the return voyage to evacuate some of the wounded to hospital in Cairo, including five officers and eighteen other ranks from the Black Watch. Four hours out of Tobruk, the action stations alert sounded, and almost imme-diately the ship was hit by an aerial torpedo. She sank in less than five minutes, taking with her many of the wounded who were below decks. Survivors who managed to get over the side before she went under were in the water for up to three hours before they were picked up. Of the Black Watch men aboard, only seven survived. For the time being, the 2nd Battalion were done for, although, as we will see, were certainly not out! The pity, too, was that Tobruk would not remain in British hands for many months.

The sounds on the Western Desert were those of repairs and training. In theory, or on paper, or in the media, the 8th Army had returned an impressive victory over Rommel in Operation Crusader. The 'tally' that is ever present at the end of a particular series of battles was horrendous but seemed to bear out the claims of Allied triumph: the British lost 17,700 killed, wounded or captured out of a force of 118,000, the Germans lost 14,600 out of 65,000 and the Italians lost 23,700 out of a force of 54,000. But this was only a beginning in the new round of battles. In May 1942 London became aware through the decrypts that Rommel was planning an early strike back. Armed with this information, Auchinleck began moving his own troops towards what was known as the Gazala Line, setting up positions behind a 40-mile-long minefield stretching from the coast out into the desert. On either side of this division of territory was being mustered the largest army ever assembled by the British, with its Indian, Australian, New Zealand and South African units, to which were added soldiers from the Free French, Poland and a number of other nations. The Black Watch, having retired badly hurt from the previous encounter, would not be engaged in this one, although they would become, little did they know it, the precursor for the return to mainstream fighting of the new 1st Battalion, at that moment in training and preparing to leave Britain for North Africa.

Rommel was preparing his own Operation Venezia, which he had assured Hitler would this time secure possession of the Western Desert, enabling him to go on to Cairo and Suez. On 26 May the great column of his main striking force of 10,000 vehicles, including 600 tanks, came thundering out of Tripoli while Stukas and bombers began attacking the British positions, which consisted of a series of defensive boxes into which whole brigades were accommodated. As the Axis troops reached their battle zone, the huge mass of hyped-up troops and weaponry around and beyond the Gazala Line exploded into a mass of flame, dust and blood, and Rommel's tactics allowed him to cut and divide the defences, and in the end overcome this defensive system the British commanders had set up. Rommel was in a hurry, and he rushed on, pushing the retreating British units ahead of him like a snowplough until they had fallen back to an area known as the Cauldron. Here the Allies were to make a stand, but again in a murderous battle in which huge losses were recorded: an Indian brigade overwhelmed, another lost, two battalions destroyed, four regiments of artillery overrun and the entire stock of the 8th Army's medium tanks reduced to fewer than a hundred and thirty.

The retreat continued, first to Mersa Matruh, and then right back to El Alamein – the place that was positively the last point beyond which there would be no return. If Rommel progressed beyond, then Egypt would be lost. But now he was suffering the same problem as the British had had when they headed towards Tripoli. He had a 600-mile-long supply line, and, with the RAF carrying out daily bombing raids on his supply ships, fuel dumps and the Italian Motor Brigade on which he relied absolutely, Rommel was forced to pull back. With his own forces substantially weakened and tired, he suspended operations and retired to Tripoli to begin planning the next round.

At the height of the battle, Churchill was in America for discussions with President Roosevelt and on 21 June, during a meeting at the White House, an aide came into the room bearing a telegraphic message which he handed to Roosevelt who read the contents and, grim-faced, passed it to Churchill. The message reported: 'Tobruk has surrendered: 25,000 men taken prisoners.' Hastings Ismay, Churchill's Chief of Staff, recalling this incident later, said the 'blood drained from Churchill's face'. He could not bring himself to believe that this news could be true and asked Ismay to telephone London immediately. Ismay went out of the room to make the call, and returned a few minutes later with a message from Admiral Harwood, commander-in-chief of the British naval forces in the Mediterranean, confirming that Tobruk was now in German hands and that the situation in Egypt was 'deteriorating rapidly'. Later it emerged that the true number of men in the Tobruk garrison who had surrendered was 32,000, along with massive amounts of stores, ammunition and fuel that had been stockpiled there for the 8th Army's hoped-for journey on through Libya towards Tripoli. Churchill later wrote: 'This was one of the heaviest blows I can recall during the war, a bitter moment . . . Defeat is one thing; disgrace is another.'

Developments that were put in hand almost immediately would see the Black Watch back in action. Four battalions, including the re-formed 1st, were already preparing to sail for North Africa.

CHAPTER FOURTEEN

Every Major Battle

Rommel's success in North Africa was bad enough, but now there was another crucial element entering the equation that injected a new and vital sense of urgency for the British to regain control, and indeed kick the Axis allies out of the region. On 1 August Churchill received confirmation from the Americans that they were prepared to participate in the joint operation to land a substantial force across French North-West Africa, which would eventually go under the codename he had chosen, Operation Torch. It was scheduled for the first week of November 1942, and the key to its success was that the British forces would, by then, have fought their way back across the desert, on to Tripoli and then Tunis. In order to ensure American participation, Churchill had all but promised it would happen.

It was a decision that in turn substantially affected the immediate future of the all-new 51st Division, which included three battalions of the Black Watch, the 1st, 5th and 7th. The division sailed from Britain in June 1942, destination unknown, in the largest military convoy ever put together, and rumour had it that they were heading for the Far East. That was true when they sailed, but as they travelled up the coast of Africa towards the Red Sea, these plans were

247

changed. The 51st were being diverted to North Africa – and, little did they know it, but Churchill would be there to greet them.

The imperative situation that had arisen prompted General Sir Alan Brooke, Chief of the Imperial General Staff, to go to Egypt to get a first-hand view of what was happening in the North African campaign. On receiving the news from America, Churchill decided he would accompany him. They set off from Lyneham airfield in a draughty four-engine Liberator bomber which had no bed, unlike the exceedingly comfortable Boeing Clipper in which Churchill had flown the Atlantic a few weeks earlier. They flew first to Gibraltar, where the 4th Black Watch were still guarding this ultra-important gateway to the Mediterranean and whose role would be even more vital with the launch of Operation Torch. Then, after a brief stopover, the Liberator carried on unescorted (had the Germans only known it) to Cairo, arriving on 4 August. The following day, the Prime Minister and Brooke met the Chiefs of Staff, including General Wavell, who had flown in from India, where he was overseer of the British Empire's Far Eastern jewels now being systematically plundered by the Japanese. Churchill had already informed Wavell that the 51st Division were being pulled off the ships to strengthen the 8th Army, and that afternoon the Prime Minister was driven out to personally welcome the first arrivals into Egypt. He was given a rousing reception. The following day, Churchill revealed to the personalities concerned that Auchinleck had been sacked from GOC, Middle East, and was being transferred back to his old job as GOC, India. The present incumbent – Wavell – was getting a knighthood and would be made Viceroy, a task he subsequently performed admirably in the difficult years prior to India's independence.

General Sir Harold Alexander was to become GOC, Egypt, and General Bernard Montgomery was selected to head the 8th Army. Churchill cabled London before he went to bed: 'Pray send him by special plane at earliest moment.' He was in Egypt within days, and was badly needed, as Captain (later Colonel) John McGregor of the 5th Battalion, Black Watch, recalled in his memoir for the Imperial War Museum Sound Archive:

When we first arrived, morale was very poor. Troops already there despaired at the fact that they had been up and down the desert twice and could not sustain the fight because they did not have sufficient [military hardware] to carry it off. The fall of Tobruk had a very adverse affect on many of them. They felt very depressed. Most of us had never heard of Montgomery, but within a very short space of time we learned about this general who was going round talking directly with the men. We first met him when he came to our area early in September. In the Highland Division, our general was very well known because the division was run like a family. Douglas Wimberley, who was the divisional commander, had trained us back in Scotland, and we went into Egypt knowing people in every other unit of the division. We knew the Seaforths, the Camerons, the Gordons and so on. But we also knew the gunners, who our sappers were, who the signals were. We exchanged jobs in training days and understood what was involved when you got a twenty-five pounder into action or set up a signals station. Douglas Wimberley was one of those inspired leaders who led from the front. Apart from our own divisional commander, we hadn't seen many generals and so in a way it was a pleasant surprise to see this new army commander, Montgomery, coming round and talking to the men, full of confidence, in language that was straightforward and simple.

His greatest impact was when we went into battle at Alamein. It was probably the last time in history that we fielded a British Empire team. Apart from the 51st Highlanders, there were the 50th Northumberland and Tyne and Tees Division, 9th Australian, 2nd New Zealand, 1st South African and 4th Indian Division and lots of other troops from various parts. It was vital in order to get such a diversity of people working together to have inspiration from the centre, and Montgomery did that better than anyone I can think of.

Before Montgomery came along, Australians talked in derogatory terms about British troops. We on the other hand tended to be accepted upon the legend of our forebears, but the Australians in part had to be convinced about the hardiness of others. Montgomery's basic theme was that what had gone on before was a great effort by great people with limited resources. He had the Prime Minister's backing that we would have the supplies, the troops and the resources. This time, we would knock the Germans for six. He used a lot of cricketing metaphors. This seemed to be borne out by the amount of stuff flowing up the desert, bigger tanks and guns, and the number of aircraft with the RAF roundel on them. There was definitely visual evidence that all the promised materials were arriving.

The division had much to do, not least in acclimatising to desert warfare, the heat, the flies, the rationed water, the sores that welled up from the slightest scratch and, of course, the mile after mile after mile of dust and sand. Montgomery immediately recognised the problems facing both newcomers and old hands, and initiated an immediate fitness and training programme for all troops, with an emphasis on the newcomers – who included tank crews, gunners and sappers, many of whom, like the 51st, were totally untried in battle. They had to face the rigour of new training that was possible only on site, as it were, to build up stamina to cope with the desert and even the basics of how to cook and take precautions against all the side effects of the climate and conditions.

Then the Black Watch battalions were moved with others towards the battle areas, for their main training for what was to come. They now knew that they would be in the front-line positions when the fighting began. They were put into defensive positions known as boxes, which were constructed to hold a battalion in each box, surrounded by barbed wire and minefields for protection. From there they sallied forth to their real desert training, learning how to advance night or day over a largely featureless landscape through an incredible fog of dust kicked up by the battle, a factor that they were yet to experience. The exercises were designed to set the pattern for what was to happen in the Battle of Alamein itself, two companies forward,

he 2nd Battalion, after heroic action in the North African campaign, left for India before ining the controversial Chindit Operations in Burma against the Japanese.

Back in North Africa, a Black Watch Pipe Band leads the advance into Sfax, the first town reached in Tunisia, where they werc met by cheering throngs.

Journey's end, the Black Watch lead a victory parade nto Bremerhaven, 15 May 1945.

Post-war guard of honour for General Dwight Eisenhower, Commander-in-Chief of NATO forces, reviving wartime memories of the day he was 'captured' by the 4th Battalion during his secret visit to Gibraltar and held for two hours until his identity was confirmed.

The Black Watch often policed the troubled regions of the declining British Empire they had helped to build, as here in Cyprus in 1958.

Changing the guard. The 1st Battalion under Lieutenant-Colonel Rose take over from the Americans at the site of their most famous post-war actions, the Battle of the Hook in Korea.

By presidential command. John F. Kennedy asked to be 'serenaded' by the Black Watch so the Pipes, Drums, Regimental Band and dancers gave their performance on the South Lawn of the White House in November 1963, nine days before his assassination.

Renewed experiments with protection from chemical weapons brought this invention from the Porton Down research station: a mask that allowed pipers to play on regardless.

Always a popular element of Black Watch displays, the Highland dancers, here performing the Argyll Broadswords.

Welcomed and applauded in times past, Northern Ireland tours became progressively demanding for the Black Watch, as in this confrontation in Belfast. Weapons had long since been upgraded from truncheons and shields for crowd control: the soldier in the foreground is carrying both a Federal Riot gun firing plastic bullets and a rifle.

End of an Empire. Fittingly the Black Watch played the pivotal role in the handing over of Hong Kong to the Chinese in June 1997 – a ceremony that was performed in torrential rain

Black Watch wives launched a 150-mile walk from London to the battalion base in Fallinbostel, Germany, to raise money for children in Kosovo where their husbands were serving in 2001.

Reflections on times past… men of the Black Watch in desert uniform gather at the monument at Aberfeldy, built to mark the raising of the regiment in 1739. And *(below)* in Basra, at the memorial to those who fell there during the First World War.

Advancing into Basra, 2003. Officers plan their strategy at a staff meeting while under an alert for a possible chemical weapon attack.

A Black Watch soldier is mobbed by children during 'hearts and minds' operations in Basra.

Before and after …the demolition of a portrait of Saddam.

...n patrol in the dust and the danger of operations in support of American troops near ...aghdad in November 2004.

In memory of Lance-Corporal Barry Stephen, 31, from Perth, killed in action on 24 March 2003 while on operations near Az Zubayr.
[both Empics]

two companies behind them, with a central spine of command, intelligence, signals and supplies. John McGregor went on:

I was taken away from the rifle company and made regimental intelligence officer and had to master the new method of setting a centre line tape to control the direction of the battalion's advance, with hurricane lamps every 200 yards. It was a most extraordinary sight. All my section carried large wooden cable reels on spindles, and these unwound, as you went forward, white tape. That meant you had to plot the course it was to run, by compass, so that people who followed the front line had to follow the tape. Your support arms, guns, tanks, ordnance, supplies, ambulances would follow that line across otherwise indistinguishable desert and know that they would come to the heart of the battalion. When that system was evolved, there were subsidiary tapes going off to the right and left, going in the required direction, which were the wings, and even in the dark the whole battalion could move in a controlled fashion across ground that had very few features. It worked extremely well, and did so because we practised over and over again so that we were able to do it when shellfire was coming at us . . . These things were vital to the future life of any battalion.

There was clearly much to learn in a very short space of time, and in such a massive arena of battle preparations there were accidents, as Major Gerald Osborne recalled. He had joined the 4/5th Black Watch in 1935 and was a lieutenant when the war broke out, but subsequently was among those who transferred to the new 1st Battalion, now in the desert with the 51st:

We were doing exercises and night exercises [with live firing] and in one of them Major Sir Arthur Wilmott, our second in command, was killed and five other Jocks with him. The guns had fired short. It was a very nasty jolt for us. I was a company commander at that time, D Company. However, we pressed on

[and] the orders finally came out on 21 October. We were moved up into the slit trenches on the twenty-third, which was part of the deception plan to see what the enemy was doing. We were drawn up to our start line, marked out by the tapes, with the 5th and 1st Battalion going forward and the 7th in reserve. We had our piper playing us into battle, with our company march, 'Scotland the Brave', which gave the troops a tremendous morale boost. It had a blood-curdling effect on the Germans and the Italians to hear the swirling of the pipes, coupled with the pipes of other companies being played into battle. Our barrage started at about ten o'clock at night, and we were then given the order to advance, following along behind the barrage, although again we had difficulty with some of the guns falling short and once again we had a number of casualties. The next thing we came to was the enemy's wire, which had been cut by our sappers. At that point I lost my batman, Thompson. He was shot as we went through. We followed on behind B Company, and when they reached their objective and consolidated there was a pause to reorganise and then we were to leapfrog through and take the next objective, moving forward on our compass bearing. As we went on, we came upon strongpoints inhabited by both Germans and Italians, and we had to make a bayonet charge in some cases and in others we threw hand grenades when they refused to come out.

We carried right on to what was called the black line, and we heard shouts coming from Germans about a mile beyond our original objective, so we decided to go forward and take them on. We ourselves had very light casualties. The enemy soldiers had clearly been shattered by the bombardment of about 1,000 guns followed by our creeping barrage, which we went in behind. In taking the German position, we managed to capture machine guns and an eight-millimetre field gun and found a large quantity of field ambulance stores. We also captured a number of Germans and then occupied a position which had been taken by the Italians. We were there the whole of the next day and had to keep our heads down. Then, about four in the afternoon, a battalion of Seaforths came through us and went ahead. They took a lot of casualties. At the same time the tanks were coming through on the central lines between the divisions, and they were having quite a nasty time of it, attacked by enemy anti-tank guns. After that second day, we were withdrawn, our part in the first stage having been completed. Brigadier Holdsworth, the brigade commander, who lived in Murrayshire, appeared with his cromack [walking stick] in his hand as if he was walking over his moors. He went round all the Jocks and congratulated them.

The 5th Battalion, meanwhile, had been through similar machinations, as John McGregor recalled:

The initial assault on the German lines had been a tremendous shock to them, but there was not a great deal of close-quarter fighting. It came mostly from their fixed lines, and so all our objectives were reached and obtained without great losses. At first light, we took stock of what we needed in the way of reinforcements and ammunition. We found that our tanks who followed closely behind us were beginning to pick up on their targets. We spent that first day consolidating, digging slit trenches and dug in the guns to be ready for a German counter-offensive. It was on a ridge that we began to suffer casualties to snipers, and we lost two officers and several men until we did what we had always been taught to do. We put out two fighting patrols spread wide across the ground with their bayonets fixed and their fingers on the triggers; they advanced and the snipers came out of the slit trenches with their hands up. We took nine prisoners. Then we had tanks milling around and other operations going on, which made the battalion's operating area more like Piccadilly Circus. Although in our training when we had been in slit trenches a tank rolled over the top of us to show how safe it was, it was not a pleasant experience to find a Sherman tank roaring up when you were lying on the ground, whereas they were supposed to follow their tracks until they got clear of our lines.

We were holding our first position for nearly a week, and next Montgomery was going to punch two holes in the German lines and send in the armour. So he feigned an attack in the south, while in the north the pushed a second channel. That effectively broke through and released the armoury into the German positions, and they were on the run. It was necessary that the front-line positions had to be maintained in case Rommel mounted a counter-attack. Units like ours were relieved by troops who had not been so heavily involved, and we were pulled out of the line after ten days. Our Battle of Alamein, from the 5th Battalion point of view, had lasted for ten days. We had 68 killed and 250 wounded out of 800 men on the ground, but we had brought up our own reinforcements so we were soon up to strength again. However, time was needed to sort ourselves out and to re-form. B Company, for example, had very heavy casualties. Then we were ready to follow the chase up the coast. I think it would be right to say there was a tremendous elation among all the divisions involved. They had had a stunning victory, and that was just on the first phase of it. As we went on we saw, day after day, droves of prisoners, long, long lines of them, coming back; there was the evidence. The battlefield showed the rest – burned-out German tanks, ammunition lorries, shattered positions and so forth. The fighter squadrons of Hurricanes had been brilliant, and the heavy aircraft were bombarding enemy positions further up the coast.

A focal point came on the first Sunday in November, by which time the battle had moved 100 miles up the coast. The corps commander was coming to see us, and our signal regiment had been able to tune in to the BBC and we heard the most remarkable sound – that Churchill and the King had arranged for the church bells to be rung across England to celebrate Alamein. We then went on to a drumhead church service, and the names were read of the sixty-eight who had been killed and we sang our Scottish hymns. It is also worth mentioning at this point the pipes going into battle . . . A Company had a piper, called Duncan McIntyre, as all the company pipers did, and he was playing their march 'The Black Bear'. As they went in on the final assault, he was struck by a piece of shrapnel but carried on playing. He was struck again, the second time fatally, and in the morning, when they found him, his pipes were still under his arm and his finger still on the chanter – typical of the spirit that everyone did what they could until the last possible moment.

The sound of pipes in circumstances like these was a great thing. In the Highland Division it had been long established that we represented the clans of Scotland and their traditions. The Black Watch, with three battalions in the division, was the senior regiment, but all the other regiments have an equally proud history. In fact, as a Scot from a Highland bloodline I can remember when I joined the 5th Black Watch I was shocked to find that my sergeant-major was a Cockney, and there were several Englishmen in the battalion, but I quickly learned that the non-Scots who joined us became as Scottish as the Scot, as did the several Irish who joined us. They learned the regimental history, they wore their kilts as well as any Highlander could do, and they were fierce in their proclamation of the fact that they were Highlanders. The official figures would show that at one time in the desert in the Highland Division, eighty-two per cent of the officers were Scots, the other eighteen may have had a link with Scotland but that might be all. Among other ranks, seventy-one per cent were Scots and the rest were English or another nationality.

The British regimental system inculcates spirit and produces results that no anonymous number such as the 1st, 2nd or 3rd Regiment could ever achieve. When we got into the centre of Tripoli, which had fallen that day when the 7th Armoured Division got in, the fighting cleared quickly, and we were in possession of the whole town within the target time set for us by Montgomery. We were allocated the governor's palace and the grounds, which was quite something, walking through the marble-floored hall and great pillars. We pitched up in the grounds and mounted the guards and set up for life in the city. Within a few days we knew we were preparing for a very special occasion, and each unit was told to detail a number of men and get them into the best possible shape. This was carried out, and we put on a tremendous parade – pipes, drums the lot – for a salute taken by Winston Churchill, standing on a carrier as we marched down the main thoroughfare of Tripoli. I've heard since then of the effect it had on many men. We had the 23rd Brigade of Tanks in close support with us right through the desert. They were a wonderful lot. One of their survivors lived not far from my home, and when he discovered I was in the Highland Division he told me when they had come in from a fairly battle-strewn area into Tripoli they were told that the tanks had to be scrubbed down, painted, polished and so on because a VIP was coming to look at them. They weren't pleased at all at the time. But they got themselves into position right opposite the saluting dais. And he told me when they saw this distinctive figure with his cigar and wide-brimmed hat that really cheered them up. At the time, he told me, they had no idea what form the parade was going to take and suddenly away to the right they heard the massed pipes and drums of the 51st Highland Division. I looked around and I wasn't the only one with tears in my eyes. When you get units cooperating under good leadership, the mutual respect and affection that grows is a very potent force.

It wasn't long before we were on the move once again. The routine varied little day to day: push on, push on. We then came up against a formidable barrier, the Mareth Line, which was heavily fortified and heavily defended, and it was obvious by this time that Rommel realised he was being caught in a pincer. The 1st Army [having landed under Operation Torch in the first week of November] was moving down the coast, the 8th Army coming in the opposite direction, and he had obviously decided that he would make a stand and slog it out. It was quite a battle and cost a lot of lives. Sad things happen. We now had the term 'friendly fire', which the Americans have invented, and we had an incident in our own battalion, one that showed that understandable mistakes are made. In our sector of the Mareth Line, it was decided we had to push forward. We had some very strong opposition ahead of us that had to be dealt with, and it was decided that two companies, A and B, should go forward. We went through the drill and the rehearsal with the usual creeping barrage in front of us with, prior to that, a softening-up of enemy positions. Our own gunners would zero in during the day so that they would have the calculations absolutely right. But somewhere along the line, a known fact had not been taken into consideration. When a field gun, or any gun, fires in the heat of the day and then has to fire on the same range at night, the change in temperature makes the night firing landing much shorter; in other words the shell doesn't go so far in the cold. This had not happened, and as we prepared to leave the start line, my Company, B, were released early to go on the flank and A Company were on the line ready to move when they were devastated by salvo after salvo of shells, and as it turned out these were from our own guns, where the mistake had occurred.

Now I think it is interesting to note that although the news came around very quickly, the Jocks were completely understanding and forgiving. There was no bitterness, and it was understood that it was one of those things, and that included the wounded. After some days of battling, the enemy pulled out on their way north, and we followed. It amazed us at the time, because the fortification was so strong and complete that very few men could hold it. The next event for the battalion was the advance and capture of a small town, Sfax, on the Tunisian coast. Although we came into Tripoli, we didn't capture the city. Now we were going to take a town. The CO said: 'Let's do it in proper style.' His order was to halt the company and everyone was to smarten themselves up. The pipes and drums were quickly assembled, and with them playing and with our bayonets fixed and shouldered we marched into Sfax. We were not prepared for the reception we received. The streets were lined with cheering people. We were, of course, into French territory now, and they gave us a terrific reception. We were later invited to an official reception for which Montgomery turned up. There were many pretty girls, and when the time came we had a little difficulty in rounding up our lads.

In battles the lulls do not last long, and we were soon on our way to reach another enemy position, at Wadi Akirit, where the Germans held a high position dominating the coastal plain. The battle was quite vicious and difficult, because we were facing a strong unit with Tiger tanks with a complete vision of every-thing, and we had to put in a series of attacks to reach the top. Colonel Lorne Campbell, who commanded the 7th Argyll and Sutherlands, won the only VC that came to the Highland Division in this war. We moved on and headed now for the mountains in Tunisia, where the roads higher up were unsuit-able for vehicles and we had to use mules for the first time.

There was yet one more Black Watch battalion to join the action in North Africa. The 6th Battalion, after their withdrawal from France at the outset of the war, had held numerous stations within the UK since. On 15 March 1943, however, the battalion sailed from Liverpool to join the 1st Army as it fought its way towards Enfidaville, the last major hurdle before Tunis. Hitler had hurriedly reinforced the area with divisions withdrawn from Russia in a last, but vain, attempt to hold on to that north-west region, and there was still a couple of months of heavy fighting ahead when the 6th Battalion arrived. After a delay while waiting for transport, the battalion went into battle on 6 April, operating in hills known as the Djebel Remel. Almost immediately, they found themselves in a position below German artillery on higher ground and took heavy shelling and many casualties. Among them was the battalion's commanding officer, the popular Lieutenant-Colonel Pat Barclay. Lieutenant-Colonel Brian

Madden took command and led the battalion into a month of heavy fighting, notably an early encounter with the renowned Hermann Goering Division at Sidi Medienne. There, in a classic operation committing one company after another, the battalion took the position after a drawn-out but close-run fight in which both sides were progressively weakened by losses. The battalion were given time to recuperate before the famous battle for Enfidaville, which finally brought the 1st Army and divisions of the 8th together. It was the final confrontation, and over the following two weeks the Germans were edged out of North Africa, hostilities ceasing on 11 May. The 6th Battalion paused now but were destined for harder times in the infamous Battle of Monte Cassino.

The 1st, 5th and 7th Battalions, meanwhile, were heading for Sicily, although a brief sojourn in Malta, where they were warmly welcomed, had amazing restorative powers. Now they were introduced for the first time to LCIs – Landing Craft Infantry – flat-bottomed boats developed on an idea from Louis Mountbatten. Each one would take a company aboard to land troops on the beach, supposedly dry. Subsequent experience showed that when attempting to land troops in the heavy seas and appalling weather that dogged the invasion of Sicily on 10 July, dry landings were almost impossible. One soldier even died of seasickness. The three Black Watch battalions were among the lead groups. The 154th Brigade with the 1st and 7th Battalions of the Black Watch went ashore with the main assault force, and the 5th Battalion followed in the second wave. Their objectives were to secure the beaches for the loading of supplies and incoming troops and then move quickly inland. John McGregor, with the 5th, takes up the running:

We had no real opposition and got established across the beach and on to the cliffs beyond and then started to move north towards the town of Puccino. The first opposition we met was a strongpoint and roadblock manned by Italians, but they came rushing out with their hands up. We were all ashore, and reports everywhere were that troops were pushing inwards. We had been given a central line to head north to the plain of Catania, and we achieved that without much problem until the town of Vizzini came into view. It was a key point to capture, although it was strongly defended by the Germans. We were ordered to make an assault on the left flank. It was a long slow climb, but we got into the streets with two companies and started to move through when suddenly we were held up by heavy Spandau fire from Germans entrenched in the main square, firing down the alleyways and streets. We decided to try using our 2-inch mortars with a range of 250 yards, fired vertically, in the hope that the bombs would land in the square. But they weren't reaching the enemy, and at that moment an American platoon came up with bazookas. This was a new word to us; we had never heard of them. They looked like a drainpipe. So they got this man to move forward up the street and aimed their bazooka in a blast of flame, and the Germans stopped firing. We then put down a mortar smoke bomb to find that the Germans had pulled out. The 5th/7th Gordons came in via the other end of the town, and so it was safely in our hands.

The advance into the Catanian plain and on to the slopes of Mount Etna proved altogether more challenging. The Highland Division initially made good progress, but as Divisional Commander Major General Douglas Wimberley himself acknowledged: 'Emboldened by the speed at which we had gone forward, we were now too hasty and took rather a bloody nose.' The 1st and 7th Battalions, with the 7th Argylls, were tasked to capture a position near Gerbini airfield at night, but they ran straight into German lines, and heavy fighting followed in a mêlée of changing fortunes. In the process of the battles, Private John Travena came across a wounded Argyll officer and carried him as far as he was able, but he was forced to halt well away from the 1st Battalion's new position. Unable to risk a further dash in daylight, he hid the officer in a dugout and remained with him, although twice went to fetch water while dodging German patrols. When darkness fell, he managed to reach the Black Watch command post and seek help to carry the officer to safety.

The 5th Battalion and the Gordons pressed on to take positions on the slopes of Mount Etna, securing the key village of Sferro, which they held to allow other units at brigade strength to move forward to take the higher ground in the surrounding hills. It was during this movement on the western slopes that the 7th Battalion took heavy losses. One company was completely cut off and under murderous fire, from which only four men were recovered. The battle went on through the night and into daylight before the battalion forced the Germans back with a barrage of mortars and an anti-tank gun, which had been moved forward to almost point-blank range. It was a key moment in the occupation of Sicily, which was completed on 16 August, well ahead of the anticipated time frame Montgomery had allotted. On 8 September the 154th Brigade joined the 8th Army invasion of Italy across the Strait of Messina. It was an unopposed landing, the Germans having evacuated north to form a more solid defensive line. At that point the 51st Division were withdrawn and prepared to sail back to England in readiness for the next major challenge.

The 6th Battalion spent months in limbo after the end of fighting on the North African coast, much of it in training in combined operations. Now they were going to make up for lost time in a big way. In March 1944 the battalion sailed for Naples and onwards to take over a position at Monte Cassino, where two bloody battles had already been fought between the Germans and the Allies, with commanders of the opposing forces all under severe pressure from above: for both sides, defeat was simply unacceptable. The battalion arrived just as the third battle opened up on 15 March, with more heavy bombing of this holy site. In the front line, British, Indian, Gurkha and New Zealand troops were going through hell trying to get possession of Cassino, held down by German parachutists and elite troops dispatched by Hitler with instructions not to allow the Allies to get beyond it. It was not until May that the Allies at last brought their full might to bear by moving much of the 8th Army from the Adriatic coast. The whole region was a mass of fighting, ground lost, ground won, casualties in high numbers and haggard, battle-weary soldiers who just kept going until they dropped or were removed by the stretcher-bearers. Faulty American policy from the outset had not helped.

The new offensive was launched under the codename Operation Diadem, aimed at crashing through the Liri valley by sheer weight of numbers, while the Polish Corps were to lead in the Monte Cassino assault, which had stoutly refused to budge against all previous attempts. It was behind this attack that the 6th Battalion came in and discovered a battle arena of sheer madness. The historic town and the even more historic abbey had been flattened, and now they were levelling the rubble. There were no secrets, either. German positions overlooked the Allies and vice versa. Observers on both sides were screaming down the telephones every time someone moved, and shelling and mortar fire was exchanged without let-up. Even Vesuvius, sixty miles away, joined in. Throughout the remainder of March and early April, the battalion was close to the action, moving on three occasions, the last to a bridgehead four miles north-east of Cassino, which they took over from a French battalion. They were relieved from that position on 8 April, but they came back from their break to discover that they were now going into Cassino town itself, which was in the unusual position of having both sides *in situ*, the Germans in one half and the Allies in the other. It was overcrowded with hardware and no place for the shell-shocked.

The British had three battalions holding Cassino and when the 6th Battalion moved in to replace one of them, an incredible coincidence of brethren meeting occurred: Black Watch officer Archie Callender, who had just rejoined his battalion after being wounded, found himself taking over from his younger brother Robbie, a platoon commander in the Coldstream. There was, however, a tragic ending to this story. The brothers were not destined to come out of the war together. Archie was killed by shellfire during an action near the Savio river, in north-east Italy, on 19 October.

There was also another remarkable incident there that wholly demonstrated what the Black Watch were all about, if anyone ever needed reminding. Lance-Sergeant William Wilson, aged fifty-three, shouldn't have been at Cassino at all. He had originally joined the regiment in 1908 and had been invalided out in the First World War, severely wounded, but had managed to persuade his original battalion to take him back in 1939, three months short of his fiftieth birthday. He was severely wounded at Cassino by one of his own side's shells, which fell short, and after being carried away for treatment sent a message to his commanding officer, Colonel Madden, apologising for falling out without permission.

The battalion remained *in situ* and in the midst of the fighting around Cassino until 18 May, when the Germans finally gave up and made a fighting retreat. It had been a long, hard struggle for all concerned, and the 6th Battalion had not come out of it lightly. Casualties totalled 246, 40 of them fatally wounded. Officers and NCOs among them had been especially badly hit this time, and the Transvaal Scottish (see Appendix II) were called to help fill the gaps. Drafts were brought in to replenish the ranks, but thereafter the battalion were never able to field more than three full companies. Even so, there was to be no let-up in the demands for their services, not in the slightest. After a brief rest, they were back among the front-runners in the fighting advance to Rome on 6 June followed by another tough journey, skirmishing virtually all the way to Florence, which was reached on 6 August.

The battalion, by then struggling to maintain even three compa-nies, were given a brief rest as their involvement in the Italian campaign switched to the north-east region of Italy, where the last gasps of the fighting in this almost-forgotten arena of the war were being played out, unnoticed and without fanfare in the shade of the great advances in Western Europe. It was a long, hard slog, a grinding succession of fighting and skirmishing and, in the towns, they had to resort to house-to-house fighting in which at least another seventy casualties were recorded en route towards the point where they pulled up for a breather at Forli, forty miles south of Bologna. There were another couple of moves after that before the battalion were pulled out at last and ordered to Taranto. From there, they were to be shipped to Palestine for a three-month rest, or at least that's what they thought.

The weary soldiers arrived at the port to await their transport, and in fact the battalion's second in command and an advance party had already been sent on ahead to Haifa when the news came: Palestine was off.

Instead, they were being sent across the Adriatic to Greece, or Athens to be precise, where the early stages of the Civil War were already breaking out. The battalion, along with elements of the 2nd Parachute Brigade, the RAF Regiment and the SAS Boat Squadron under the command of Lieutenant-Colonel Lord Jellicoe, were dispatched post-haste to intervene in a political war. As soon as the Germans pulled out of Greece, fighting had erupted between the Greek Communists (ELAS) and the Royalists (EDES). At least 5,000 Communist guerrillas were operating in and around Athens, and, even with the war in Europe reaching a desperate point in December 1944, the Allies had no option but to attend the Greek crisis. The Russians were already in Yugoslavia and Bulgaria, and if ELAS gained a foothold they would be in control of Athens in no time. The task was considered so urgent that the Paras were dropped just outside Athens. It was a hard landing, in which eight were killed and thirty-seven injured.

The Black Watch ship *Bergensfiord* anchored off the Greek coast by 15 December and the men were moved on to the mainland over the next two days. They were now to adopt the role of armed policemen, conducting house searches and vehicle checks on the route into Athens, which was their lifeline for supplies and also a rat run for the terrorists. They were billeted in a number of houses close to the main thoroughfare, and ELAS welcomed them on the first night by lobbing hand grenades in their direction. The next day, the snipers were out and two Jocks were killed. After the ordeal of the past few months, resentment among the Jocks set in, especially as the Greeks had just been rescued from the German jackboot. Over the coming days, there were numerous skirmishes with the Communists, and another soldier of the battalion was killed and two wounded. However, the Greek people began to show their support for the British soldiers, hanging the Greek flag from their windows to indicate that they rejected the Communists, and gradually the situation calmed. The battalion kept up vigilant patrols and unearthed a number of large ammunition dumps. In the New Year, however, their role transferred to that of a mobile one, travelling the length and breadth of the country on the same brief, patrolling and searching, a task that they fulfilled for another eighteen months. There were a number of further incidents, in one of which two Jocks were killed and nine wounded. By the middle of 1946 they could boast to have travelled to every corner of the country. But on 8 June they paraded in Athens for the last time. The Second World War was finally over for the 6th Battalion, Black Watch, and they returned home to be disbanded and consigned to history.

Now we must catch up with events surrounding the 2nd Battalion, which we last saw leaving North Africa for Syria and then India, after the tragedies at and after Tobruk. What came next, as already indicated in regard to General Wavell's return, was another fine mess that saw casualties aplenty, and men dying from disease and suffering in dire, almost inhumane, conditions in the jungles of Burma. Many of those who survived – and the percentages were akin to something out of the nineteenth century – were affected by their experiences, in one way or another, for years. Yes, the battalion were heading for what proved to be one of the most controversial of all campaigns in the Second World War, that of the Chindits, so-called Special Forces brigades formed to get behind enemy lines and disrupt the Japanese.

Deep penetration behind enemy lines wasn't a new idea. Many had tried it in the past. Some units survived, including that formed by the ambitious David Stirling. Having acquired fifty parachutes that fell off the back of a truck, Stirling used them as the basis for the formation of the Special Air Service and made a name for himself racing ahead of the herd and getting inside enemy lines, raiding and pillaging, stealing and killing and causing general mayhem among the outposts of Rommel's Afrika Korps until his luck ran out. He was hauled off to Colditz, but the SAS went careering on without him.

Orde Wingate's scheme was much more grandiose and controversial. He was a difficult, colourful and complex man. The son of a British officer, he was born in India and brought up in a family with strong Christian beliefs. He received a military education and was commissioned in 1923, later serving in India and then in the Sudan. He was transferred to Palestine in 1936 as an intelligence officer at a time when small bands of Arab rioters were regularly attacking both the British and the Jews. Wingate organised and trained special 'night squads', which successfully employed the tactics of surprise and mobility. His support for the Zionist cause was heavily frowned on, and in 1939 the British succumbed to Arab pressure: Wingate was transferred from the region that eventually became Israel and was barred from returning. He went back to Britain briefly before being transferred to Ethiopia, where he was a major figure under General Wavell's command in liberating the country from the Italians. It was from this posting that he moved directly to India under Wavell. There, Wingate developed his idea for a guerrilla force to attack the Japanese in Burma, and the London powerhouse needed little convincing. Churchill was very keen on swashbucklers. Wingate came up with the name Chindits for his force, which was a corruption of the Burmese word 'chinthe' for 'winged stone lion', the guardians of Buddhist temples.

The original Chindit formation was officially known as the 77th Infantry Brigade, brought together for Wingate's first expedition. Under the title of Operation Longcloth, he assembled British commandos, the 13th Battalion, King's Liverpool Regiment, 3/2nd Gurkha Rifles and 2nd Battalion, Burma Rifles, in all about 3,000 men, with hundreds of mules, oxen and elephants carrying their supplies. The first expedition had three objectives: to cut two main railway links from Mandalay and generally harass the enemy in the Shwebo area, 180 miles to the east. The Chindit columns were launched from Manipur in February 1943, and the main force reached the railway in two weeks without encountering any Japanese. They were to be re-supplied by the RAF. However, at the railway line two columns were ambushed and suffered heavy casualties. They managed to blow up the railway line in numerous places over a distance of thirty miles, which would be heralded by war reporters as a brilliant achievement but, in truth, was overstated and the damage not sufficient to hamper the Japs seriously. Nor did the media report the horrendous situation confronting the Chindit troops.

The Japanese were now alerted to the presence of a large British force, which they believed was a division of commandos. They acted accordingly, piling troops into the area. The Chindits had managed to cross the Irrawaddy, but then, under heavy fire, Wingate had to disperse his force, so they were unable to take the RAF drops, as arranged. The columns faced desperate weeks ahead: starving, lost in dense jungle, hundreds falling sick, wounded or killed under ambush; they were a sorry sight and many suffered psychologically. A disorganised retreat became the only solution, many of them under the command of an efficient ex-sapper officer, Major 'Mad Mike' Calvert, later of the SAS.

Even so, Wingate finally had to split his force into groups of forty with instructions to get back to India as best they could. Overall, Wingate lost almost a third of his force. They had spent twelve weeks in the jungle, and most had marched almost a thousand miles. And now they were going to do so all over again, this time with a much larger force, including the 2nd Battalion of the Black Watch, partly under pressure from the Americans. They wanted action from the British and from the substantial reservoir of Indian army manpower, which the ebullient US General Joe Stilwell, commander of US forces in the Chinese-Burma theatre, claimed was being left idle, which was hardly true. The real reason was that Stilwell was getting some stick from the Japs and did not have the answers himself. He wanted the Chindits to disrupt Japanese lines of communication and to attack troops moving towards him. At the summit conference in Quebec in August 1943, Churchill took along Orde Wingate, who revived his theories of long-range penetration. Although Stilwell raised objections to some of the more unmilitary ideas, such as that the men should never shave and that rank was of little importance in the jungle, Wingate was given the go-ahead by Allied commanders for a second expedition. In addition, the Americans offered help by forming their own Long-Range Penetration Group to be trained and commanded by Wingate (this group later became known as Merrill's Marauders). When the British requested a supply of American light aircraft for evacuating the wounded, the Americans instead offered to provide an air task force consisting of light bombers, fighters, transport Dakotas, light aircraft and gliders. As they discovered, however, landing planes and gliders over such a treacherous landscape was fraught with difficulties.

His vast new 'special force' would be formed for what was to become known as Operation Thursday, a complex and meandering proposal involving six brigades, each made up of columns that were to be deployed by air into jungle locations. The object, according to Wingate, was 'to insert a substantial force into the guts of the enemy'. Unfortunately, Wingate did not survive to supervise the operation. He was killed in a plane crash on 24 March 1944. His body lies in Arlington National Cemetery, Virginia. Brigadier Joe Lentaigne, a former Gurkha officer, succeeded him, and meanwhile the 2nd Black Watch had joined battalions from more than sixteen British regiments supplying troops for the Chindit operations. The brigades had their own base close to an airstrip from which their columns would be sent to harass the Japanese communication lines and troops. Lieutenant-Colonel G. C. Green, leading the Black Watch contingent, commanded one of the columns and Major David Rose the other. The colonel is quoted by Bernard Fergusson, who was also there, as saying: 'This ought to confuse the Japs. We don't even know where we're going ourselves.' An additional embarrassment, as they moved away, was caused by the large numbers of British troops in the area and, for most of one tense day, Green's column played hide-and-seek with what it took to be a Japanese column but which turned out to be equally nervous Gurkhas. Once they got on the move, however, the columns began flying around the jungles in small aircraft and gliders loaded with men, mules and equipment to sustain them for up to thirty days at a time with resupply directed by radio. Early in April both Black Watch columns carried out successful ambushes of

Japanese columns and supply lines. Much of the time, however, was spent marching in terrible conditions.

In May 1944 the British handed control of the Chindits to Stilwell, which survivors of the British expeditions have said was tantamount 'to a death sentence to many of the Chindits'. A high proportion of casualties – some put the figure at ninety per cent – occurred in this final phase of the campaign. Under Stilwell, the whole concept changed, and the men were required to operate as normal infantry, for which they were neither equipped nor trained. The Chindits put on a brave face and began what was to become an imprecise movement of men, machines and animals across the most challenging terrain under the worst weather on earth. Casualties were amplified by sickness from typhus, malaria, dysentery and foot rot. Major R. J. Bower, then one of the young newly qualified and commissioned doctors with the Chindits, and at one time attached to Black Watch columns, recorded in his long and detailed diary of events:

> The day starts before dawn when everybody stands to . . . usually moving off at 06.00 hours. Breakfast is K rations – chopped ham and egg yolk, some biscuits, fruit bar and coffee. There would probably be some porridge or rice available. This may sound very nice, but after several months each meal almost made one sick . . . Ground covered depended on the weather and country. On flat in the dry, columns could easily do thirty miles a day, but on a wet day with hills of three thousand feet to climb, three to five miles would be good. It needed good men for the job [but even then] the rate of sickness and debility among them was high . . . My main recollection over the hills was the slow progress due to deep mud and the number of cases of men left behind by the preceding column (Yorks and Lancs) which had passed over several days before. Some of them were in a pitiful condition with severe infections. One was completely demented. We attempted to carry some of them but there were several deaths. Undoubtedly their discipline had become slack.

They had been noticeably slovenly. As a contrast, the Black Watch was always tidy and clean-shaven.

The troops were exhausted. As reports of these inadequacies reached Louis Mountbatten, by then Supreme Commander of South-East Asia, he ordered a team of doctors to evaluate the conditions of the Chindits. They made an inspection of four and a half battalions, almost 2,500 men, and found only 119 truly fit for duty. Mountbatten ordered Stilwell to evacuate all the wounded, and the rest of the Chindits retreated. The last Chindit left Burma on 27 August 1944. Casualties for this phase of Chindit operations amounted to 1,496 killed or missing presumed dead and 2,434 wounded. Almost half of the survivors had to be hospitalised. Some were permanently affected, while others took years to recover.

Military commentators continue to argue over the value of the Chindits. Field Marshal Slim at first praised their efforts, but later, in Britain's Official History, was highly critical of the whole concept. Most of the arguments, however, were clouded by the extremes of views for and against Wingate himself.

Finally, in this chapter of the finest hours of the Black Watch, we turn to D-Day for the conclusion of what can be no more than a summary of the varied and substantial contribution in life, limb and sheer brute force that the Black Watch made to the Allied effort in the Second World War. To strike a perspective, the Normandy landings saw the transfer of 156,000 men and thousands of tons of heavy metal from southern England to the beaches in the first 12 hours between the Orne estuary and the south-eastern end of the peninsula: 83,000 British and Canadian troops on the eastern beaches, 73,000 Americans on the western. They were followed in the coming weeks by more than 2 million, a movement that involved some 7,000 seagoing vessels and 11,590 Allied aircraft, of which 5,510 were from the Royal Air Force, with a large contingent of air-sea rescue aircraft from Coastal Command, plus 406 British and 1,200 American transport aircraft used to drop paratroops and to tow the gliders of the airborne units.

The principal action involving the Black Watch came through the three battalions, the 1st, 5th and 7th, which remained part of the 51st Highland Division. They had been training hard since leaving North Africa in readiness for the advance across Europe. Just as the desert required specific and rigorous attention to detail in the methodology of mastering the landscape, so did north-western Europe, in perhaps an even more determined and detailed way. The desert was a great slab of sand, perilous of course, while the countryside of Europe held so many more intricacies in the potential for attack, not to mention the other major obstacle: sixty divisions of German troops to get past. There was also brand-new weaponry to master: the battalions generally carried the normal infantry rifle, one Bren gun for each section with nine sections in a company, four two-inch mortars, which were also good smoke producers for screening, eight anti-tank guns – two-pounders, six-pounders and later seventeen-pounders – six mortars in the mortar platoon, and such new toys as flame-throwers, with a range of a hundred yards, mounted on carriers. Then there were all kinds of new kit, never used by the Black Watch before, for crossing rivers and minefields, none of it of the pick-up-and-go variety; all had to be learned and appreciated.

The 5th went on the first day of the invasion, landing in the afternoon, and the 1st and 7th followed over the next seventy-two hours. All were engaged in early encounters with the Germans on reaching their target areas and beyond. The 5th met the enemy at Breville village, close to a château, owned by Lord Derby, which the forward units used as an observation post. Soon, mortar bombs and shells were falling thick and fast, and in between voices were calling for the Jocks to give themselves up. A particularly nasty battle developed and a flank section was overrun and captured: they were taken out to a yard and shot in the back. One of them, feigning death, escaped to tell the story, although the Jocks had trouble believing him. Months later, Bernard Fergusson tells us, came official confirmation.

At the helm of the 1st Battalion was Lieutenant-Colonel (later Brigadier) John Adam Hopwood, a popular member of the officers' corps who had chosen a military career after his Eton education and, as he said, 'living in St Andrews, there was only one regiment you could possibly go into and that was the Black Watch. Every chap you met had either been in the Black Watch or had a relative killed in the Black Watch or had a younger relative serving in the Black Watch.' He took command of the battalion in Sicily, and his lively recollections and memories of the journey into Germany add another dimension to the saga:

The battalion was to all intents and purposes a TA battalion [when formed after the surrender of the first 51st Division in 1940] but had trained very hard indeed for D-Day, endlessly practising the attack and advancing, which we'd become pretty good at. All our training was based on practical experience in North Africa and Sicily, but, of course, it was totally different from what we would face in Normandy. When we landed in France, everything went very smoothly, a wonderful sight of everything being offloaded and troops and vehicles going ashore very efficiently. As a follow-up division we landed unopposed and moved off very quickly. By then, the Germans had already been pushed back. Our job, as we thought, was to follow up the first wave, but there was still much work to be done.

The fighting was initially in bocage country, very closed in. The shells would burst in the trees above you, scattering their splinters from above downwards. That was one of the nasty shocks we had, and even before we went into attack we'd had about 100 casualties from these overhead shell splinters in this terrible area known as the Triangle. Very unpleasant. We had one dreadful day when we had the Moaning Minnies [multiple-barrelled mortars firing thirty bombs in one go] on to us in a really big way. We were digging into a new command post and there was a hell of a stonk, which landed practically on top of us and killed my adjutant, who was standing beside me. I climbed into the remnants of the command post, the last in, and finished up protecting the chaps who were underneath me.

Everyone looked around for the adjutant and saw that he was dead. He was a charming young man: Ronnie Milligan, aged just nineteen, excellent adjutant. John Benson, one of my company commanders – an enormous chap – got an axe and went into the orchard, saying: 'I'm going to chop these bloody trees down.' And he did, and it did help resolve the problem. But, of course, we couldn't go through the countryside chopping down trees.

We were also strafed pretty heavily by our own people. I waved my map board at the buggers. The boss of the brigade actually got on the blower and said he wasn't prepared to advance until they called the fighter boys off. But, of course, it was difficult for them, especially in bad weather. Once we'd got that sorted out, they were magnificent, especially later on when the Typhoons, attacking singly and severally, dived at tanks and saved our bacon many times.

On 7 August we were preparing an assault along the road to Falaise, with the intention of capturing three villages, with the 1st Battalion on the left and the Northamptonshire Yeomanry, 7th Argylls, on the right and the 7th Batallion, Black Watch, following up. We had all the chaps mounted in armoured personnel carriers, which were anti-tank guns with the guns taken out. No one was on their feet; they were all riding in these vehicles and we motored on very quickly. The operation was in the darkness, and we got right on to our objectives without any severe opposition. Our left flank was covered by the Strategic Air Force, who made a terrific row with those great bombs coming down only about 4,000 yards from us. We had enormous artillery support, which was also coming down like hell. They'd put everything they could into this attack. In the meantime, the Northamptonshire Yeomanry motored up, formed up on our left and got their Beazers out and shot up everything they could. They really were bloody marvellous. I went to the agreed rendezvous to meet my company commanders, hardly expecting to find them all there. But in fact none had got lost, and I simply said: 'Right – go on and attack!' They were wonderful. They'd gone through this long attack in the dark under a hell of a lot of noise and turned up on time and in good order.

They pushed on. The leading companies cleared up the enemy in the village and were dug in by dawn. Next morning, the counter-attack came in but didn't get very far. The Northamptonshire Yeomanry brought their tanks in and knocked out nine or ten of the other side's straight away, then pulled back. This attack was the best the 1st Battalion had pulled off so far. By that time also, the much-respected General Tom Rennie had returned to command the division, a man of immense self-confidence and much loved by the men of the Black Watch. He 'put the division back on its feet', said Colonel Hopwood, because up to that time they had had rather a black period: several attacks had failed, one in particular where four battalions were sent in, leapfrogging each other to eliminate the element of surprise. It was a 'hopeless business' and the Camerons suffered the brunt of it. But now they were back on course.

Their route was from Falaise, hooking round up to Le Havre, which was successfully attacked by the 51st and 49th Divisions, but there were many casualties. The port was, according to Hopwood's description, 'strongly defended, one of these damned places where the Bosche had decided they couldn't give it up without fighting. Thus we were lured into attack.' In fact, although the division were moving swiftly forward behind the great sweep of the mechanised units ahead, trouble spots required great stamina and courage of the men to overcome.

As we approached the Ardennes, the weather virtually grounded our air force, and the Germans were able to push their armour forward. Directly the fog lifted, the armour got smashed up by the Typhoons, and we got on the move again swiftly. We were not involved in Arnhem, but instead went up through a corridor towards Nijmegen, and the Bosche were holding out on both sides of the road and eventually we had various battles and

274

pushed them back. Going up one day, there was a hell of a lot of shooting going on, and I discovered that a German patrol had had the temerity to put in a raid on the battalion, rather a stout-hearted effort, actually. They even grabbed three prisoners, but we got them back.

How? During the mêlée, as the raiders ran into a forward company of Jocks, the three who had been kidnapped took matters into their own hands, attacked an officer and three guards and escaped. The battalions reached the corridor between Eindhoven and Nijmegen in the first week of October, and the first task of the 1st and 7th Battalions with the 154th Brigade was to line the Wilhelmina Canal to provide a protective cordon on the approaches to Eindhoven airfield for a visit from King George VI, who arrived on the fourteenth. He also carried the good wishes of the Black Watch Colonel-in-Chief, Queen Elizabeth. Duty done, the men then moved off again in a north-west-erly direction towards the Maas, an area still infested with Germans. Much heavy patrolling was called for by all three battalions. The 1st liberated the town of Baarlo, whose residents kept in touch with the Black Watch after the war, and by the end of the month the division were within striking distance of the Dutch–German border.

Ambitions for a post-Christmas advance over the German border were halted by the surprise launch of Hitler's last-ditch effort to blast the Allies back from the border, divide their armies, cut communications and force a Dunkirk-style evacuation. This was the Ardennes Offensive, otherwise known as the Battle of the Bulge. The German attack was launched with a spearhead of V-1 rockets against Liège and Antwerp, while 2,000 guns were ranged against the southern-most positions of the American forces. A massive wall of firepower from five Panzer divisions came up behind, followed by four powerful Waffen-SS armoured divisions. With thirteen infantry divisions and five armoured now moving on Allied positions, Hitler expected his troops to be in Antwerp within four days, and it seemed possible that they might achieve this, given that the Americans had clearly been

caught on the hop during severe weather that had prevented reconnaissance. In fact, few of Hitler's generals believed the plan could
succeed, but they carried on out of loyalty and fear.

The Allied commanders quickly recovered and their defences
remained solid, despite the huge German assault. On 20 December
Montgomery took command of all Allied forces north of the German
push, while General Patton commanded the troops to the south, where
the main thrust of the attack was directed. The weather was appalling,
with deep snow, frozen ground and then mud and slush in this cauldron of heavy and bitter fighting. The battles spread across the bulge,
with the Allies calling up the equivalent of thirty-five divisions and
a huge air bombardment. Even so, casualties were heavy as the Allies
gradually pushed the Germans back to their start line, and by the end
of January the salient had been closed off. This six weeks of fighting,
mainly involving American units, cost the Germans more than
100,000 men and around 1,200 tanks. The Allies were equally hurt,
losing 70,000 men, while the British, who were not seriously engaged,
lost only 1,200. Hitler had lost the gamble, and the Allies were ready
to begin the advance into Germany in the sure knowledge that the
last lines of defences inside Germany itself had been seriously, if not
fatally, weakened.

So the surge forward began again, and in February the Highland
Division had reached the Reichswald Forest, through which ran the
Siegfried Line, a defence system stretching more than 390 miles with
more than 18,000 bunkers, tunnels and tank traps. It went from Kleve
on the border with the Netherlands, along Germany's western border
to Switzerland. The Americans should have joined them in the assault
but their arrival was delayed and the British went ahead without them.
The battles, which lasted three weeks, were costly, especially from
enemy snipers specially trained for the defence of the area. The 1st
Battalion, however, managed to find themselves on a route where the
opposition was manageable. They shot their way through, took a
hundred prisoners for twenty-three casualties, and second in command
of the battalion, Major Peter Taylor, deputising for Colonel Hopwood,

who was away from his desk at the time, became the first to set foot on German soil, an event that was marked by a complimentary message from General Sir Brian Horrocks, commander of the 30th Corps, and which earned an eternal place in Black Watch history. The 1st and the 7th Battalions went on to punch a hole in the Siegfried Line itself at Hekkens, took almost 300 prisoners and again went into history as the destroyers of this shrine of the German military.

The way was open now to the Rhine, but the road ahead was heavily defended and the casualties mounted. At the river, the 7th Battalion, Black Watch, and the 7th Argylls were the lead battalions of the 51st Division to cross; the 1st came in afterwards. They crossed in Buffalo armoured tracked vehicles, each boat taking about three minutes to get to the other side. There was a high bund on the opposite bank, which the lead battalions held while the 1st pushed on through with the intention of moving ahead while the 7th consolidated. The 1st ran straight into German armour, and one of their forward positions was almost overrun. The enemy also had to be kept away from the bund, so Colonel Hopwood, back from his break, pulled in his troops to make a stand. The Jocks behind rushed forward to assist their isolated comrades and heavy fighting broke out. 'One company commander, 2nd Lieutenant Henderson, carried out a series of wonderful gallant acts,' said Hopwood, 'including charging a Spandau with a shovel after his weapon had been knocked out of his hand and killing those who were firing it. Then he got the rest of his platoon into a building and called out for the Bren gun [firing at the incoming German soldiers]. I recommended him for a VC, which he didn't get, I'm afraid, but won a DSO instead. The Germans fought stout-heartedly at the Rhine.'

Henderson was cheered as he regrouped his patrol and again went forward, holding out in the village of Speldrop against attacks by artillery and armour until the rest of Hopwood's battalion caught up with them. The 5th Battalion had crossed further upriver, and the Jocks there had to resort to house-to-house fighting in the village of Rees, where they were confronted by Spandau teams. A 'lively' confrontation followed for a couple of hours before the remaining

Germans surrendered. General Rennie, the much-admired, straight-as-a-die commander of the 51st Highland Division, was among the casualties in the battle for Rees. But even as he died, Rennie knew that the north-west campaign was won, and that the war was as good as over. His troops now began fanning out through northern Germany, still fighting as they went, in the great dash of the Allied forces to secure the key cities, and then into Berlin itself. The Black Watch had undoubtedly made their mark on this moment of history.

There was, however, one more vital task in searching for the survivors of the original 51st Division captured at St-Valéry in 1940. They found most of the Black Watch officers and a very small number of Jocks at the Laufen prisoner-of-war camp on the Austrian border with Bavaria. They included General Victor Fortune, the divisional commander who had had the unenviable task of handing himself and his men over to Rommel whom, incidentally, he had outlived. The German field marshal was allowed to commit suicide after being accused by Hitler of plotting against him. Soldiers of the Black Watch battalions captured were scattered across Germany, and weeks passed before all the survivors were located and identified. Some were discovered in harsh military prisons for making disparaging remarks about Hitler.

Well, they would, wouldn't they!

CHAPTER FIFTEEN

On the 'Bloody Hook'

The end of the war was also the signal for the emergence of nation-alistic conflagrations that would dominate the military scene around the world for years hence, and the Black Watch were among the fire-brigade troops rushed to the scene of several of them. The first priority for them was India, where the voice for independence had grown stronger, if somewhat muted, during the war years and had now emerged with new impetus and violent internal strife.

Clement Attlee's new Labour government immediately promised home rule, but that wasn't enough. Independence was the only route for the activists, and even then a bloody civil war loomed between the Muslims and Hindus over plans for a joint governing body, which would please neither side. In the run-up to the final dislodgement of the cornerstone of the British Empire, the 2nd Battalion were among the British troops attempting to hold the fort as negotiations for parti-tion and the creation of two new nations proceeded. Indeed, the battalion barely had time to complete their own re-formation after Burma before they were required in the hot spots of protest and uprising across India.

Among the early post-war troubles was a threatened mutiny by the

Indian Navy – effectively still under British control – which was viewed with great concern both in India itself and in London, where fears were mounting over increased violence between the warring Muslim–Hindu factions. The Indian Navy had given sterling service during the war, when its manpower was increased from 2,000 in 1939 to almost 30,000 by 1945. Mutinies had occurred in Bombay in February 1946 and at the naval base near Karachi. It was to the latter that the 2nd Battalion were dispatched as part of the 44th Airborne Brigade. The battalion were to lead the ground force in to capture the base in a dawn raid, first by surrounding the central area and then preparing to storm the base. On witnessing this approach, the mutineers agreed to negotiate and ultimately to call a halt to their actions, and the mutiny was ended without a shot being fired. Elsewhere, as violence and civil unrest spread through the country, the battalion were again on the move, this time to a place resonant in Black Watch history. Peshawar in the north had been the scene of exchanges between the Jocks and the murderous Pathans, scourge of the British army's legendary endeavours on the North-West Frontier. It was nearby, too, that a Black Watch graveyard was located at Cherat, containing the remains of those who had died in the cholera epidemic of 1867. Joe Fairhurst from Wigan, who so wanted to be in the Black Watch that he lied about his age when he was sixteen and said his grandfather was a Scot (which he wasn't), now found himself in this historic place as a lance-corporal in the 2nd Battalion in those trying last weeks of Empire in India:

At that particular time, I went to A Company, which were high up in the hills at Cherat. There was nothing there by then, just three sets of barrack rooms, a guard room, a massive parade ground and a canteen run by an old Indian. There were still all the old wallahs. The cha wallah used to come around with a long bamboo pole across his shoulders. On one end he had a big tin box and on the other end he had an urn with a charcoal fire underneath. In the box he carried different kinds of sandwiches, cakes and boiled eggs. When he arrived, at a certain time every night, he banged a gong and everyone would come out with their tin mug and get what they wanted. He also had a tick book for those who had no money. Some of the newer fellows would try it on, of course, and sign Mickey Mouse or Donald Duck. What they didn't know was that he had an arrangement with the sergeant-major, who would have the offenders on parade for a right rollicking. We were up there to do patrols, and right on the top of that position we could see the trails and villages below. We built a series of gun pits, then we went on patrols for two or three days at a time, two mules, twelve men, a lance-corporal, a corporal, a sergeant and an officer. We would go through the trails to make sure there were no dissident Pathans around. Then we would alternate by coming down from the hill station and in trucks go straight up the Khyber Pass, where there was one thing I will always remember: we came across a cutting in the rock on which had been etched the badges of all the regiments that had served up there, going back many years. A bit further on, there was a huge fort, by then occupied by the police, and then on to the border with Afghanistan, which we also patrolled.

To remind the present-day inhabitants of their fortitude in the region during this era of deployment to India, the battalion's pipes and drums were brought to bear, and, as the regiment's history records, demonstrators who had taken to lying on the railway lines in silent protest rose quickly to their feet on hearing the strains of the pipes. There was, in this country of superstition, something mystical about their arrival, and the tense situation was lightened and calmed. This traditional ending without serious violence brought a temporary peace to the region, and on that note the Black Watch retreated to become the last battalion of the British army to serve on the much-vaunted North-West Frontier, which carried so many memories and such great history for soldiers. The battalion marched out of Peshawar in August 1946 on a note of peace, albeit a temporary one. Within a matter of weeks, the region had descended into a crescendo of civil strife that had spread across India as preparations to end British rule and divide the country reached their climax.

In that period, and indeed for some time previously, the presence of British soldiers at riot scenes could have the red-rag-to-a-bull effect, but even so the British troops remained on peacekeeping duties, although turning out to a riot situation, as they had done so often in the past, was now an exceedingly sensitive issue, as Joe Fairhurst recalled:

We were formed up into internal security companies, which were intended as back-up for situations that the police could not handle. When we were called out, say to a riot, we had a section of men, led by a lance-corporal in front, with an officer and a sergeant at the back. We would proceed forward in a straight line with rifle and fixed bayonet. We each had five rounds of ammunition, all to be kept in your pouch and nothing in your rifle. As we closed on the rioters, we were supposed to halt, four men would advance and at that point the sergeant and officer would come forward to begin the show of strength. But we could not do anything further; no weapons could be used unless there was an Indian magistrate on the spot or a superior police officer who had to first give his permission. Even then all we would do was put two rounds in and wait for the order to fire over their heads.

On 20 February Lord Wavell, Viceroy of India since 1942, vacated his post in favour of Lord Mountbatten of Burma after disagreements with the Labour government on the manner of the handover. Wavell was given an earldom and sailed from India, as did the 2nd Battalion of his old regiment, the last battalion of the British army to leave Pakistan on 26 February 1948. It was more than the end of an era for the Black Watch. The independence of India and the resultant release of a large number of British troops, along with the general need for economic belt-tightening after the war, had meant a reduction in most regiments, including the Black Watch. The TA battalions were demobilised and languished for many years thereafter. The 2nd Battalion suffered a similar fate at the end of their Indian assignment. After home leave, and the departure of those who had completed their term, the battalion went to Duisburg in 1948, there to be amalgamated with the 1st Battalion.

The 1st Battalion had remained in Germany at the war's end as part of the British Army of the Rhine, set up under a strict regime of non-fraternisation drawn up by Montgomery. The Black Watch and other regiments that made up the vast contingent of British servicemen in Germany at the time also began taking National Servicemen, the compulsory two-year conscription of young men over eighteen which was re-introduced in 1948 in the wake of a significant slump in recruitment across all the services and which remained in place until 1960. This form of recruitment existed for longer than had been anticipated when the Cold War emerged and a counter-force was required in Germany against the mighty Russian armies as Stalin gathered up the Eastern-bloc nations in the Soviet Union and slammed down the Iron Curtain. This massive presence was to continue in various forms for the next forty years, until the formal ending of the Cold War, and at its peak the BAOR strength exceeded 40,000 troops.

Over the years the Black Watch would be regular contributors to that force, and none more so than immediately after the war when the regiment formed part of what was then an occupying army. Furthermore, as various threatening emergencies developed in British interests and protectorates around the world, the 2nd Battalion were re-formed in Colchester and posted to Hubbelrath in October 1952. Colonel Robert Gurdon, a young platoon commander with the new 2nd Battalion in 1952 in the early stages of what became a thirty-two-year career with the Black Watch, noted:

It was principally a National Service battalion, and in fact most of the regiment was made up of two-year servicemen. Little did I realise that as a newly commissioned officer who trained at Sandhurst how little I really knew about running a platoon. For one thing, one had to learn Jockese [a language like no other,

with words that many a southerner found impossible to deci-
pher]. You also had to understand their way of working, their
thoughts, how they behaved and generally getting to know them.
It could be quite hard work. Life in Germany was [at that point]
very relaxed. We had freedom of movement; we could do
anything we liked: knock down fences, go through cornfields,
whatever. Training was imaginative and interesting out in the
countryside. The soldiers themselves varied enormously. With
a National Service army, you get an enormous cross-section of
people ranging from the very intelligent to those who could not
read or write, all muddled together. One had to show a certain
amount of imagination to make sure that the right people did
the right job. The most frustrating business was that no sooner
had you got your platoon to a certain level than people were
leaving and new people were coming in. Also, the less good
National Servicemen were only interested in doing their time
and getting out. Even so, the National Service soldiers did begin
to establish an identity with the regiment, and very much stood
with each other. And, of course, the stories were legend about
when they all went off duty down to Düsseldorf, with the Welsh
Fusiliers in one part of the town and the Black Watch in another,
and when they met they certainly showed their pride in wearing
the Red Hackle. In fact, life in Germany was very good for
soldiers at that time, socially and within the regiment itself.

The 2nd Battalion were, however, destined for peacekeeping duties
in British Guiana (now Guyana), the South American protectorate
which was under threat from insurgents. They were to remain there
for almost eighteen months. The 1st Battalion were also bound for
foreign parts, heavily reinforced for duties that would soon put them
in world headlines when the new flashpoint of Korea emerged. Britain
was to make a significant contribution to what was to be the first-
ever allied operation under the auspices of the United Nations – and
indeed the first conflict in which the UN had sponsored the use of
military force against an aggressor. Although it was largely driven

by the Americans, who also supplied ninety per cent of the troops, hardware and equipment, all the British service arms were heavily involved.

In fact, such a conflict was the last thing that hard-up Britain needed, and the causes were linked once again to colonialism. Japan had ruled Korea since 1910, but, when the Russians and the Americans kicked them out in 1945, Soviet troops occupied Korea north of the thirty-eighth parallel while American troops controlled the country south of this line. In 1947 the UN General Assembly declared that elections should be held throughout Korea to choose one government for the entire country. The Soviet Union refused to sanction elections in the north, but on 10 May 1948 the people of South Korea elected a national assembly. The north responded by forming the Democratic People's Republic of Korea. Both claimed the entire country, and the Communists made their move and invaded South Korea on 25 June 1950.

Sixteen UN countries, including the UK, sent troops to help the South Koreans, and forty-one countries sent military equipment, food and other supplies. The North Koreans had the backing of the Soviets for equipment and advisers and the Chinese for additional manpower, of which they had a vast reservoir. Apart from being, at that point, one of the most brutal and dehumanising conflicts in modern history, the war was unique for a number of reasons, not least that it was a forerunner of Vietnam and thus its horrors soon became somewhat overshadowed by even greater controversies. Issues beyond the battle lines included the brainwashing techniques used by the North Koreans and Chinese Communists on prisoners of war as well as other atrocities. There were also allegations that germ warfare was used by the Americans, which was never substantiated but is not beyond belief, given what happened later in Vietnam.

In Germany, the 1st Battalion were placed on a ready-to-move alert, as Norman Potter, one of the Black Watch southerners, from Reading, recalled:

One morning a rumour came round that we were going to Malaya, but then we had a CO's parade in the afternoon and he confirmed that we were going to Korea. [Some of us] came back to Scotland from February to May, reorganising and preparing the equipment for Korea. We were issued with new weapons, rifles, Sten guns and so on and went out on the ranges to zero them in ready for what was to come. We also took in a large number of reinforcements from different regiments, including the Seaforths, Gordons and Camerons, people who had volunteered to go. I must be honest: I also wanted to go. I had volunteered for the army, and as a trained soldier there was a certain excitement about going to Korea, and I was looking forward to it. I didn't know any different, and it is only when you get there that things change. You grow up. A lot of the chaps were looking forward to going, and the things they were saying, you'd never think they were going off to war.

Everybody was happy and talking about things. No one gave it a thought that they might not come back. The journey out was typical army. We were on the boat for six weeks and the routine was rigid: up at six, PT, shooting practice, map-reading, drill, weapon training lectures, films. They kept you busy. We went ashore at different places: Aden, Colombo, Singapore and Kowloon. There, our pipe band met up with the Argylls' pipe band and they were at the harbour playing together. They'd all had a few drinks, but they still managed to put on a show. The next stop was Pusan [on the south-eastern tip of South Korea], about six-thirty in the morning. The sun was shining as we glided into the harbour. There was an American band playing ['St Louis Blues', of all things] on the shore to welcome us. But despite that, the place, from the ship, looked a dump. We went ashore the next day and marched to the railway station and, since we had a three- or four-hour wait, the pipe band kept us entertained. On the next platform, a beautiful train came in with United States Army plastered all over it. Then, after another hour or so, ours arrived. I don't think the train had been cleaned out since the day it was put on the track. It was filthy.

The floor was thick with dirt, hard wooden slat seats, half

the windows were missing – that was our transport for the next eighteen hours. The only food we had until we arrived was a packet of sandwiches, an apple and an orange, which we were given when we got off the boat. We then moved to a tented transit camp, which was the only accommodation they had in Korea at the time. From there we went off to relieve the Leicesters, taking over their transport, which was diabolical, incidentally. I was posted to C Company in early July, and we moved into the line later that month, taking over from an Australian unit. You realised then what it was all about. The shells came over every two or three minutes. At first it was exciting, but as the days went on it affected your nerves. We had a single Centurion tank up with us, and on one particular day it was hit seventeen times and had to be replaced. A couple of days later, there was an air strike coming in, with the Australians flying Mustangs dropping napalm. The commander of the new tank, a sergeant, was standing on the engine cover looking at something ahead. Just at that point we heard a mortar bomb coming over, and we ducked down into the trench, but there was no explosion. We looked up and the tank commander had apparently dived off and the mortar bomb had gone through the engine cover exactly where he had been standing, and it had shredded itself. So that tank was also written off. We remained in that position for two weeks, going through the same procedure, shelling every day. We were then relieved by another unit. Two weeks of shelling was considered sufficient in one go for one of our sergeants. It turned him; he totally lost it. Whether he had suffered before, perhaps during the Second World War, we never knew, but his nerve went. There was a private, too, who had to be brought out.

Veteran campaigner Lieutenant-Colonel David Rose, who had taken command of the 1st Battalion in May after the present incumbent Lieutenant-Colonel Pat Campbell-Preston suffered a heart attack, brought his World War II experience to the task now at hand. By mid-July he had noted in his diary 'the inevitable first casualties – very sad – but it has made them realise that all the noises aren't our own. I have got them digging hard. They are really working well and cheerfully.' He also reported a visit to the battalion by the US 'bigwigs', including General Mark Clark, General Collins (Chief of Staff, American Army) and divisional commanders. They were met by a small guard in kilts, and two pipers played while they were served tea, apparently 'tickled to death'.

Then it was down to business, and fortunately in this battalion of young men there were enough experienced soldiers to help instil reality. Among them was Major George Paterson, then an NCO with C Company. He had been in Germany for eighteen months prior to their removal to Korea, and pointed out the family issues that had to be resolved by those married soldiers whose wives had joined them in Germany. Most now had to go into married quarters near Aberdeen while the rest either had to find private accommodation or move in with relatives. This background activity is, of course, one that seldom reaches the newspapers but was a necessary adjunct to all overseas deployments to which the Black Watch as a whole seemed more prone than most regiments. There were also the issues of the National Servicemen and the many young soldiers and NCOs who had never experienced any form of hostile fire. In his memoir, Paterson said:

We had to get them to realise this was a very, very serious affair. Many still hadn't grasped the reality of what was to come. They hadn't yet seen anything and wanted to get up to the front. Well, you just can't do that until they knew how to look after themselves. Junior NCOs, again, were very young and totally inexperienced in battle procedures outside of training routines. Though they may have been very good in barracks, [it was a totally different matter] when it came to looking after them in the field, especially in the line when they would be responsible for their own section in trenches and dugouts. They had a very serious job on their hands, and they needed to be assertive and of strong character to keep control of the men under their command. This rectified itself as time went by and they began to understand how to get the best out of their men. And that was the amazing thing about Jocks. All the way through the campaign, the way they went about things and the cheerfulness with which they undertook their work was quite incredible. When eventually we moved into our first position, an advance party had gone ahead to prepare. On the way up we passed a tank unit on the hillside. As our column began passing them, the shelling started and made us realise we were in the line now. The position there was that our front trenches of the forward platoon were very near the Chinese line, no more than 400 yards with a valley in between and a lot of wire, but we could look directly into their trenches.

The higher ground was ideal for Chinese sniping, and we had several casualties because of that, most with men just moving around. Another unfortunate thing occurred when a patrol went out under a sergeant who had already done the patrol with the advance party getting to know the track through the wire, otherwise you would never get back. And, indeed, that patrol was stranded in the wire on the way back and overlooked by the Chinese position; one man was killed and the sergeant and two others wounded. The 2IC of the company, myself and stretcher-bearers went out to bring them in, and unfortunately one of the wounded died as we carried him out. But the Chinese didn't interfere at all. They could have wiped them out but didn't, but it was an example of the danger of losing your way through the wire. It could be catastrophic.

Another thing we had to do was to search for infiltrators. A lot of that went on, with the Chinese infiltrating in the rear of our positions. This was a job you did thoroughly because there was a lot of them getting through, working individually. Often, they weren't in uniform but dressed in civilian clothes. This had caused considerable difficulties in the early stages of the campaign. One other early problem was the rain, especially when the monsoon broke and down it would come. You sloshed about along the dirt road and you had to make sure of the drainage in the trenches or you would soon be up to your knees in water if you didn't get rid of it. Continual maintenance was necessary. The dugouts were never as good as we would have liked. The water would seep down, and there was always a danger of the sides collapsing on top of you. Later on in the campaign we began to receive huge wooden beams already cut to a certain dimension that were used, like building a house. The digging was all done by the Jocks themselves, although porters had the job of bringing up the supplies of wood. The older dugouts were splinter-proof but not bombproof and had to be reconstructed. The roads were all built by the Royal Engineers, the sappers, and they cut out the roads around the rear of the hills. When the rains came, you would get subsidence if they weren't properly drained, so we did have a problem of vehicles going over the side.

The dugouts were always bothered by rats, and one night, having finished my stint at the command post, it was pelting down with rain and I had some sheeting over the door to the dugout. Inside we had small oil lanterns, and I sat down to read a couple of letters I had received. I was lying down on my bed when there was a swishing noise and a black and white shape flashed through the sheeting. Then I saw a bloody great rat followed by a wild cat which was chasing it. The rat jumped on top of me and died almost immediately, leaving this cat snarling in the corner. As I moved, it ducked back through the sheeting and disappeared, leaving me to remove this very bloody rat from my chest.

The Korean porters did all the hard work of transporting materials to our positions, many of which were up high, skyline defences. They would bring up the rations, ammunition, water and so on attached to A-frames on their backs. They would also help in carrying down casualties to the field hospitals. It was a very difficult job for them, and they were very hard-working. As to the fighting, the Chinese were very, very good at night fighting. Considering they had the American army and the Commonwealth Division there, with all its technology, they really did put up a show. We were pretty positive that they were using dope. We found opium seeds and discarded cigarette packets that smelled dreadful. When they attacked they would run round in circles, and then they'd suddenly stop, as if the effects were wearing off. The other amazing thing with Chinese: in every case they took away their wounded and their dead more or less as it happened and in the middle of the battle. We very seldom managed to bring one in alive for questioning.

We did two or three different positions and one of them was a very high feature with a very pointed summit overlooking the Hook position. While we were at one position a strong smell began to arise, and it got so strong it was decided to dig down to see what it was. The team dug down and down until they reached on old dugout in which they found four American sergeants, or what remained of them, still in their bunks. There was not a mark on them, so they must have been killed either by the dugout caving in on top of them or by a blast from a shell. They had their watches on, and all the papers were there. They were not a pretty sight, obviously, because they had been there some time. Their remains and possessions were brought out. It was an amazing discovery because the place had been handed over to the next in the line. We contacted the unit concerned, and believe it or not, they had not realised they were missing.

Through the summer and into the autumn, the rotational call to duty kept the Black Watch as busy as any unit in the war, and towards the end of October 1952 Chinese movements once again centred on the feature known as the Hook, and later the 'Bloody Hook' because of the number of casualties there. It was a key position, so called because it formed a pivotal and tactical hinge in the UN main line of defence. From there, key UN communication lines could be observed. But more important, beyond it lay the uninterrupted countryside of the

Imjin valley and the road to the South Korean capital. Any break-through at the Hook would have had severe consequences for the entire front of the UN forces.

The Black Watch had already served a month on the Hook, in August, in dire conditions under torrential rain. They had taken casualties from shelling, but that experience was no more than a prelude to the main event as the Chinese renewed their assault in October 1952 and the Hook became the main attraction. Towards the end of the month, the Black Watch prepared to take over from the 7th US Marines, who had taken a heavy toll in their defence of the feature and were shattered, physically and numerically. The arrival of Lieutenant-Colonel Rose to discuss the handover coincided with a fresh onslaught by the Chinese, with hordes of their infantry surging up the flanking hills around the Hook. Bitter hand-to-hand fighting developed, and at that point Colonel Mike Delaney, commander-in-chief of the marines, called down yet another massive air assault by fighter-bombers from the airfields near Seoul and the US carriers in the East China Sea to halt the Chinese advance. They arrived in V-formations, peeling off to slam their rockets and napalm bombs into the hillsides, before the commander gave the signal to unleash the guns of the largest artillery concentration assembled in the Korean War so far. The noise was incredible, and the landscape rocked under the weight of fire. When the smoke and dust had cleared, the marines began the counter-attack in an attempt to push the Chinese off the slopes and reclaim their positions – and their wounded and dead who had fallen to the Chinese assault.

At the command post, the debonair Lieutenant-Colonel Rose discussed the Americans' defensive layout and clearly had thoughts about what he saw as major flaws in their system of trenches, to put it mildly. Delaney, in any event, was convinced that the Black Watch would be blown off the hill in short order, and Lieutenant-Colonel A. J. Barker records a conversation between Rose and Delaney in which the latter described Guadalcanal as a walkover compared with the Hook. He then went on to ask: 'See any combat yourself, Dave?' Rose apparently winced at the shortened use of his Christian name and replied coolly: 'A little . . . here and there.' Delaney was warning him he would not have seen anything like this: 'You'll soon see I'm not kidding. It's a lousy place, and those Chinese are tricky bastards.'

Rose had already made up his mind that the Hook would need to be re-fortified. He had already taken a patrol on the slopes to examine the trenches and discovered that whatever system existed originally had been wrecked by weeks of bombardment. The front-line bunkers were unusable, partly because of human remains that still existed in some of them. The communication trenches were so shallow that anyone using them would have to crawl, but in any event most of them had already caved in. The Americans had a known aversion to digging, and many lives were lost as a result. It was clear to Rose that there was little or no depth to what defences remained. It was an appalling, unsafe mess, and he wasn't prepared to risk the lives of his men under such circumstances. The whole system needed to be re-dug with new trenches, bunkers, tunnels and communications. Rose, historically a stickler for digging, said as much to Major-General Mike West, the Commonwealth Divisional Commander. The commander asked him what he needed, and Rose replied: 'Eight hundred Korean labourers and a troop of sappers.'

He got them, although work could not start until the marines came off the position for the changeover to take place on 7 November. In the meantime, Rose sent out a reconnaissance patrol of a dozen into no-man's-land. But they ran straight into a forty-strong Chinese platoon doing the same thing and took casualties even before their shift on the Hook had begun. On the day the marines handed over the position to Rose, the Korean labourers were brought in immediately to begin digging the defensive system according to the colonel's plan. They worked straight through without a break for many hours but then, as the battalion moved on in force, the Jocks had to finish off much of the digging themselves. It was a nasty business, uncovering a number of bodies as they went about the work. The sappers and wiring parties then moved in to build a barbed wire fence over and around the defences. Finally, the signallers laid out a fairly complex array of heavy-duty communications aerials, cabling and additional radio and telephone sets so that every company commander was in direct contact with the command post at all times. Quartermaster-Captain Nobby Clark had to threaten, cajole and steal to get the amount he needed, but in the end they set up a system that could withstand heavy bombing, and it worked! It was also vital to the safety-net plan that David Rose had invented to save his forward units if they were threatened with being overrun. A codeword was worked out which would indicate that the company commander believed his position was untenable and was moving out, and this would trigger an artillery barrage of air-bursting shells directly over the trenches that had been evacuated through the tunnels. These additional measures were all being worked on furiously as soon as the battalion took over from the marines, and Rose and his superiors were agreed that they would probably get about ten days' grace before the next attack. But with so much activity on the Hook and its approaches, the Chinese decided to get back in, just four days after the Black Watch had moved on to the Hook. Under a barrage of shelling, their infantry surged forward and were soon literally in front of the battalion's forward positions. George Paterson takes up the story:

It began on the night of 18 and 19 November, and the build-up had been evident for some time before the shelling came. Just after midnight we were informed we were on the move, and soon all hell let loose. We were in the trenches, and there was a bit of hand-to-hand fighting as well. Our most forward position had already been overrun and the position was lost, as were a number of men. All through the night the Chinese began appearing from all directions, and our command post put everything across they could, firing across our own position. We had tunnels built into the trenches that the troops could get into when this happened. When it lifted they could come out and mop up. That meant you had a lot of odds and ends – a very dangerous place to be when you've got enemy running around up top and on the sides of trenches, slinging in grenades. The tunnels were a great innovation, and with a grenade shield we had added protection up to a point. It died down and then it would start up again, and again. The shelling was very bad, and we had a lot of casualties. Reinforcements were called for from a company on the right. We were going hammer and tongs all through the night. Companies were being brought up from all over the place, and overhead the shelling from our guns continued and the Chinese were obviously feeling the pressure too. Finally, at dawn, they withdrew. That battle was really something to speak about. The supporting arms were very good indeed, especially the artillery and our own arms. Colonel Rose was brilliant. Everything was for the Jock. He would get things done. You could not have asked for a better man. He came around to every unit, night after night. He was a stickler for communication, and especially during battle. He was in touch with every platoon.

The Battle of the Hook made headlines in the British newspapers, and the Black Watch were once again heroes of the hour, and rightly so. Far from being blown off the Hook, as some of the Americans had suggested, they held it, and more. Lieutenant-Colonel Barker commented:

The company and platoon commanders did everything that could be expected of them . . . Under the pressure of repeated attacks concentrated on a very narrow front, the Chinese managed to get a footing on the Hook. Sergeants like Alexander Hutchinson, who led a counter-attack on his hands and knees after he had been wounded, corporals like Robert Manning, who silenced a Chinese machine gun with a grenade after being twice wounded himself, and privates like George Coley, who bowled Chinese over like ninepins until he was killed by a grenade, did their best to hold them back. But the Jocks were [in danger of being] overwhelmed by sheer weight of numbers, and David Rose decided that a counter-attack was called for. A few of the Jocks had been captured when the forward platoons were overrun, and some of these disappeared with the casualties. Some, like Privates Macdonald and Graham, managed to escape. Macdonald, deprived of his rifle, resorted to his fists; Graham split the skull of his Chinese guard with the brim of his steel helmet.

The toll for the night's work was twenty killed, seventy-six wounded and fourteen missing, two of whom were later confirmed killed in action. On the slopes, spreadeagled on what remained of the wire, more than 100 dead Chinese, missed by the evacuation parties, were counted. The battalion completed their time in prime position on the Hook and returned again later in the campaign. The feature continued to dominate the action in their zone of operations and in any event, in spite of attempts to launch peace talks in the New Year, no sign of any let-up was apparent on the ground. The battles and the shelling continued incessantly, as did the 'psy-war' in between the exchanges of fire. Scottish songs were relayed by loud-speakers across the valley in the evenings, interrupted occasionally by the trill voices of the Chinese Communist announcers: 'Hello, Scotsmen. Are you settled in all right? Keep your heads down. Don't go out on patrol . . . Do you know we can shell you any time we like? Shells that blind the eyes?' However, at last peace talks were beginning to produce encouraging signals, and the last battle of the war took place on the Hook soon after the Black Watch had been relieved by the Duke of Wellington's Regiment, who repelled the Chinese for the last time. A truce was signed in July, and the guns fell silent after three years of bloody fighting which had cost two million lives.

The Jocks cheered up no end with the prospect of going home – at least, they thought that was the plan. But the Ministry of Defence in London had other ideas, as George Paterson explained:

The fact was when we left Korea we didn't know where we were heading next. It was a bit of a worry because we had been away for over a year and there were quite a few problems at home with families. The regular soldiers were also due eight weeks' leave, and all the people who had been abroad before going to Korea [i.e. in Germany] could have claimed a home posting. Even so, we were told we were going to Kenya, where the British army was engaged in a bitter confrontation with Mau Mau terrorists campaigning for independence. We all agreed that if our wives and families were brought out we wouldn't bother about the home posting. There were a lot of empty hotels because tourism had collapsed during the terrorist campaign. And so the higher-ups eventually agreed, provided that we understood we might be moved up and down the country. It wasn't entirely satisfactory, but we accepted it because it meant that we could see our families from time to time.

David Rose was fully in support of his men on the issue, especially as he was quite certain the battalion were in for a hard time, working in dense bamboo forests for up to two weeks at a time. They sailed into Mombasa and continued by train to Nairobi, where they received a tremendous welcome from the large expatriate community who had been following the media coverage of Black Watch activities in Korea. They were moved out into the forests and split up, living under canvas. George Paterson recalled:

It was very hard for the Jocks because of what they had already gone through in Korea, and now they were being sent upcountry, well away from any form of civilisation again. There were murmurs of dissent about that. When we were in a position where they might be bussed into a small town, having been away for so long, they had a tendency to – shall we say? – get rather merry. The Nairobi staff didn't like that, which was a bit unfair. Unfortunately, we also at that time had one or two bad hats joining us there, people who should never have been in the army. You could only classify it as being recruitment in quantity and not quality, as was our norm. The wives and families did not arrive for six months after it was agreed they could come out, and the accommodation was rather poor. We had to live as if we were staying in a hotel as guests, and the food wasn't good. As to the terrorists, they were a disgusting, terrible lot who were committing unspeakable acts. It was a thoroughly unpleasant task.

The Black Watch were the fourth battalion to arrive in Kenya as the Mau Mau stepped up their campaign of murder and mutilation, with reprisals against the Europeans, especially in the so-called white high-lands, claimed as Kikuyu lands. The settlers retaliated, and non-partic-ipant Kikuyu were massacred by the Mau Mau. The British increased the security forces in the country, eventually to over 5,000 troops and police. The initial station for the Black Watch was under canvas near Thika, where they formed patrols to go out into the jungle in search of the terrorist gangs. They were, of course, well hidden and could often only be reached on foot, by using animal trails. The troops always had to be alert to ambushes, and indeed turned that technique on the terrorists themselves, lying in wait close to suspected hide-outs. During one of these operations the battalion suffered a severe setback and loss, when Archie John Wavell, a major in the Black Watch and the only son of the former field marshal, was killed by a Mau Mau bullet. A gang of around sixty terrorists had been surrounded by a Black Watch patrol under Wavell's command and he was directing operations when he was felled by a single bullet. His father had died three years earlier, and Archie had succeeded to the earldom.

The heavy patrolling techniques began to pay off. Hundreds of the rebels were rounded up at a time and detained in special camps. The nationalist leader Jomo Kenyatta was eventually among those impris-oned as the British technique of laying on blanket coverage over specific areas brought results. The Black Watch's first area of respon-sibility was declared 'pacified' by February 1954, and the battalion moved again, to repeat the operations in an area below Mount Kilimanjaro. Later they moved to Nairobi itself, taking on the role of armed police in conducting search-and-arrest operations before finally being released from duty in 1955, when the military effort began to give way to diplomatic negotiations. The state of emergency remained in force until 1960, when Jomo Kenyatta was released. He subsequently became Prime Minister on independence from Britain in 1963 and President when the country became a republic a year later.

The Black Watch had served in sub-Sahara Africa for the last time.

CHAPTER SIXTEEN

A Policeman's Lot

While the Korean crisis was an issue that had required diplomatic and military resources at the highest international level, India and Kenya were more typical, in their diverse ways, of the problems confronting the UK in the years beyond the Second World War. The decline and fall of the British Empire was in full flight. British interests in Malaya, Borneo, Africa, the Middle East, Suez, Cyprus, Malta, Hong Kong and, closer to home, Northern Ireland, were all to erupt into some form of civil, social or military cataclysm. Over the next four decades Britain eventually exited from all those situations, apart from the last named, although for years British troops were being dispatched to deal with emergencies and to enforce the last piece of military pressure before giving way to nationalistic sway. Some, such as the anti-terrorist operations in Malaya, Borneo and Cyprus, were long and costly. Others, like the disastrous Suez raid, were political disasters.

Throughout these years, the Black Watch, whose very foundation lay in the traditional role of peacekeeping in the Highlands of Scotland, reverted to type, as it were. Having battled heavily in Korea, the Kenyan engagement had been uncomfortable but manageable, and thereafter a pattern of such operations emerged. The invasion of Suez happened during their Kenyan expedition; Malaya was also pacified during that period and, having already been assigned to Cyprus, they also missed the difficult and protracted jungle operations in Borneo in the 1960s. In fact, even Cyprus gave them a fairly quiet time when they went there in 1958 as peacekeepers after several years of terrorist activity by General Grivas's EOKA bombers as they attempted to persuade the British to pack up and go. When they reached the island, the UN Security Council was already engaged in an attempt to resolve the issue. The Black Watch, it will be recalled, had an historical interest in the island, which may also have helped in their undoubted acceptance by the local populace. They had landed there in 1878 in support of Sir Garnet Wolseley as he took possession of the island from the Turks, and, to the sound of a piper, a Union Jack was hoisted for the first time. There was also a Black Watch burial ground on the island, which included the remains of Victoria Cross hero Sergeant Sam McGaw who had died from heat apoplexy on 22 July 1878. Now the regiment arrived to bring calm to a troubled island and oversee a peaceful transference of power to the government of a Cypriot republic.

Robert Gurdon, back from British Guiana with the 2nd Battalion, was by then adjutant in the 1st. In fact, there had been another merger. Much to the dismay of many, the 2nd Battalion were again amalgamated with their senior force when the two battalions were reunited in Germany after their respective missions on opposite sides of the world. Now as one, they arrived at Limni in October 1958. By then the situation had calmed down considerably. Gurdon, who took over as adjutant as they arrived, recalled:

For many in the 1st Battalion, myself included, Cyprus was our first experience of active service, although in fact it wasn't terribly active. We did mount pickets and searches. We were armed all the time, operating initially from a tented camp not far from Paphos, in what was very much a Greek stronghold. We succeeded the Argylls, who had had a very rough time in

302

the same area that we were covering. We were busy with detached companies scattered all over the west of the island, but the height of the trouble had passed and peace was signed six months after we got there. The activities were winding down, and I don't think there was a shot fired in anger during the whole time we were there, although we remained very active throughout.

Eventually, the whole British operation was brought to an end, and the Black Watch returned to the UK in 1961 then were posted to Germany in 1964. They were forced to return to Cyprus in 1966 under the banner of the UN, now wearing the customary blue berets, when violence broke out between the Turkish and Greek populations. This proved a more demanding role than their earlier time, and the Black Watch were at times forced to put themselves between the warring factions of Turkish militamen and the Greek National Guard. Their position was such that although the Jocks kept the two sides from falling on each other, they themselves were caught in a no-man's-land and, as such, their supplies had to be helicoptered in.

The manner in which the military policed such incidents was about to undergo a fundamental change, as indeed was the general utilisation of the infantry in combat situations. In fact, Robert Gurdon had been taken out of duties in Cyprus for a move that ultimately led to his appointment as company commander of a brand-new mechanised unit in Germany, as the Cold War between the Soviets was reaching its height and NATO armies were being bolstered substantially to meet the threat:

The old days of route marches and going by train were coming to an end. We were the very first battalion to be equipped with what was then the new tracked armoured personnel carrier known as the 443 specifically for armoured warfare, which in fact lasted for twenty years. It required a great deal of training and skill, particularly for the drivers. The 1st Battalion became part of a mechanised brigade in Germany. Each vehicle carried a section of infantrymen or machine-gunners. They were complete with marvellous new equipment including communications that actually worked.

Towards the end of the 1960s, Cold War tensions began to draw in more and more British troops as NATO analysts came forward with projections that, if there was a war, it would most likely start with a head-to-head of military hardware in Northern Europe. Of course, there was always the possibility of a nuclear flare-up with both sides now equalising each other with doomsday submarines permanently sailing the oceans. The east coast of Britain was bristling with nuclear missiles pointing towards the Soviet Union, and US and British nuclear bombers on RAF bases throughout the UK were on a permanent ready-to-fly alert. In the midst of this, Britain became engulfed in pressing matters when the IRA decided it was time to resume operations.

The statistics tell the exact story: between 1956 and 1969, no soldier had been killed and just six men of the Royal Ulster Constabulary lost their lives in incidents linked to political violence. In the early months of 1969, IRA activists were exerting considerable influence on the Catholic civil rights movement, which had been formed to fight severe injustices to the Catholic population as a whole in Northern Ireland. As the IRA began to exert their pressures for civil disobedience, many in the civil rights movement left, disenchanted and feeling they had been betrayed. As the months passed, the evident tensions on the streets of Northern Ireland rose dramatically, and towards the end of the Protestant marching season they reached boiling point.

The fuse to the explosion of violence that erupted was the outbreak of the worst street fighting the province had seen for many years. Rioting flared in Londonderry towards the end of the Orangemen's Apprentice Boys' march. In three days of battles, five people were killed and more than seven hundred injured. Londonderry's Catholic population, under attack from marauding gangs, protested at the actions of the B-Specials and the Royal Ulster Constabulary (RUC), which, they claimed, allowed the Protestant gangs to go about their business unfettered. They were also angered by the IRA's failure to protect their communities from nightly attacks by petrol-bomb-wielding mobs. More than 1,500 Catholic families, compared with 300 Protestant families, would be forced to leave their homes because of firebombs, looting and intimidation from loyalist gangs.

Trouble spread to Belfast, where hundreds of rioters came on to the streets, hurling petrol bombs, backed by hidden sniper fire. As gun battles raged, the inevitable dispatch of British troops to restore law and order was approved by the British government on 15 August 1969. The first detachment from the Prince of Wales' Own Regiment arrived on 19 August for what the government described as a 'limited operation'; they would be withdrawn as soon as order was restored, but it never was. From then on, in terms of deployment numbers for British troops the only way was up, reaching in excess of 20,000 men by 1972 – Ulster's bloodiest year ever, which saw 468 killed and 5,000 injured. The numbers of troops then escalated rapidly, eventually exceeding 35,000, and the Black Watch became regulars in the rotational tours mounted by the army.

For the people of Northern Ireland, there was initially a sigh of relief when the troops moved in. But it was a temporary feeling that would soon turn to hatred in many quarters as the military floundered miserably, with poor intelligence, inexperience in handling trouble among its own people and run by a hierarchy whose most recent experience of urban unrest was in the wild colonial campaigns. The Black Watch, well experienced in difficult policing, came through the troubles better than most. They arrived for two short deployments in 1970 and were back again in 1971 for extended duties in Armagh, one of the original stamping grounds of their forebears. While clearly the troops themselves did not relish these deployments to what was becoming a nightmare for security forces, they were conscious of the fact that their relationship with the island of Ireland was long established. Indeed, it was drummed into them that some sort of continuation of their record there might be pursued. They, perhaps more than any of the units posted to the country, could at least point to

305

this historic association, and it stood them in good stead. They clearly sought to build on their earlier experiences in the present difficult climate, as was made clear in an article, written by a senior officer, in the Black Watch magazine *The Red Hackle*, in which past endeavours were proudly recalled for the benefit of the young soldiers of the day:

So here we are in Ireland once more, engaged in the difficult and exacting task of keeping the peace. But neither the place nor the job is exactly unfamiliar to the battalion, for we have spent some thirty-five years over here on similar duties at various stages of our two hundred years' existence. We have done five major tours of duty: from 1746 (after Fontenoy) until 1757 (on leaving for America); from 1767 to 1774 (between the two American campaigns); from 1814 to 1825 (although we had to return to Flanders in 1815 so as not to miss Waterloo); from 1838 to 1840 (a relatively short stay, that one); and then from 1906 to 1911, engaged in preparation for possible war. In fact, as we take up once more our unrewarding stance between jealous factions we can find in the records an example worth following and one which gives point to the homilies which platoon commanders have been inflicting on their platoons these past weeks. In 1772, on our second visit, the regiment was actively employed in different parts of the country in aid of the civil power – a familiar role, and as today, so then the basic religious conflict was complicated by a secondary one, today between Unionist and Republican, in 1772 between landlord and tenant. 'In this delicate service the Highlanders were found particularly useful both from their knowledge of the language and from their conciliating conduct towards the Irish, the descendants of the same parent stock with themselves.' The branches of the family tree seem to have grown a bit further apart since then. In 1838, on our fourth visit, that same affinity was felt, and even the invidious job of providing escorts for civil prisoners failed to produce 'any unkind feeling', and in 1911 relations reached a peak of cordiality when the battalion saved the town of Limerick from destruction by fire. A reputation for courtesy and humanity is one worth preserving, and need not conflict with one for toughness (witness the needless anxiety of the Belgian house-wives on whom the 42nd were billeted in 1815, who feared for the safety in battle of the gentle giants in petticoats who rocked their cradles and helped with the housework). Also worthy of study is the regiment's traditional attitude to discipline. General Stewart of Garth, best known and best loved of the early officers of the 42nd, writes how in Ireland in the 1770s there were few courts martial; the punishment most commonly resorted to had not much of a military complexion. The culprit was made to ride astride a wooden horse with his kilt round his neck or sometimes in a petticoat as a symbol that his conduct was deemed unworthy of a man. When, rarely, a man was brought to the halberts [i.e. flogged] he was considered, and considered himself, to have become degraded, and little more good was to be expected of him. After being thus publicly disgraced he could no longer associate with his comrades and it was a fact that on several instances the privates of a company subscribed to procure the discharge of an obnoxious individual.

There was one other postscript that linked the past and present tours of duty. In 1817, when the battalion were posted to Armagh, the soldiers were packed into their mini-barracks at the rate of twenty-four men per room. In 1971 the accommodation was not dissimilar: eighteen men sharing one tiny hut. Even so, *The Red Hackle* recorded at the end of their first major tour:

> .... relations with the locals both on and off duty have been excellent and for this credit goes to everyone and above all to the Jocks themselves for their endless good manners and good humour when on operations, often when cold, bored and wet ... We have also made a point of taking up all invitations for sporting and social occasions, and our football team

in particular have had mixed fortunes against a variety of opponents . . . and from a recreational point of view, the 8:1 ratio of single girls to single men in the area leaves little need for comment and there are few who do not take full advantage of their one free day in six.

As time wore on, the social intercourse became more difficult and often plainly impracticable. Even so, as the Black Watch returned time and time again to police the troubles over the next two decades, their relationship with the community remained excellent. The same good grace was not reciprocated by the IRA and even some sections of the population they were attempting to protect. The first significant attack on the Black Watch in 1971 was serious enough to merit a national news item when a Black Watch patrol drove into the heart of an explosion triggered by terrorists. They had booby-trapped a Mini at Rosslea in County Fermanagh, near the border.

One army truck went through the ambush but as a second truck was a few feet from the Mini, the bomb was detonated by remote control. The truck was badly damaged, hedges were shredded and a hole was blown in the road, but the two soldiers in the truck escaped without a scratch. Signs that the terrorists had waited several hours for their target to show up were found by patrolling troops. They had planted the booby trap, laid the detonating wire across a field and apparently ate sandwiches until the patrol appeared. It was the first of many such incidents on the tour, including the dispersal of a stone-throwing mob with rubber bullets. The troubles grew progressively, testing to the limit the Black Watch's long-established record of good relations with the island's communities. This relationship came under further pressure in October 1971 when the battalion returned for a further tour. This time they were posted to Belfast guarding key installations and power stations, and running vehicle checks and property searches in the wake of an IRA threat to step up the action following the introduction of internment. It was during these operations that the battalion suffered a severe blow, when Corporal Edwin Charnley was killed by a sniper's bullet on 19 November 1971.

There was also a touch of irony in that the pipes and drums of the Black Watch were heckled that year on a tour of America where, at the same time, emissaries from the IRA were canvassing the Irish communities to increase their donations in cash and kind to fund the fight against the British army and the politicians. The band was also picketed in a number of places by Irish Americans protesting against the Black Watch and the 'brutality' of the British army in Northern Ireland.

With haste, now, the battalion – and families – prepared for a well-deserved overseas posting to Hong Kong scheduled for 1974. It turned into an action-packed twenty-four months with a vast programme of exercises and training and goodwill missions staged throughout the Far Eastern theatre of British operations. There were also a hefty number of events in Hong Kong itself, associated with civilian and military protocol, along with a substantial sports programme and other non-military events that were to make their stay in the colony one of their busiest, and most enjoyable, for years.

At the time, there was still no apparent hint that the British government was already engaged in the preliminaries for returning Hong Kong to Chinese rule in 1997, and as far as the troops were concerned it was business as usual. This fact was reinforced with stone-cold reality at the end of their term in Hong Kong. On their return to Colchester, a British army briefing and training team arrived in 1974 to bring the battalion up to scratch on developments for their next task – back to Northern Ireland. After a brief leave, the men were posted to Andersonstown, a well-known troublesome area where a large Catholic enclave was sited within a Protestant area and consequently was under the protection of the Provisional IRA. The situation in the province remained tense, and the military was under constant attack, both by word and deed. Given that the average age of all privates in the Black Watch was just nineteen, and that of company commanders was early twenties, the responsibility placed on these young men was enormous, and no better demonstrated than this summary published at the time in *The Red Hackle*:

From the march in the north, the Black Mountains to the west, the motorway to the east and where the outskirts of Belfast gradually dwindle away into the country, our patch of responsibility covers an area of seven square miles. This district sounds small. However, when it is split up into company areas, the company commander finds himself to have a demanding task ahead of him. He has in a very short time to acquaint himself with everyone living there. He must also familiarise himself with all the local problems. He seems to be the only local authority, so he finds himself occupying the seat of local government, having to provide the force with which to police the area, and every other local amenity which we at home tend to take for granted. Unfortunately, the Royal Ulster Constabulary cannot work in our area without a military escort. Despite all this, the company commanders must always remember that we are working in support of the RUC and for the resumption of normality within their areas and eventually the reinstatement of the police.

It is very easy for us to sit at home in comfort, and acquire a preconceived impression of the people of Andersonstown from the continuous string of cleverly designed articles pushed at us by the reporters in every national and provincial newspaper that we read, but it is extremely difficult for the young soldier suddenly to realise that the occupants of our area are normal people. Where they differ is not in themselves but in the conditions created by the present political impasse. He is ordered into the streets of Belfast with a weapon in his hands, live rounds in his pouches, enormous powers at his disposal and then told that he is dealing with normal British subjects. He has been trained as a soldier, how to observe, how to seek out a target and how to shoot. Suddenly he is thrown into a situation where he has to make the terrible decision between being polite and firm at one moment and shooting to kill in self-defence at another. He is put through tremendous demands in his personal endurance, resulting from the long hours and the peculiar strains and pressures of his position. At the same time he must show

310

almost super-human patience and self-restraint when patrolling and attempting to help a community that to him appears only to be antagonised by his presence. Although this is our fifth visit to Northern Ireland since the outbreak of the troubles, we could never fully imagine what it must be like to live the life of an Irishman. We come and we go. The people who we now control have lived this life for five troubled years. Every four months their 'soldiers' change. The training that we do prior to a tour in Northern Ireland may be standardised, but the temperament of each and every regiment will change according to its territorial background and character . . . There will always be attempts by the terrorists to gain or create a suitable atmosphere of discontent and disruption in which their political aims might be achieved. The people of Britain are apt to turn a blind eye and deny strongly that this could be, and is, happening within their own territory.

The work of the battalion routinely involved the random stop and search of individuals, and searching hundreds of homes and thousands of vehicles. The major aim of the battalion was to prevent bombers from getting through to the city centre, and considerable effort went into maintaining this screen of checkpoints. Each company had its own intelligence cell, working on the findings of Jocks on the ground in conjunction with information received from other sources. Their log for the 1975 stint from August to October showed that the Jocks searched 37,000 vehicles and 165 houses and took possession of a large and varied haul of weapons and explosives, as well as 'putting away a great number of criminals and terrorists, all on serious charges'. Few enjoyed the experience, and the men were constantly being reminded by their officers to be on the alert for attempts to lure a patrol towards a booby-trapped car, or the approach of a sniper hidden by a sympathetic crowd that suddenly opened to allow him to fire, leaving the Jocks unable to respond without harming others. There were, in that time, 'only three fully fledged riots demanding the battalion's attention, although stoning and bottling occurred

311

frequently . . . and when school terms resumed in September, the children on their way home took great delight in stoning Glassmulin Camp and vehicles on the Andersonstown road. Bottles filled with paint were popular missiles.'

The battalion's intermittent service in Northern Ireland did not stop even when the Jocks learned they were being given a five-year posting, with their families, to Germany as part of the British Army of the Rhine. This was a major move, involving all aspects of operations. It also represented new departures in terms of gearing up for the battalion's future role in potential battle scenarios, which in turn meant learning many new skills and involvement in numerous major and gruelling exercises embracing all aspects of the army's capability in a war situation. Training in Germany was one particular aspect that proved to be far more varied and demanding than even many officers had anticipated as they confronted the battalion's increasing expansion into mechanised and chemical warfare. In the five years ahead, they faced many tough and rigorous deployments across the German landscape, often close to the Iron Curtain, utilising a vast array of heavy metal. Initially at least, company commanders became painfully aware, as one put it, 'that the hours spent on such skills as terrorist recognition and other Northern Ireland training were not highly relevant in a General War scenario in North-West Europe'.

The reverse was also the case when, after almost two years of heavy training in Germany, as well as extensive preparations for an expedition for live firing exercises in Canada to further master the intricate arts of mechanised warfare, the battalion were re-roled for another four-month experience of street warfare in Belfast. But this was seen as an opportunity to present a fresh challenge to the battalion and in particular to the junior ranks, who did not, in mechanised warfare, have the same opportunities for individual action. On return to Germany from Belfast, the Black Watch companies had ten weeks in which to re-polish vehicles and to begin learning other skills – this time to become experts on chemical warfare in preparation for a major exercise with the soldiers cocooned in full chemical protection kit at the hottest time of the year. They spent three weeks on a very hot

312

and dusty training area at Soltau with scientists monitoring the effectiveness of protective gear and that of some of the machines under chemical warfare conditions.

Of all the various exercises, undertakings and commitments to test the Black Watch as a complete battle group during this five-year posting, one in 1984 was particularly gruelling and brought great admiration from the army commanders. Exercise Baseplate was the first corps-level mortar concentration exercise, and it was run by C Company of the battalion, in conjunction with the HQ Company, combining a tough four-day tactical exercise with live firing. All the British army's mortar platoons in Germany, whether mechanised, air mobile or ground role, passed through what became a treadmill of feeding, briefing, accommodating, inspecting, lecturing, exercising and debriefing for the participating units. During the exercise, the Milan Platoon loaded and unloaded over 35,000 rounds of 81-millimetre mortar ammunition, handling some of it up to four times.

Away from military training, the soldiers also had excellent opportunities for adventure training. In fact, a summary of these events provides no better advertisement for recruitment. Each winter, 200 members of the battalion spent a fortnight skiing, langlauf or downhill, in Bavaria. There were also climbing expeditions to Switzerland and hill walking in Norway, France and Morocco. After two training exercises in Canada, the soldiers also had the chance to climb, walk, canoe, raft and cycle in the Rockies, at their own expense. Much nearer their base at Werl, the soldiers took sailing lessons on the Mohnesee, with adventurous ones travelling to Kiel for offshore experience. As *The Red Hackle* recorded, it was a 'tour full of opportunity and experience' and a great deal of hard work. The pipes and drums also went to Japan and, with the Band of the Scots Guards, carried out a very busy tour of North America, playing in over a hundred cities. In fact, the years immediately ahead were full of activity and the relocation of their operational base which of course affected not only the troops themselves, but wives and families too. On completion of the tour of Germany, the battalion returned to the UK for a further five-month assignment in Northern Ireland, followed by a two-year posting to Berlin amid signs that the Cold War was defrosting. This was finally confirmed with the momentous event soon after the completion of the tour in 1989 when demonstrators crashed through the Wall.

The battalion was also selected to participate in another major international event of the 1990s. After a successful two-year posting to Hong Kong in 1993–4, the Black Watch was then selected to help organise and participate in the delicate matter of transferring the colony back to Chinese rule in 1997. The handover had long been in negotiation – or not, as far as the Chinese were concerned. To them it was simply a fact that on the appointed day, their troops would march across the border and install the new administration. The journey towards a satisfactory conclusion was further troubled by events in Tiananmen Square on 4 June 1989, during demonstrations by student dissidents.

Up to 2,500 people were believed to have been killed and 10,000 injured as the Chinese People's Liberation Army advanced through the streets of Beijing, firing indiscriminately. Ignoring international protests, the Chinese pursued the demonstrators over the coming days in a savage crackdown on the young rebels across the country, throwing hundreds of their leaders into jail. The effect in Hong Kong, already preparing for the Chinese takeover a few years hence, was dramatic, as shares crashed amid fears that the colony would suffer similar consequences if it did not come to heel when the time came. However, stiff negotiations with the British team in Hong Kong followed and, even though the situation remained tense, the count-down to the handover moved inexorably to the final curtain. The Black Watch moved in to take over formal garrison duties in February, knowing full well that they would play a major role in one of the major political events of modern times, one that required the equi-librium of firmness and delicacy with the eyes of the world on the scenario in which they were to perform. Although there were indeed some tense incidents, the whole event, overseen by Chris Patten, went smoothly and was capped by the massed bands of the Royal Marines, the Scots Guards and the Scottish Division (the Highland Band) with the pipes and drums of the 1st Battalion, Black Watch, and the Brigade of Gurkhas. Finally, the Guards of Honour came through – the Royal Navy, the Royal Air Force and, to tremendous applause, the Black Watch, marching to 'Highlan' Laddie' – in celebrations that were marred only by torrential rain. The finale came with the lowering of the Union and Hong Kong flags to the accompaniment of the solitary Pipe-Major Stephen Small playing 'Immortal Memory'.

CHAPTER SEVENTEEN

Into Battle Again

As the first year of the new millennium approached, plans were already afoot to change dramatically the operational possibilities of the Black Watch. Over the previous decade, the battalion had gradually slipped away from the role of mechanised warfare that the men trained so hard for in Germany. Since then, the versatile companies had been progressively brought back into the arena of infantry operating in a civilian environment, mostly in Northern Ireland, because they were good at the job. As a consequence, a number of military operations, including the Falklands, the first Gulf War and Bosnia, came and went without the Black Watch's participation. It was not a situation that the battalion, from officers commanding to privates, had either wanted or enjoyed. They campaigned to get back to the real business of soldiering and duties more in keeping with the traditions of the Black Watch, and the recovery of that situation would soon begin.

In 1999 elements of British and NATO forces were mustered for the possible invasion of Yugoslavia, where President Slobodan Milošević had engineered the ethnic cleansing of Kosovo, resulting in wanton killing and the displacement of 330,000 civilians. After the sixty-seven-day NATO bombardment of key Yugoslav cities and installations, Milošević finally caved in and agreed to negotiate, thus signalling the entry of multi-national ground forces, of whom 11,000 were supplied by the British army. They did not include the Black Watch, whose companies were, at the time, scattered across Scotland on public duties from their base at Fort George.

Later that year the Black Watch finally received the news their officers had been waiting for and which had been a long time in coming. The battalion were to revert to the armoured infantry role. The first steps towards that achievement began in the autumn of 1999, when the battalion were booked for what is commonly known as a TESEX – a Tactical Engagement Simulation Exercise. This is a tough and intensive scenario carried out over three weeks on Salisbury Plain, where a battalion is tested as it would be in war using Direct Weapons Effect simulators. It was completed in January 2000. The battalion then moved lock, stock and barrel later in the year to Fallingbostel, just south of Soltau in Germany, the long-time home of the 7th Armoured Brigade, bearers of the famous Deserts Rats' insignia. It was to this brigade that the battalion would be assigned on completion of the conversion procedures for the armoured infantry role. The last time they were together was, it will be recalled, in 1942–3 with Montgomery's 8th Army when the Deserts Rats led the charge against Rommel's Afrika Korps across the North African coast after the Battle of Alamein, with the Black Watch mopping up behind.

After the TESEX and subsequent conversion packages were concluded with a two-week gunnery course and a week on final test exercises in Germany, the battalion completed the configuration process as a complete battle group. It was the first time they had achieved that status since 1984, and no sooner was that exercise over than the battalion's immediate future changed. In 2001 the Black Watch were bound for Kosovo as part of Britain's contribution to NATO's Kosovo Force (KFOR), set up post-war for peacekeeping and stabilisation within the country. The battalion were based in Priština, the capital of Kosovo, with responsibility for maintaining the safety of its inhabitants, in cooperation with the UN police. It was a daunting task, given that Priština was a city of 200,000 people before the war, and, post-war, an additional 400,000 had moved in, mostly from the Albanian community whose houses had been destroyed during the war or who had moved in from the countryside. The rule of law was tenuous and barely maintained by a legal system still in disarray. One problem confronted the Black Watch. Like many other British regiments at the time, there was a manpower shortage – in signals, for instance, fewer than twenty men covered thirty-three stations – and D Company had to be disbanded completely, albeit on a temporary basis, until new recruits were found and trained. Until that happened, the battalion had to be reinforced by 16 Battery, 32nd Regiment, Royal Artillery. The shortage was exacerbated by another problem confronting the army, that of drug-taking. The Black Watch, on their move to Germany, discovered an increase in the number of soldiers having to be discharged after being found to have taken drugs. Germany was rife with cheap drugs, and young soldiers on a weekend pass were an obvious target for the pushers. The battalion, vigilant to such practices, resolved to stamp out the problem whenever and wherever it arose.

Despite these negative factors, the battalion arrived in Priština under Operation Agricola VI on 14 July and took command of the UK Battle Group 1 Area of Responsibility from the 1st Battalion, the Duke of Wellington's Regiment. At that time, the city was divided into five multi-national brigade sectors controlled centrally by KFOR commanders. The Black Watch portion was broken down into three company areas. The preparations were immense, given that the battalion's stock of hardware and transport had to be brought in by sea. Once in place, they had barely had time to settle when fresh orders began arriving thick and fast, and by the end of the first week they had conducted most types of operations that would confront them throughout.

The situation was tense and dangerous. Apart from the general patrols, duties included everything from escorting public buses to and from sensitive areas, search operations, vehicle checkpoints and VIP security operations. The tasks were manpower-intensive and were carried out against a backdrop of an ever-present air of menace and threat to vulnerable personnel from extremist groups. In property and vehicle searches, they made a significant find of weapons and bombs every four days. As an adjunct to the military operations, the battalion also undertook a number of community projects, such as rebuilding an orphanage.

The battalion's tour ended in November 2001 and was followed by the transfer of all men and vehicles back to Germany for the beginning of what was to become one of the busiest and most significant periods of activity for the Black Watch for many years. It so happened that the rotational clock that ticks around annually for the selection of the sections of the British military who spend the next year in training in a state of High Readiness (HR) had stopped on the 7th Armoured Brigade (Desert Rats), of which the battalion was part. They were to become the HR brigade for 2003, and in turn the Black Watch were the lead Armoured Battle Group within the brigade: in other words, the first to go if an emergency arose.

There was already much discussion about the developing situation in Iraq over the issues of weapons of mass destruction and the speculation that, by the time their HR year came around, there could be a war. How right the speculators were! But that was months away, and in the meantime intense training started for the battalion and all those involved as the nominated units worked to reach their point of High Readiness. The year saw the battalion in major exercises on the ranges of Canada, Poland and Germany that tested them to the limit. As one sergeant put it: 'We hit the ground running and never stopped. It was a fantastic year, absolutely packed with stuff. Some of it we had never tackled before. Terrific soldiering.'

It needed to be. By the year's end, the possibility of trouble in the Gulf was becoming a racing certainty. In Germany, the Black Watch and colleagues in the 7th Armoured Brigade were banned from using vehicles to save spares in the event of deployment to Iraq. Outside the preparations that could be done, the commanders worked out a programme for reinvigorating some of the regimental activities that had taken second place to the demands of the Training Year. It was obviously a management decision to give the troops a break with recreational activities – the lull before the storm, as it were. These included football matches, sports and social events and a battalion concert followed immediately by an all-ranks dance. Finally, the battalion had a good leave and managed Christmas and the New Year in peace and quiet, although Burns Night celebrations had to be cancelled as the order for deployment was confirmed. Work began immediately on the preparations, and the number-one priority was to transform the entire stock of hardware and vehicles into desert colours. That meant painting everything. The work was carried out around the clock in order to get the vehicles to the docks in the short time available. The task was made all the more difficult in that the paint was designed to be sprayed on to the vehicles in a heated environment. In the sub-zero temperatures of the garages, the paint was freezing in the air before it could stick to the surface of the vehicles. Eventually, work was completed only by working day and night to get the vehicles loaded on to the ships at Emden.

Saddam Hussein was still refusing to reveal where he was hiding his weapons. He kept telling President George Bush that he hadn't got any, and that those he'd had previously had all been destroyed. Bush didn't believe him, and nor did the British Prime Minister, Tony Blair, whose office put out an outrageous claim that Iraq was capable of launching their ballistic missiles at forty-five minutes' notice. What the politicians didn't tell their respective nations was that Saddam only had four ballistic missiles capable of carrying chemical warheads and they would fall well shy of even the Israeli border. Hans Blix, head of the UN Weapons Inspectorate, had already concluded that this was not a threat and repeated early in 2003 that his team had not found any WMDs. Bush said they were not looking in the right places. Well, perhaps not, but Blix was proved right in the end, although, of course, the incoming troops who were to confront all these possibilities were not to know that. Indeed, they went in expecting to be hit by nerve gas and other chemicals. From experience, it would have been foolish in the extreme not to have prepared for the worst.

After the last Gulf War, the WMD inspectors found the following haul inside Iraq: 13,000 155-millimetre shells loaded with mustard gas, 6,200 shells loaded with nerve agent, 800 nerve-agent aerial bombs, 28 Scud warheads loaded with nerve-agent sarin and 75 tons of nerve agent. Between 1991 and 1998 the UN Weapons Inspectors also discovered 48 operational long-range missiles, 14 conventional missile warheads, six operational mobile launchers, 28 operational fixed launch pads, 32 fixed launch pads (under construction), 30 missile chemical warheads, other missile support equipment and a variety of assembled and non-assembled components for the construction of Saddam's much-vaunted 'supergun'.

In the area of chemical weapons, the inspectorate discovered 38,537 filled and empty chemical munitions, 690 tonnes of chemical weapons agent, 2,900 tons of precursors chemicals, 426 pieces of chemical weapons production equipment and 91 pieces of related analytical instruments. The biological finds included the main biological weapons-production facility at Al-Hakam and a variety of biological weapons-production equipment and materials. Of course, all this information was already available had there been a closer check of the records of Western companies and governments, which for years had been supplying Saddam with all the materials and components required for the manufacture of such weapons, along with other hardware. It was all legal and above board, approved by government departments of France, Germany, Great Britain and the United States, which then even lent Saddam the money to buy the stuff.

This was the background, then, for the troops going in, a deployment that the British and American media spinners said was to put further pressure on Saddam in the hope of convincing him to comply with 'international obligations'. Sceptics said it had more to do with oil and the Americans gaining control of the Iraqi production, and with timing, i.e. that Bush would be running for re-election in November 2004, and he wanted the matter all over and done with long before that. Blair raised no objections, although many of his MPs did. Nevertheless, UK deployments to the theatre began in earnest in early January, initially with the Naval Task Group and

Amphibious Ready Group, which arrived in the Gulf on 12 February, integrating with US and coalition maritime forces to commence operations by 15 February.

A UK force of four Mine Counter-Measures had conveniently been 'in theatre' since November on a 'routine training deployment'. Land force deployments began with the flow of enabling equipment and stores by sea and air. The first troops began arriving in the theatre in late January, the lead grouping of the 7th Armoured Brigade comprising HQ and Signal Squadron, Royal Scots Dragoon Guards equipped with Challenger 2 tanks, 2nd Royal Tank Regiment (also with Challenger 2s), 1st Battalion, Black Watch, with Warrior infantry fighting vehicles, 1st Battalion, Royal Regiment of Fusiliers, also with Warriors, 3rd Regiment, Royal Horse Artillery, equipped with AS90 self-propelled guns, 32nd Armoured Engineer Regiment, Queen's Royal Lancers (Challenger 2 tanks), 1st Battalion, Irish Guards (with Warriors), and 1st Battalion, the Light Infantry (also with Warriors).

The Black Watch doubled in strength for the deployment, with reinforcements from other units and elements from the above to field a powerful All Arms battle group which, in addition to the 1st Battalion, Black Watch, included A Squadron, Royal Scots Dragoon Guards, Egypt Squadron, 2nd Royal Tank Regiment, J (Sidi Rezegh) Battery, 3rd RHA, 26th Armoured Engineer Squadron and 32nd Engineer Regiment. Hardware in the Black Watch battle group included 28 Challenger 2 tanks, 50 Warrior Infantry fighting vehicles and a mass of other heavy duty equipment, and of course 1,275 personnel. The group then began to move to Kuwait by stages from the middle of February until early March, which meant that the last men to arrive would barely have time to acclimatise to conditions before the shooting started. This was exacerbated by a very fluid timetable for the arrival and departure times of flights and ships. In fact, it was something of a relief to finally get into Iraq. This euphoria was short lived. In his summary of events in *The Red Hackle*, Black Watch Operations Officer Captain N. E. Ord commented:

323

The Kuwaiti desert came as quite a shock. Our vehicles immediately became our homes, the temperature came as a surprise,
ranging from being positively cold at night at first to scorching
during the peak of the day, and simply living in the desert was
a challenge. A training package was thrown together to enable
us to have a run-out with the vehicles and to test the weapon
systems, but ammunition was severely limited. A range package
[training routine] took place north-west of our concentration
area, only a few kilometres from the Iraqi border.

By 18 March 46,000 men and women from the British services and
their equipment had been deployed over 3,400 miles to the Gulf in
10 weeks, half the time it took in 1991. The British army relied largely
on tented accommodation for pretty well every situation; given the
extremes of the weather, which also included torrential rain, this was
not always the best solution. By contrast, the US, with significant
numbers of troops already based in Kuwait, had permanent camps
with high-quality facilities. A complaint much to the fore in early
deployments in the last Gulf War related to appalling toilet arrangements and delays in establishing adequate shower facilities. Similar
problems arose again, with insufficient contracts for portaloos. Air-
conditioning units were also in short supply, all of which the MoD
admitted had 'caused some hardship for our soldiers'. The food –
always a contentious issue – did show an improvement on the last
Gulf War by all accounts. The mainstay of catering for UK troops
was the Operational Ration Pack, of which three million were available for distribution for the period prior to and during the war. The
pack provided three full meals a day and a snack, with a variety of
menus, containing substantially more calories than the NATO
minimum requirement.

A few other statistics provide an indication of the sheer hard labour
involved for a good many folk. Of the total personnel, 15,000 were
engaged purely on logistics, a considerable undertaking using 670
aircraft sorties and 62 ship journeys, up to the point of deployment.
Four C-17 aircraft and other air transport were used twenty-four hours

a day to carry more than half the personnel and stores, the rest going by sea. Vehicles shipped to the theatre, if laid end to end, would have stretched the eighty-two miles from London to Southampton, while general stores and equipment, normally measured in lane metres rather like supermarket shelves, would have covered seventy-seven miles. Thereafter, the daily operational requirement at its peak involved the daily delivery of 254 metric tonnes of stores. The speed at which this pre-war movement of stores had to be carried out was little short of a logistical nightmare, but by and large the deliveries were completed on time and in good order. But there were shortfalls in a number of key areas, as was later confirmed in a post-war report from the National Audit Office that examines public expenditure.

From the outset, these issues became pertinent to the progress of the war and to the safety of the troops. The concerns may well have raised a wry smile for Second World War veterans of the Black Watch, who had had nothing. But in a modern army facing such diverse probabilities there is absolutely no reason – as the Americans constantly demonstrate – to expect anything less than a full complement of decent equipment with the safety and wellbeing of the troops as assured as possible. Questions as to whether that was achieved became a matter of some controversy. Keeping track of everything that was required for operational purposes – given the extent and rapid pace of deployment – was, of course, something of a nightmare, and vital equipment did go astray, or was not ordered in the first place. The National Audit Office disclosed that lack of supply confidence at divisional headquarters 'led to a considerable degree of misappropriation of equipment and stores moving through the supply chain, items including desert combat clothing, boots and nuclear, biological and chemical (NBC) protective clothing'. There was also a 40 per cent shortfall in the number of nerve agent detection systems, and as many as 4,000 sets of a vapour detector used to monitor residual chemicals after an attack were unserviceable. There were also insufficient supplies – in some cases none at all – of NBC defence filters for armoured vehicles to help protect the crew and soldiers inside. This may well have been an especially worrying discovery by the troops, given the publicity the government gave to claims in its intelligence dossier in September 2002 that Iraqi forces could attack soldiers with them within forty-five minutes of an order to do so. Another shortage that concerned the brigade resulted in a quarter of their force having to wear black boots and green uniforms rather than desert kit throughout the war. David Clarke, the director of the audit team that visited Iraq in summer 2003, said that while this particular problem had not affected combat effectiveness, it had had a profound impact on morale. Soldiers were quoted as saying: 'We're out here fighting, and you can't even be bothered to buy us a uniform.'

One of the most controversial elements in the National Audit Office report related to the discovery that thousands of body armour sets went missing, and consequently many of the troops did not receive a set of their own. Up to 200,000 sets, costing £170 apiece, had been issued since the 1999 Kosovo war, but they 'seem to have disappeared', the NAO commented. This became an especially poignant issue after Samantha Roberts, the widow of Sergeant Steven Roberts, who was shot near Az Zubayr, near Basra, while trying to quell a riot, discovered that he did not have a flak jacket because he had lent it to a colleague.

The coalition campaign began on the night of 20 March with an opening bombardment that was to be a dress rehearsal for the 'shock and awe' bombing that followed twenty-four hours later. A substantial aerial attack on key sites was the prelude to a dramatic storming of southern Iraq, with Desert Rats in the vanguard. As cruise missiles fired by American ships and Royal Navy submarines in the Gulf and the Red Sea slammed into Baghdad, RAF Tornado GR4s took off from the Ali al-Salim airbase in Kuwait to join the assault with US Air Force F15 Strike Eagle and US Navy FA18 Hornet ground-attack aircraft.

In the south, the 3rd RHA opened up across the border with their 32 AS90 155-millimetre self-propelled guns, which fell heavily on Iraqi front-line positions, while the Royal Navy ships *Marlborough*, *Chatham* and *Richmond* and the Australian frigate *Anzak* provided heavy bombardment, hitting targets coordinated by Special Forces and Royal Artillery spotters. Then a contingent of about 8,000 British troops in 120 tanks and 145 armoured vehicles began the move into southern Iraq from Kuwait, aiming for Iraq's second city, Basra, eventually travelling up the notorious Highway 80 to a point south of Basra with the protection of Apache attack helicopters. The roadside was dotted with Iraqi tanks blackened by direct hits on their dug-in bunkers. White flags flew over some deserted barracks, including a white cloth draped over a portrait of Saddam Hussein. Roads were lined with groups of Iraqi men in civilian clothes, although many were soldiers who had changed from military uniforms. This turned out to be a common trick among the more ardent Iraqi soldiers, who then turned on the coalition forces.

US Navy Seals and a company of Royal Marines moved towards their first major objective, to secure the vital Kwahr al Amaya and Mina al Bakr oil terminals, as reinforcements were airlifted in by helicopter troop carriers containing the three companies of 40 Commando, Royal Marines, from their base in Kuwait. Other units were deploying from *Ocean* and *Ark Royal*, that had steamed into the waters of the northern Gulf. The Iraqis responded by firing Scuds into Kuwait, forcing the alert for NBC suits, although no chemicals were detected. With memories of 1991, when Saddam had ordered the destruction of the Kuwaiti oil industry by setting fire to 730 wells that took five months to put out, the oil terminals were their first objective. With 1,000 well heads in the southern oilfields, the potential for destruction was enormous.

While the marines dealt with those objectives, the 7th Armoured Brigade's battle groups of the Black Watch and the 1st Battalion of the Royal Regiment of Fusiliers began the ninety-mile journey that would eventually take them towards the outskirts of Basra, a movement supported logistically by helicopters flying from *Ocean* and *Ark Royal* and carried out under air cover provided by the US Air Force and by the Royal Air Force, whose Tornado GR4 aircraft attacked enemy artillery in the area with precision weapons, along with other military installations as far north as Al Kut.

The Black Watch were given immediate missions to be enacted

on arrival at the target area. The first was to join elements of the 7th Regimental Combat Team of the US Marine Corps and block Iraqi troops at Az Zubayr and Basra. The preparations were made through extensive liaison between Black Watch commanders and the Americans prior to the move north on 21 March. The Americans had crossed into Iraq roughly twenty-four hours ahead of the 7th Armoured Brigade, which began the move across the border from Kuwait in the early hours of 21 March, advancing towards Az Zubayr. There, the British force was to relieve the Americans, allowing their continued advance north.

Black Watch D Company recorded this somewhat momentous occasion in their battle report, as follows:

The Engineers breached the border, and the Royal Regiment of Fusiliers secured a bridgehead. At 0102 hours D Company were called forward to become the first Black Watch company in fifty years to cross the line of departure in general war. We pushed hard on to main supply route . . . We linked up with the American 7th Regimental Combat Team, and D Company formally took over the battle space at 1430 hours. During the night we had several small-arms contacts, and just after midnight the nuclear, biological and chemical warfare dress state went up long enough to put on the suits but thankfully dropped again shortly afterwards. The following day began at 0325 hours when Captain Hedderwick took the pipes and drums [that revert to armoured infantry in times of combat] on a clearance of the area at daybreak . . . Meanwhile Lieutenant Dallard took two Warriors to escort some Engineers into the southern part of Az Zubayr so they could destroy a large arms and ammunition cache. As they approached the periphery of Az Zubayr they came under heavy attack from Rocket-Propelled Grenades (RPG) and small arms, but all drivers put their feet to the floor and miraculously drove straight through to emerge intact on the other side. Soon thereafter Battle Group Headquarters informed us that two British Royal Engineer's Land Rovers had been ambushed in Az Zubayr and that we were to move in to recover casualties or dead. With the company already heavily committed, the company commander put together a task force from 13 and 15 Platoon and four armoured ambulances, which set off into Az Zubayr via the main road that became known as RPG Alley. They were met by a company strength of Fedayeen, who had occupied the rooftops along both sides of the road. Again the only option was to punch through to safer ground on the other side of town, along a route that was about two kilometres long, throughout which there was a constant hail of incoming RPG and small-arms fire.

Despite numerous direct hits and the disconcerting fact that the enemy were using the red crosses on the side of the ambulances as an aiming point, all vehicles made it through to the quieter eastern side of the town. Eventually, Sergeant Allan spotted one of the Land Rovers upside down and burned out but very much still in the enemy killing area. The second Land Rover was then spotted nearby . . . Both vehicles were checked, but were empty, the occupants presumed to have been killed. Having ascertained there was nothing that could be done, the troops extracted themselves, still under fire, to the Warriors and the group pulled back. Three vehicles sustained direct hits with RPGs, and one still had a live RPG stuck in its back bin, but it was very heartening to see this was the only damage done.

The enemy were still active when the main British contingent caught up, and there were a number of exchanges as the Black Watch established control of their area and captured a vital bridge between Basra and Az Zubayr. The sniper platoon and the mortar lines were particularly busy and were caught up in a large firefight in the vicinity of the mosque on the outskirts of Az Zubayr very soon after arrival in the vicinity. The mortar men had taken position just to the north of the town, five miles from Basra, and first took enemy fire on the morning of 23 March, when, in another historic moment, the platoon began their first fire mission in anger since the Korean War. The platoon battle report noted:

> A real feeling of achievement and fulfilment emanated from the whole platoon . . . [but] these moments in war are short lived, as we were to continue to find out throughout our deployment. On the next day at 1934 hours Lance-Corporal Barry Stephen was killed in action while protecting the lives of the other members of the armoured vehicle in which he was travelling. This is something that training cannot prepare any man for. His loss is one that the platoon will never get over but one that we will have to learn to live with. For the next four days the Mortar Platoon fired many more missions before the battle for Az Zubayr was won and Basra had been contained. Within a week the Mortar Platoon was split into two patrolling multiples and had adopted a dismounted role in order to secure the streets of Basra, putting all its years of experience in Northern Ireland to good use. The people of Basra kept us busy demonstrating all of their qualities; both their overwhelming hospitality and the harshness that the Saddam regime had taught them.

On the morning of 24 March the battalion moved into a new concentration area from which the Battle Group's total encirclement of Az Zubayr began. In the early evening it became clear that elements of C (Support) Company had met some strong resistance, and the quick reaction force was deployed as a new offensive opened up at midnight to prepare for a raid into Az Zubayr itself. As this was happening, the battalion received an intelligence report that the two missing Engineers had been taken to the house of a prominent Ba'ath Party official, and clearance was given for a Special Forces rescue attempt supported by D Company. The rescue mission was launched just before dawn on 25 March, when the company commander led 15 Platoon into Az Zubayr with the Special Forces team, while 13 Platoon secured the extraction route, with 14 Platoon in reserve in case of trouble. The company commander's Warrior drove through the six-foot-high compound wall of the target house, then the SF team under Sergeant-Major Anderson and a team commanded by Sergeant Shaw dashed to the front entrance, which was heavily bolted. As they attempted to break down the door, rifle and RPG fire erupted from inside the house. Sergeant Shaw and one of the Special Forces soldiers were wounded, though not seriously.

At that point a heavy firefight opened up between the defenders of the house and D Company outside, but the combined team broke into the property in less than five minutes. The Ba'ath Party official was arrested and stowed in the back of a Warrior. One report suggested that up to twenty of his bodyguards were killed, but unfortunately there was no sign of the two missing Engineers. The extraction of the rescue team was covered by 13 Platoon, which had been fighting all along to keep the escape route open.

Later on that morning of 25 March, D Company, supported by a troop of tanks from the Scots Dragoon Guards, moved into the town to secure a foothold. Resistance was lighter than expected, and the company moved so fast that it put them at risk, being overstretched from the main force. However, they were quickly reinforced by the Anti-Tank Platoon, which cleared and secured an old and very dirty prison compound, where they set up camp. By three in the afternoon, an aid convoy was motoring into the town, bringing a welcome response from the townsfolk as they came out for water and food. The area was, however, under constant watch by the troops and, as was anticipated, the distribution point came under attack from snipers and RPGs. Even so, the remaining infantry elements of the Battle Group occupied positions in Az Zubayr from which they conducted further peace support operations, attempting to restart the local infrastructure, escorting food and water convoys and gaining the support of the population.

Conditions were such that the decision was taken on 1 April to remove helmets and body armour and patrol downtown in tam-o'-shanters. By 5 April the Black Watch, which had secured the confidence of the locals, handed over their positions in Az Zubayr to the Duke of Wellington's Regiment to give the troops some rest and recuperation before moving into Basra. In fact, some elements of the Black Watch, along with other units in the 7th Armoured Brigade, were already probing the Iraqi defences in and around Basra after receiving intelligence of a popular uprising among the Shiite population inside Iraq's second city. The first UK intervention to help the uprising began on the afternoon of 25 March, when AS90 155-millimetre self-propelled howitzers of the 7th Armoured Brigade silenced an Iraqi mortar firing at demonstrators in Basra. The level of respnse, however, suggested that a heavy force still existed in this sprawling city in which the available teams of British infantry could be lost within a very short space of time. At one point heavy firing broke out from the brigade units when a force of up to fifty Iraqi T-55 battle tanks made a dash southwards towards Al Faw. While British tanks engaged their targets, Harrier air support was called in, leading to the destruction of twenty Iraqi tanks immediately and the rest under pursuit.

On the southern outskirts of the city, B Company of the Black Watch tested enemy positions and met incredibly staunch resistance from the militia. In one incident the British troops looked on incredulously as a Fedayeen militiaman began attacking a tank with a shoulder-launched rocket while mounted on a donkey and cart. Trouble also flared again back at Az Zubayr when D Company's prison compound was attacked at dusk on 27 March. The battalion's snipers once again took the lead in halting this assault, although soon afterwards the Battle Group Headquarters and surrounding troop positions came under multi-barrel rocket fire from which there was no alternative but to pull back. These were temporary setbacks in Az Zubayr, where D Company continued to surge further forward, and the aid convoys were reintroduced. A Squadron was also in action, this time in a dawn raid into Basra itself, on the way accidentally knocking down a statue of Saddam Hussein at the main crossroads and destroying the state television mast.

The Battle Group had planned a limited raid into central Basra for 6 April, but this time the brigade commanders were convinced, after the initial fierce fighting, that entry to the city was now a fighting possibility and that more could be achieved. The Black Watch raiders had secured far more than their planned objectives by mid-afternoon and then continued to consolidate their position, allowing two other parts of the Battle Group, the 2nd Royal Tank Regiment and Royal Scots Dragoon Guards, to pass through and push on into the heart of Basra. Thus, by the end of 6 April the 7th Armoured Brigade had occupied Basra, and the Black Watch were poised to introduce the stabilising and peacekeeping operations that had already proved highly successful in Az Zubayr.

As already demonstrated in that town, this was a welcome task but not without its dangers and challenges. Apart from the strong presence of Ba'ath Party officials and troops and snipers, there was lawlessness on a wide scale as the regime's administration and infrastructure in Basra collapsed. The scenes were evident to all, shown on worldwide television, of widespread looting as this repressed population turned out in their thousands to pillage government buildings and even schools and hospitals. Many looters were armed and presented a threat to the incoming troops. In addition, the population, perhaps not unnaturally, began to view the British troops who had crushed Saddam's rule in their city as the source of immediate humanitarian aid and civil organisation, on a scale for which the Black Watch, or anyone else on the ground, had no real experience. In Basra, expectations of rapid drastic improvements were running high, far higher that the troops and administrators would be able to deliver for some time. The entry into the city had been so swift, and the collapse of the defending troops so complete, that the Black Watch had to attempt to quell the looting before attempting to tackle any wider issues. Once again adopting the soft posture, wearing their Red Hackles, they quickly established a rapport, demonstrating that they were not there to continue the repressive actions of Saddam but to help the people to recover and rebuild. But the need for a strong patrolling presence was ever present, and the Black Watch, in addition to handling the security of the city, had to start from scratch, training and developing the new police force. In his overview of the Black Watch's performance, Operations Officer Captain N. E. Ord wrote in the *Red Hackle*:

It is hard to capture the richness of the experience of entering Basra by force, then stabilising a lawless society, and ultimately trying to encourage development across political and economic boundaries, all after some fierce fighting in the first two weeks. The extremely warm welcome we received from most of the population was unexpected. Perhaps this is to do with the fact that there is no shortage of signs of previous British presence in Basra. One of the first Iraqis to come to our camp in Basra was a man called Hameed who had previously been employed as a messenger boy at the Royal Air Force base in Shaibah in the 1950s. A dependable man, he had a wide range of contacts in Basra – as a result he became the de facto fixer around camp, capable of dealing with any odd job or task. Our headquarters was situated a few hundred metres away from the Maqil Commonwealth War Graves Cemetery, which accommodates British and Commonwealth and Indian dead from both world wars. Sadly, there is not a headstone left standing, and many lie broken in the dust, but the bulk have been saved by the caretaker and his family.

There was another postscript to the story, in that when the rule of law initially collapsed, the management of a state-controlled steel company at Basra fled, and looters poured in. The sheer size of the place required a large number of troops to take control until a security force could be formed. Then the situation changed again when local intelligence suggested that weapons of mass destruction had been buried in the compound and that the huge piles of steel had been placed on top to conceal the excavations. The specialists came in with ground-penetrating radar equipment to scan the area, and also conducted some excavations, but nothing was found. It was a curious omen to what was to follow; indeed, the aftermath was filled with controversy and violence, the first in regard to weapons of mass destruction or, more precisely, the lack of them. But that was a political issue. That none had been discovered in no way detracted from the *possibility* of the presence and use of such weapons prior to and during the conflict as far as the military was concerned. The questions as to how British and American intelligence had overestimated that possibility, or that it was exaggerated by the politicians to justify the war, became a central focus of numerous commissions of inquiry that wasted everyone's time, notably in the UK the much-criticised report by Lord Hutton following the suicide of government WMD expert Dr David Kelly.

As these controversies raged following the so-called liberation of Iraq, the supposed peace fell into deep disarray, largely, it was being said, because of the lack of post-war planning by the US administrators in Washington whose ultimate lead the British had to follow. One thing was certain. The manner in which the British military had taken their objectives in the south could barely be faulted. They were confronted by a more responsive population in that region, but in the American-run north a massive problem of insurgency was emerging. And although they were due to end their Iraqi engagement in July, the Black Watch would yet, famously and tragically, become involved in that end of the business.

CHAPTER EIGHTEEN

Forward the 42nd!

Even before the battalion left Germany for the deployment to Iraq as part of the 7th Armoured Brigade, officers were aware that, on return, the Jocks would be moving house again, even though they had completed only three years of the planned five-year posting to Fallingbostel. Initially, the news was received with some dismay. Apart from having to leave what was considered the 'first-division' environment of the British army, the move entailed considerable upheaval in terms of repositioning the entire battalion physically and operationally. It also meant a sooner-than-expected removal for the service families living in Germany and for the soldiers themselves as they worked towards improving their career prospects. The new posting was back in the UK, to the Warminster Garrison, Wiltshire, where they were due to remain for two years. But the battalion's new commanding officer, Lieutenant-Colonel James Cowan, picked out the positives in notes to his troops, outlining the moves in *The Red Hackle*.

At Warminster, he said, the battalion would enjoy virtually unlimited resources and suffer none of the track mileage bans and other obstacles to training that were now in force across the German countryside through which they once rampaged with few restrictions. Consequently, when the battalion completed the Warminster tour, they would rank as probably 'the best trained and most experienced battalion in the army'. The colonel did, however, acknowledge that the battalion needed more than just the prospect of high-quality collective training: 'All ranks have worked exceptionally hard in the last few years. Time with families has been short and single Jocks have missed out on leave. The next few months provide an opportunity to put this right through more leave, sport, adventure training and travel. At Warminster, we will certainly work hard, but people will lead a structured life that will allow them to book holidays and enjoy weekends. In Warminster we know jobs are much more available [for wives].'

He also predicted that a period of relative stability for the battalion would enable the Jocks to develop professionally with additional training and courses to provide opportunities for promotion. But by the time his remarks were published in November 2003, new challenges and dark clouds were gathering. The Jocks were about to be thrown back into the military headlines, busier than ever and right at the sharp end of their business. And if that wasn't enough, this coincided with strong rumours emanating from Whitehall suggesting that a new round of defence spending cuts could spell the end for a number of Britain's finest infantry regiments, and the Black Watch were among those being mentioned as possible candidates for the chop. As we will see, an almighty row was in the offing as campaigners inside and outside the regiment joined in a vociferous nationwide campaign to try to save the Jocks from oblivion.

Soon after Christmas 2003, with the troops and their families now settled at Warminster, the Black Watch were summoned for another six-month tour of Iraq. Little did the Jocks know it then, but their old stamping ground of Basra would provide them with the opportunity of displaying their exceptional prowess – possibly for the last time. Initially, the challenge seemed no greater than the regiment had faced many times as peacekeepers. Although not without considerable risk, the task was in theory manageable, if a trifle unexpected and unwanted, after so recent a journey through that hot, dusty and uncomfortable landscape. In fact, the Jocks were being held hostage to their own fortune. When the Black Watch completed the tour of active service in Iraq in July 2003, Basra was a model of relative calm, and so different from the north of the country, where the Americans were under severe pressure. The Black Watch's post-war peacekeeping and stabilisation work in the area had been exemplary, based on years of hand-me-down experience and training. They successfully brought the looters under control without undue pressure or publicity and, although many groups and religious leaders were still violently opposed to foreign troops on their soil, the Black Watch had nonetheless established a unique rapport with the diverse communities. Historically, the Black Watch ran a very successful double act in the 'raid-and-aid' mode, or what in the aftermath of battle the Americans call their 'civil affairs soldiers' – specially trained units brought in after battle. The British, and especially the Black Watch, who are past masters at this task, simply changed hats. They made real contact with the population, and, after setting up an efficient supply line for food, water and utilities, they went out into the communities to begin the 'hearts-and-minds' contact. They did enormous good works – most never reported – repainting and even partially rebuilding schools, hospitals and other public buildings. They helped improve hospitals and numerous public services, including road repairs, and they staged football matches with local teams.

Of course, there were still huge dangers and violent confrontations, but the transfer from warfare to peacekeeping was far less painful than in the north, where scenes of street violence and killings soon began to shock television viewers in the West and to scare hell out of Americans watching at home. In the south, as the weeks and months passed, the British continued in the manner set up initially by the Black Watch and their colleagues in the 7th Armoured Brigade. Their policing operation was quite clearly defined as being relatively low key, even to the point where the soldiers wore soft hats whenever possible, as opposed to the vision of American forces of heavily armed and armoured troops whose eyes were generally hidden by face-clutching mirrored sunglasses, sitting with cigarette drooping from the mouth behind the barrel of 65-ton Abrams tank bearing hand-scrawled legends such as 'I'm a motherfucking warrior'.

In the anarchy, terror and confusion that developed in Iraq when the so-called war was brought to an end, the distinct differences between the modus operandi of the American and British soldiers continued to be apparent to observers. The areas under the post-war control of the 7th Armoured Brigade and the Black Watch, centred around Basra, continued to show a marked and progressive calmness, albeit interrupted by inevitable outbreaks of violence. The same degree of reluctant acceptance of the invading force was never apparent in Baghdad and the north under a vastly numerically superior force installed by the Americans. The guidelines to the conflict and those set in place by the 7th Armoured Brigade in Basra were by and large followed by the British peacekeeping force, as far as any particular approach could be sustained in a war, and they were in stark contrast to the hyped-up 'Go get 'em' directives issued by the American commanders, especially in view of what developed later. Furthermore, whereas the use of the Union flag remained low key, the Americans made sure that everyone was aware of their presence and intent, for example, by famously hoisting the Stars and Stripes over the statue of Saddam before it was demolished.

This pattern continued when, in the months following the war, the 7th Armoured Brigade were replaced by other units. But in July 2004 the 1st Battalion, Black Watch, were recalled to continue the brilliant work the soldiers had instigated during and immediately after the capture of Basra. The success of their tactics was evident for the world to see, and was even more vital now in the months leading towards the elections to form the first democratically elected government of Iraq.

Of course, there was a distinct difference between the situation that the Americans faced in the north and the calmer lands of the Shiite majority in the south. In the former Saddam heartlands, the Sunni majority as a whole now despised the occupying forces, and the increasing activity of local and imported terrorist groups combined to raise the stakes to nightmarish proportions. As the insurgents kept up a campaign of suicide attacks, car bombings, kidnappings and execution-style killings, the frustration of law-abiding Iraqis was further enhanced by the deaths of many innocent civilians and by reports of abuse of prisoners by coalition forces. Towards the end of the summer of 2004, and with the election campaign already under way, the Americans revealed that they were to embark on what they termed 'decisive action' against insurgents in northern Iraq. It soon became apparent that these would entail large-scale attacks to clear out the lawless areas of terror cells, notably Fallujah, along with other towns mainly in the province of Babil, formerly Babylon, which were the havens of the most notorious of the terrorist gangs and ruthless tribes.

The Black Watch were already preparing to pack up and return to England as the end of this latest six-month tour approached when rumours began circulating in Westminster that the Americans had asked for help in the north, and specifically that the Black Watch were to be kept on for that purpose. Parliament was suddenly in uproar, and the nation – and especially Scotland – was brought to a seat's-edge position when Prime Minister Tony Blair went to the Commons to announce that the Black Watch would indeed remain in Iraq if the British military commanders deemed it necessary. In the final analysis, he said, they would make the decision. Some said he was passing the buck, but there was little doubt among the analysts that the deal was already done. Blair subsequently confirmed that the Black Watch would be transferred north to assist in the American operations but, he promised, they would be home by Christmas. The timing of the operation, just before the US presidential election, also led to loud speculation that Blair had agreed to send in British troops to help George W. Bush by demonstrating British support for his policy in Iraq with some hands-on, side-by-side action.

MPs, commentators and soldiers' families demanded to know why else the Americans especially needed 850 British troops at a time when there were 137,000 US troops in Iraq. Further, they were destined for an especially hostile area, where nine US Marines had been killed and 197 injured in the previous three months. Blair, forced on the back foot, insisted that it was a military plea for help, not a political one. 'This is nothing to do with the American elections. It has everything to do with the Iraqi elections in January,' he told MPs. But there was real concern among the military, and senior Black Watch officers, that neither the Prime Minister nor Defence Secretary Geoff Hoon fully appreciated the risks. One further element of consternation was that even as the Black Watch were being called into what the newspapers had dubbed 'the Triangle of Death', the regiment's very future was in the balance. The Ministry of Defence had already decided to cut infantry regiments from forty to thirty-six. In fact, the decision had more than likely already been made – that the Black Watch were among those to be abolished and the battalion placed into an amalgamation of Scottish regiments.

And so, amid a distinct air of distaste and anger among the regiment's many supporters and followers worldwide, Operation Bracken swung into action at the end of October and the battle group's lumbering ten-mile convoy of hardware began its two-day journey north by road. It would, as a senior Black Watch officer commented, be a sitting target for any terrorist attack en route. Fortunately, most of the soldiers were flown up to Baghdad, but that wouldn't stop the insurgents and criminal gangs promising a hot reception. The complete battle group comprised 530 Black Watch soldiers with 40 Warrior armoured personnel carriers, 100 reconnaissance soldiers from the Queen's Dragoon Guards with 12 Scimitar tanks, 100 troops from 40 Commando, Royal Marines, 50 from the Royal Engineers and 100 from support units. A wide range of US air combat were also available to the Black Watch commanders, including Spectre gunships, ground-attack aircraft such as the A10 tankbusters, and attack helicopters.

Camp Dogwood, twenty miles west of the town of Mahmudiyah, was a desolate place, located on a wilderness of sand and mud. En route, the battle group was forced to stop four times by roadside bombs planted by insurgents. Although there were no casualties during the journey, Private Kevin McHale, twenty-seven, was killed when his Warrior armoured personnel carrier overturned in a road accident. At the camp itself, the anticipated welcoming activity arrived even before the troops had begun to unpack, with incessant mortar and rocket attacks on their new base. The soldiers were forced into immediate action as well as doing a spot of labouring, stacking sandbags in windows and doorways to block the shards of shrapnel from the incoming shells. Such was the continuing bombardment that it wasn't long before the soldiers re-christened the place Camp Incoming. The greatest danger was the tactic that they were unused to in the south, that of suicide bombers, the reason now why the Americans stopped no one and stopped for no one in the desolate ghettos of these areas that were soon to feel the full force of the US counter-attack. Here, the Jocks were to be given the task of policing the terrorist rat runs into and out of Fallujah, which was being vacated by its 250,000 inhabitants ahead of the US onslaught to clear the city of insurgents, including Abu Musab al-Zarqawi, the terrorist leader whose men kidnapped and beheaded a number of Westerners, including the Liverpool engineer Kenneth Bigley.

They went to work immediately, first venturing on a patrolling mission in Mahmudiyah, one of the towns nearest Camp Dogwood, which itself was not in the so-called Triangle of Death, although the battle group would in time make forays into that area. Initially, however, they adopted a deliberately low-key approach, handing out leaflets to identify themselves as Scottish soldiers, and explaining their presence. However, on 3 November the troops began preparations to move across the River Euphrates into rebel-dominated areas to the east. A team of Royal Engineers erected a metal reinforcement over a crumbling bridge across a tributary of the river to allow Black Watch armoured vehicles to move into their area of operations to patrol the land from which mortar and rocket fire was emanating. This again brought protests of 'mission creep', but the Ministry of Defence firmly rejected that allegation and instead labelled it as 'mission essential'. The Black Watch's commanding officer, they said, had made a tactical decision to move his forces across the river to take the battle to the insurgents and added firmly that the 'Black

Watch should be left alone to get on and do their job instead of every single tactical decision being microscopically examined'.

Later, as two Warrior armoured personnel carriers, carrying twenty soldiers, made their way towards villages six miles north-east of Camp Dogwood, a roadside bomb was detonated in what turned out to be a carefully orchestrated attack. The first of the two thirty-ton vehicles was thrown off the track and was badly damaged at the front end, although apart from a few bruises none of the troops was injured. They radioed Camp Dogwood to report the incident while the second Warrior moved in to secure the area. As it did so, that vehicle came under mortar fire and ended up in a ditch, although again there were no serious injuries. The Black Watch soldiers jumped out of the back of the vehicle to check on their colleagues and to secure the area around the scene. The troops managed to get the serviceable Warrior out of the ditch and took the crew of the first one aboard to await orders from Camp Dogwood. They were told to tow the first vehicle to a more secure point until it could be recovered the following morning; in the meantime they set up checkpoints on the road to Baghdad. At that point the attackers sent in a suicide bomber in a vehicle loaded with explosives which was aimed at the northernmost checkpoint. Lieutenant-Colonel James Cowan, in a statement afterwards, explained what happened next:

A suicide bomber drove his vehicle at the soldiers, detonating the device. The troops then came under sustained mortar fire. Three soldiers and one civilian interpreter were killed and eight soldiers were wounded. The wounded were evacuated by helicopter, and I'm pleased to report that they are all making a good recovery. Sergeant Stuart Gray, Private Paul Lowe and Private Scott McArdle were all killed instantly, as was the patrol's interpreter, whose name cannot be released for security reasons. For a close-knit family such as the Black Watch, this is indeed a painful blow and all three of these soldiers were our friends. But as we mourn their deaths, so we remember their lives and give thanks for their contribution to the life of our regiment. Stuart Gray was a sergeant of great experience in the mortar platoon. Paul Lowe was a talented drummer in the pipes and drums. Scott McArdle was a rifleman in the elite reconnaissance platoon. As brothers in arms, we extend our love to their families in Warminster, in Scotland, to their cousins and brothers serving in the battalion here. The whole of the Black Watch is saddened by this loss. But while we feel this blow most keenly, we are the Black Watch and we will not be deterred from seeing our task through to a successful conclusion.

News of the deaths brought renewed angry reaction across Britain, and Tony Blair's message of sympathy to the relatives of the dead soldiers did little to defuse the situation. A number of commentators and MPs were highly critical of government motives for sending the Black Watch into the danger zone, a theme also used by Alex Salmond, the Scottish National Party leader, one of the few senior politicians to criticise the government over the deaths. 'Today's events are an absolute tragedy for all involved,' he said. 'The bravery of those soldiers in Iraq contrasts sharply with the chicanery of the politicians who sent them there in the first place.'

At Battlesbury Barracks in Warminster, Wiltshire, current home of the 1st Battalion, there was grief, of course, but a resigned acceptance of the consequences of being a soldier in a battle zone. However, many local residents paid their respects by laying flowers at the entrance. Back at Camp Dogwood, as the Black Watch prepared to set out again on their mission, a lone piper walked across the Jurf al-Sukhr bridge, which links the west and east banks of the Euphrates, playing a lament for his three comrades. Wearing body armour and helmet and still carrying his own rifle, Pipe-Major Scott Taylor, thirty-four, from Glasgow, stood on the bridge piping 'Flowers of the Forest' and 'Highlan' Laddie'. Visibly moved by the lament, the Black Watch pressed on, stoically rejecting media assessments of their plight. Anyone with even a cursory knowledge of their history would know that they never shirked from a fight, and that adversity would be quickly turned into a weapon. A spokesman for the regiment told assembled journalists:

> This is a setback, not a disaster. It's tragic, but these things happen in war. Calls for us to pull out are nonsense and smack of defeatism. What sort of message would that send to our enemies and our allies? We were unlucky. We have been attacked every day, sometimes several times a day, sometimes without any serious injuries. We will readjust our tactics to try to eliminate the risk. The insurgents are trying to alienate us from the civilian population. They want us to treat all Iraqis as the enemy and we won't fall into that trap, but that does mean accepting a level of risk. It is not easy to spot a suicide bomber, especially when he has his wife and children in the car with him, as has happened in Iraq. I know it's difficult for the public to understand sometimes, but this is life for a soldier in an infantry unit – you join up, go to war, fight and sometimes soldiers get killed. That's what we get paid to do.

Twenty-four hours after the attack, they were out on patrol handing out leaflets to passing motorists, ever mindful of the threat of suicide bombers, and thereafter events were more demanding of their soldiering skills, as this diary of the action, compiled at the time by the author, clearly demonstrates:

> *6 November:* Soon after midnight, 14 Warrior fighting vehicles moved out of Camp Dogwood with 120 troops and intelligence experts aboard. They were bound for the first of a number of raids on the homes of suspected rebel leaders in small riverside townships on the west bank of the Euphrates, formerly a prosperous area under Saddam Hussein. Now, the townships were riddled with heavily armed insurgents whose modern weaponry was used for attacks on the Black Watch base. Alpha Company was accompanied by two US Marine Corps liaison officers to call down strikes from Harriers flown by marine pilots. The

principal targets were three houses of known insurgents and any other opportunities that might arise. The Warrior crews had half an hour's drive before reaching the target area, where they formed into units and, while keeping radio silence, walked the remaining couple of miles towards the houses in order to maintain the element of surprise. They were ordered in just before 4 a.m. with the troops divided into three, each to hit their target simultaneously, crashing down the doors. Unfortunately, none of the people on the list of the intelligence officers was found, but in each house Kalashnikovs and handguns were found, but, of course, possession of personal weapons is not illegal in Iraq. Later that day, three companies of the Black Watch were back in action, sealing off key routes used by insurgents ahead of the imminent and much-publicised assault on the city of Fallujah by a task force of 12,000 American troops.

7 November: Two bomb-disposal experts from the Black Watch battle group were very severely wounded when a suicide car bomber ploughed into their Warrior. The men, one serving with the Royal Logistic Corps and the other with the Royal Signals, were airlifted to an American military hospital. Despite this setback, the battle group continued with its mission that day, moving once again to cover the rat runs and supply routes for terrorists prior to the assault on Fallujah.

10 November: Black Watch Private Pita Tukatukawaqa, twenty-seven, was killed and two others wounded when a wire-controlled roadside bomb was detonated as the Warrior they were travelling in passed by north of Camp Dogwood. Pita had been a popular member of the battalion since joining from his native Fiji, one of more than 2,000 young men recruited into the British army from the island since 1998. The Warrior had swerved off the road when its wheels were blown off on one side. It was a bad start to what was to become one of the busiest days of action since the battle group arrived at Camp Dogwood,

347

with heavy incoming bombardment and prolonged firefights with a tough and able insurgent force. Royal Marine Commandos attached to the battle group on patrol in Warrior armoured fighting vehicles came under mortar fire. After taking shelter, they returned fire with mortars of their own. Two hours later, four rockets landed in quick succession in Camp Dogwood. The first three exploded on the ground, but the fourth hit the helicopter pad. Another helicopter was hit and a soldier injured by shrapnel.

12 November: A Black Watch patrol intercepted a suicide bomb squad after a running battle with ten insurgents who traded heavy fire before attempting to escape. They jumped into three cars and headed out into the desert. The Black Watch called in an Army Air Corps Lynx helicopter, which joined the Black Watch troops in pursuit. Again in a running gun battle, the soldiers halted one car. The insurgents scattered, leaving inside a booby trap that was safely disarmed. A second car was also halted and a large arms cache was discovered, while the helicopter tracked a third car so that the troops were able to pick up the insurgents outside a mosque.

16 November: A Black Watch soldier was seriously injured by another roadside bomb as he drove a Warrior armoured vehicle on patrol near his Camp Dogwood base south of Baghdad. In a separate incident in the area, six soldiers from the Queen's Dragoon Guards escaped injury when a suicide car bomber blew himself up as they approached his vehicle at a checkpoint.

22 November: Hundreds of Iraqi insurgents were said to be trapped inside the Triangle of Death following the American assault on Fallujah and the blocking of key escape routes by the Black Watch, according to a British military intelligence officer. He said a 'hornets' nest' of insurgents had been stirred by the arrival of the Black Watch and the Queen's Dragoon Guards. The Black Watch continued to man roadblocks to confine and entrap insurgents.

24 November: Defence Secretary Geoff Hoon was accused of 'simply brushing aside' pleas of Black Watch campaigners after making it clear that MoD plans to scrap historic regiments would go ahead. He maintained that threats from international terrorism, the proliferation of weapons of mass destruction and the demands of stabilisation and peacekeeping operations required the forces to adapt and become more flexible. This was a clear rejection of the pleas of a delegation he met from Scotland, consisting of former members of the regiment and civic officials from its principal recruiting areas in Scotland. They had presented the Defence Secretary with a paper arguing for the retention of single-battalion regiments. Brigadier Garry Barnett, the chairman of the Black Watch campaign committee and the colonel of the regiment until he retired in 2003, said: 'These are tribal regiments and one of the reasons that they are so successful when they go to war is that the soldiers believe in their regiments. The links to their home areas and their families contribute to their operational success.' Owen Humphrys, a former captain in the Black Watch and grandson of Field Marshal Earl Wavell, quoted the foreword his grandfather wrote to Bernard Fergusson's regimental history: 'It is the fashion today in some quarters to seek a soulless uniformity in all things. It will be a sad day and an evil day for the British infantry if the reformers ever succeed in weakening or destroying the regimental tradition.'

23–25 November: The Black Watch battle group took part in a major American-led offensive aimed at rounding up Sunni fighters who fled from Fallujah during the onslaught to clear the city of insurgents. Early-morning raids captured about thirty-two suspected insurgents, including several men believed to be senior figures. On 25 November, in their biggest raid yet, Black Watch soldiers crossed the Euphrates to arrest more insurgents. In the middle of the night, houses were entered and scores of males were arrested. More than 700 soldiers and 116 vehicles, including 42 Warrior armoured assault vehicles, were involved in the operation, which lasted 12 hours. The mission, codenamed Operation Tobruk, had been planned for a week and was in rehearsal for two days before the off. It was timed to coincide with two simultaneous attacks by American soldiers on other villages. Lieutenant-Colonel Cowan rallied his officers with a speech in which he made clear reference to the plans to scrap the regiment: 'This may be the last attack for the 1st Battalion, the Black Watch. Let us make sure it goes as well as anything we have done in the past and is one that we can be proud of.' The same theme was picked up by A Company commander Major Alastair Aitken, who yelled the countdown into his radio: 'Five-four-three-two-one . . . Forward the 42nd!' Loudspeakers blared out Scottish pipe songs, including 'Scotland the Brave', as the Warriors sped along the main road and turned down lanes leading to houses near the Euphrates, targeting properties nominated by intelligence sources. As in the previous, smaller raid, soldiers were wearing night-vision goggles as they went mob-handed through the area, each platoon working to a designated list of houses to search. They drove through walls, kicked down doors and threw stun grenades into houses in villages on the eastern bank of the Euphrates. When it became clear that there would be little or no resistance in some of the houses, the assaults were downgraded to a straightforward search operation, and it was left to junior officers to decide if they felt that those inside should be arrested or not.

One quoted case was that of Lieutenant Alf Ramsay, a platoon commander whose men had detained a father and his twenty-year-old son. As the man's wife and eight daughters began pleading for their release, Ramsay made an on-the-spot adjudication that the men were unlikely terrorists and sent them back to their family. In all, twenty-six people were arrested, of whom sixteen were later released. There were no extensive weapon finds, either. After the soldiers had returned to Camp Dogwood, Lieutenant-Colonel Cowan said: 'If you can achieve a military objective without firing a single shot, then that has got to be a good thing. We had the elements of surprise by arriving at night, travelling five miles without the enemy expecting us – and it was a bloodless operation.'

26–30 November: The row about the future of the Black Watch and other single-battalion regiments continued. The Defence Secretary made clear in the Commons that the cut in the number of infantry battalions would go ahead. Anabelle Ewing, the SNP MP for Perth, said it was a disgrace that while the Black Watch were in the line of fire in Iraq, Blair and Hoon were preparing to stab them in the back at home. The Defence Secretary was also lampooned for his 'contempt for the tradition of the Black Watch' by criticising those who put sentiment above the national interest. Meanwhile, in the US, Colonel Ronald Johnson described the Black Watch soldiers in Iraq as 'awesome' for the way in which they had handled their mission in cooperation with the Americans.

5 December: The Black Watch returned to Basra. Warrior driver Lieutenant-Corporal Lewis Montague, twenty-three, from Kirkcaldy, told the media on hand to witness their return: 'It's been quite a privilege to be chosen to go up to a part of Iraq where none of the British army has been before. It was the first time we had experience of suicide bombers, but there was never a feeling among us that this wasn't worth it. We have made a difference just being here. It's our job and we had to do it.'

16 December: The amalgamation of the Scottish regiments is confirmed, to form the Royal Highland Regiment of Scotland, a five-battalion regiment with a single cap badge. The Royal

Scots and the King's Own Scottish Borderers would henceforth become one battalion. The Royal Highland Fusiliers, the Black Watch (keeping their hackle), the Highlanders, and the Argyll and Sutherland Highlanders would each become one battalion within the new regiment, retaining their names as battalion identity.

There is too much history to let them go. But that is not the end of the story. What has gone before will ensure there is a future for the Black Watch, in whatever form, for years hence.

APPENDIX I

Victoria Cross Awards

The Black Watch (Royal Highlanders) and as the 42nd Regiment

Indian Mutiny

Lt Francis Edward Henry Farquharson, twenty years old, on 9 March 1858 during the Indian Mutiny at Lucknow led a portion of his company and stormed a bastion mounting two guns and then spiked them. This meant that the advance positions held during the night were rendered secure from artillery fire. Lt Farquharson was severely wounded while holding an advanced position the following morning.

QMS John Simpson, thirty-two, on 15 April 1858 during the attack on Fort Ruhya, India, volunteered to go to an exposed point within forty yards of the parapet of the fort under a heavy fire and brought in first a lieutenant and then a private, both of whom were dangerously wounded.

LCpl Alexander Thompson, thirty-four, on 15 April 1858 during the attack on Fort Ruhya volunteered, with Edward Spence, to assist a Captain William Martin Café in carrying in the body of a lieutenant from the top of the glacis, in a most exposed position under a very heavy fire.

Pte Edward Spence, twenty, on 15 April 1858 during the attack on Fort Ruhya volunteered, with others, to assist a Captain Café in bringing in the body of a lieutenant from the top of the glacis. Private Spence deliberately placed himself in an exposed position, so as to cover the party bearing away the body and received a severe wound from gunfire. He died on 18 April.

Pte James Davis, twenty-three, on 15 April 1858 during the attack on Fort Ruhya, with an advanced party, offered to carry back to the regiment the body of a lieutenant who had been killed at the gate of the fort, performing this act under the very walls of the fort.

CSgt William Gardner, thirty-seven, on 5 May 1858 at Bareilly, India, saved the life of his commanding officer who, during the action, had been knocked from his horse when three rebels rushed upon him. The colour-sergeant ran out and bayoneted two of the assailants and was in the act of attacking the third when he was shot down and killed by another soldier of the regiment.

Pte Walter Cook, twenty-five, on 15 January 1859 at Maylah Ghat, India, when fighting was most severe and the few men of the 42nd Regiment were skirmishing so close to the enemy that some of them were wounded by sword cuts, the only officer was severely wounded and the colour-sergeant was killed. Private Cook and another private (Duncan Millar) 'immediately went to the front and took a prominent part in directing the company and displayed a courage, coolness and discipline which was the admiration of all who witnessed it'.

Pte Duncan Millar, thirty-four, skirmishing to the enemy who were in great numbers that some of them were wounded by sword cuts, the only officer was severely wounded and the colour-sergeant was killed. Private Millar and another private (Walter Cook) 'immediately went to the front and took a prominent part in directing the company and displayed a courage, coolness and discipline which was the admiration of all who witnessed it'.

Ashanti War

LSgt Samuel McGaw, thirty-six, on 21 January 1874 at the Battle of Amoaful, Ashanti (now Ghana), led his section through the bush in excellent manner and continued to do so throughout the day, although badly wounded early in the engagement.

Egyptian Campaigns

Pte Thomas Edwards, twenty, 1st Bn, the Black Watch (Royal Highlanders), on 13 March 1884 at the Battle of Tamaani, Sudan, when both members of the crew of one of the guns had been killed, after bayoneting two Arabs and himself receiving a wound from a spear remained with the gun, defending it throughout the action.

First World War

Cpl John Ripley, forty-seven, in the 1st Bn, on 9 May 1915 at Rue du Bois, France, led his section on the right of the platoon in the assault and was the first man of the battalion to climb the enemy's parapet. From there he directed those following him to the gaps in the German wire entanglements. He then led his section through a breach in the parapet to a second line of trench. With seven or eight men he established himself, blocking other flanks, and continued to hold the position until all his men had fallen and he himself was badly wounded in the head.

Sgt David Finlay, twenty-two, of the 2nd Bn, on 9 May 1915 near Rue du Bois led a bombing party of twelve men in the attack until ten of them had fallen. He then ordered the two survivors to crawl back, and he himself went to the assistance of a wounded man and carried him over a distance of ten yards of fire-swept ground into cover, quite regardless of his own safety. He was killed in action in the Persian Gulf on 21 January 1916.

Pte Charles Melvin, thirty-one, of the 2nd Bn, on 21 April 1917 at Istabulat, Mesopotamia, while his company were waiting for reinforcements before attacking a front-line trench, rushed on by himself over ground swept by rifle and machine-gun fire. On reaching the trench and having killed one or two of the enemy, he jumped into it and attacked the rest with his bayonet. Most of the enemy then fled but not before Private Melvin had killed two more and disarmed nine men before taking them prisoner.

Lt-Col Lewis Pugh Evans, thirty-six, on 4 October 1917 near Zonnebeke, Belgium, took his battalion through an enemy barrage, and, while his troops were working round the flank of a machine-gun emplacement, rushed at it himself, firing his revolver through the loophole and forcing the garrison to capitulate. Although severely wounded in the shoulder, he refused to be bandaged and again led his battalion forward and was again wounded. Nevertheless he carried on until the next objective was achieved, and then collapsed. As there were numerous casualties he again refused assistance and managed unaided to reach the dressing station.

APPENDIX II

Affiliated Regiments Overseas

The Black Watch (Royal Highland Regiment) of Canada

The Black Watch of Canada have a proud history dating to 1862. Volunteers were sought following the rise of American military strength during the Civil War. Each of six Montreal Scottish chieftains raised a company for the 5th Battalion of the Canadian Royal Light Infantry. It was the beginning of a proud military heritage in which thousands of Canadian citizens have served in the Black Watch. The Canadian offshoot was formally affiliated to the Black Watch after the battalion's contribution to the British effort in the Boer War, and, as has been outlined in Chapter Ten, the 42nd Royal Highland Regiment (the Black Watch) of Canada won numerous battle honours through their three battalions in the First World War. They were mobilised again 6 August 1939 when men of the 2nd Battalion of the regiment were called to the Armoury from their homes by radio and messengers, and within a few hours, armed and uniformed, they were guarding fifteen miles of the vital Soulanges Canal, which links the St Lawrence River with the Great Lakes. The 1st Battalion were mobilised on the day war in Europe was declared, and when volunteers were being enlisted for the Canadian expeditionary force to sail to England hundreds of men from both battalions arrived at the Armoury in Montreal to sign on, including every single serving officer.

The regiment saw their first action in May 1940, when they captured an Italian ship which had tried to escape from Montreal on the day Mussolini declared war on Britain. On 22 August, after three months spent in guarding airfields in Newfoundland, the 1st Battalion, along with a large number of reinforcements, sailed for England, arriving at the height of the Battle of Britain, and went straight into action guarding British installations during the invasion scare.

Meanwhile, the 2nd and 3rd Battalions, both holders of outstanding honours and medals from the First World War, were in training for the call to Europe, although in fact they never made the journey and instead were engaged in duties in Canada. The 1st Battalion, meanwhile, were engaged in vital work guarding the British Isles and also provided one company and a motor mortar detachment for the Dieppe raid, organised by Mountbatten under the auspices of his Combined Operations command. The operation involved 6,100 troops, of whom 4,963 were Canadians, and was intended as an experimental invasion of the French coast, as well as giving the enemy a bloody nose. Highly criticised in some quarters, the Dieppe assault fared badly. Of the Canadians who embarked on the journey, only 2,210 – many of them wounded – returned to England. Of the remainder, 907 were killed and 1,946 became prisoners of war. Of the Canadian Black Watch, the ship carrying the mortar detachment was hit and forced to turn back while the men on the second ship were hampered by an accident on board, when grenades exploded, killing one and injuring eighteen others. In the attack, four out of the five officers did not return.

The battalion remained in England until D-Day, when they joined the southward attack on Caen and were engaged in heavy front-line fighting throughout north-west Europe for the next four months, operations that took them through places of historic interest and important in the regiment's history, including St-Julien, where in 1917 their forebears had helped withstand the first gas attack, and Walcheren, scene of the decimation of the Black Watch in 1809. This time, the casualties were also heavy. The Black Watch of Canada lost 80 officers and 1,400 other ranks in the battles towards Germany.

After the Second World War, as Canadian forces contracted, the Black Watch battalion remained with a creditable profile, fighting in the Korean War and contributing to NATO operations in Europe and UN peacekeeping worldwide. The men took part in aid to civilian operations, including the Quebec and Eastern Ontario ice storm disaster. In the year 2000 the Black Watch battalion earned the distinction of being selected as the best unit in Quebec's 34 Brigade for the Dubuc trophy, and was again the winner in 2002.

The Transvaal Scottish

There is also a strong affinity between the Black Watch and its South African affiliate, the Transvaal Scottish, which, as we have seen, provided reinforcements and especially officers for the 6th Battalion, Black Watch, during their murderous engagement at Monte Cassino. The Transvaal regiment was formed immediately after the Boer War, raised from volunteers from Scottish units whose members chose to demobilise and remain in the colony. Lieutenant-Colonel the Marquess of Tullibardine, heir to the dukedom of Atholl, was among the co-founders, and his family tartan was used. In the First World War the regiment joined the invasion force that swept into German South-West Africa in late 1914, where they were joined by a new battalion, the 2nd Transvaal Scottish; using the 2TS as a supplier of men, the 4th South African Infantry (SA Scottish) were formed specifically for service overseas. They were among the forces that fought an Arab attempt to invade Egypt in 1915 but their main action came when they were sent to France, fighting at the Somme, in particular the battle of Delville Wood in July 1916. In just seven days three-quarters of the battalion had been cut down, with only four officers and thirty-eight other ranks surviving unscathed. The battalion were re-formed after Delville and continued on the Western Front fighting in key areas, including the Somme again and the terrible third Battle of Ypres.

359

The SA Scottish were disbanded at the war's end, but many men rejoined the Transvaal Scottish, involved mainly in civil protection, including the Rand Rebellion of 1922. It was an encounter against heavily armed white miners in which twelve members of the Transvaal Scottish were killed. As the Second World War began, the Transvaal Scottish were running three battalions. The 1st Battalion were assigned to the British forces against the Italians in Somaliland and Ethiopia, and then to the North African campaign, including operations around Tobruk, where a portion of the battalion was taken prisoner. In October 1942 the battalion joined Montgomery's offensive, and when the Axis troops were finally defeated the Transvaal Scottish returned home to be converted to armour.

The 2nd Transvaal Scottish also joined the 8th Army and helped construct the famous Alamein Box, before moving up the coast to the Libyan border. There, on 11 January 1942, they attacked the fortified town of Sollum in a bitterly fought battle that has ever since been commemorated by the battalion. Meanwhile, their colleagues in the 3rd Transvaal Scottish also joined the Ethiopian campaign before going on to North Africa under Wavell and Auchinleck. The battalion were hit by disaster at the famous battle of Sidi Rezegh where, on 22 November 1942, the brigade, of which 3rd Transvaal Scottish formed part, was overrun by German armour. As many men were killed that day in the one battalion as died in each of the other two Transvaal Scottish battalions throughout the war. Lance-Corporal Bernie Friedlander was awarded the George Medal in most unusual circumstances. The recommendation came from a German officer after an Italian ship carrying prisoners of war was torpedoed off the Greek coast. Friedlander stripped and swam ashore with a rope, so that many lives were saved which would have been otherwise lost. Sidi Rezegh was the end for the 3rd Transvaal Scottish, which were temporarily disbanded, but other Transvaal Jocks fought through Italy either as part of a composite unit or forming fully one-third of the strength of Prince Alfred's Guard, an Eastern Cape regiment. A number also served with the 6th Battalion, Black Watch, including Captain R. M. Honey, 2nd Transvaal Scottish, who was taken prisoner at Tobruk but later escaped and joined the 6th Black Watch north of Cassino. Another 2TS officer, Major A. A. Hope, commanded a small mobile group known as Hope Force before being sent on missions to the partisans in Yugoslavia and Italy, where he was finally killed.

The war over, all three battalions were reconstituted in 1946, with the 3rd Battalion being converted to artillery as the 7th Medium Regiment (3TS). But the latter was disbanded at the end of 1959, when many members transferred to the Transvaal Scottish. Earlier, in 1953, the 1st and 2nd Battalions had been amalgamated. The post-war change in government brought difficult times for the Transvaal Scottish, whose apparently 'foreign' ethos made it difficult for the nationalist government to understand that the regiment's loyalty was always to South Africa. In 1968 training moved into a new phase, that of counter-insurgency warfare. Three years later, the 2nd Transvaal Scottish were once again revived as South Africa's traditional regiments were in the limelight and peacetime soldiering ended abruptly with the Portuguese withdrawal from Angola in 1975, which resulted in the 1st Transvaal Scottish being deployed into southern Angola from South-West Africa (Namibia), the start of an involvement that was to last until 1989. As a result, guerrilla activity showed a marked decrease where the battalion operated.

From the mid-1980s the 2nd Transvaal Scottish became the first Citizen Force unit to deploy on the western Transvaal borders with Botswana and Zimbabwe as well as to undertake peacekeeping operations in the townships and rural areas around Pietersburg in northern Transvaal. The battalion were highly commended for their efforts. During much the same period, the 1st Transvaal Scottish were transferring their focus to peacekeeping operations in the black townships, often operating on the Witwatersrand, but on occasion as far south as Port Elizabeth, as well as in Natal. The regiment's last major service was to provide troops for, and remain on standby throughout, the country's first all-race general elections on 27 April 1994. The Transvaal Scottish thus helped assure their country's peaceful transition to full democracy, and with it signalled their own readiness to contribute fully to the new South Africa.

The New South Wales Scottish

The tradition of the Scottish and Highland soldier found its way in to all the dominions in the nineteenth century and none more so than Australia, where the Black Watch affiliate arrived in the shape of the New South Wales Scottish Regiment. Formed in 1885, the regiment became part of the Union Volunteer Regiment in 1897. The 5th NSW Infantry Regiment (Scottish Rifles) expanded into two battalions in 1903, and in 1912 they were drafted into the 16th and 25th Infantry. The latter in turn split into two battalions, and all three served in the First World War, laying claim to a number of battle honours, including the second Battle of the Somme, Passchendaele and Egypt.

The New South Wales Scottish (30th Battalion) were mobilised a month after the outbreak of the Second World War, and the CO on parade called on all those willing to serve overseas to slope arms. Everybody did. Government policy at the time, however, was to assign militia units to home defence, although individual members were allowed to go overseas. Many did, as demonstrated by the fact that the first Australian officer killed and the first six Australians decorated in this war all came from the 30th Battalion. Later, the Australian government decreed that any unit in which two-thirds of the men volunteered for overseas could do so, and the battalion immediately placed themselves in the frame. Late in 1943 the battalion moved to Queensland, to spend three months in jungle training as a preliminary to active service in New Guinea to fight the Japanese. After American troops arrived in January 1944, the battalion were tasked to clear coastal areas and link up with the Americans advancing in the opposite direction. As with most of the fighting in this region, conditions were appalling, with incessant rain, thick vegetation and crocodile-infested rivers. Despite strict precautions, the sick list – as opposed to casualties – was more than thirty per cent of the total strength when the battalion linked up with the Americans in Saidor. The battalion then pressed on under similar conditions to Madang and Alexishafen and Hansa Bay, where the men remained for the rest of the war engaged on heavy patrolling in the bush. Three months before V-J Day, the battalion were withdrawn to take part in the final assault against the weakened Japanese garrison in the hills above Wewak, operations still going on when the surrender came.

The New Zealand Scottish

New Zealand had a strong and varied military presence formed from its Scottish and Highland populations dating from the middle of the nineteenth century, out of which came the New Zealand Scottish Regiment, another formal affiliate of the Black Watch. Various units drawn from the Scottish community were engaged for the First World War, sailing in October 1914 as part of the New Zealand Expeditionary Force. Diverted from their original destination in Europe, the New Zealanders were landed in Egypt, where they helped to repulse a Turkish attack on the Suez Canal in February 1915. On the fateful day of 25 April 1915, as part of the New Zealand and Australian Division, the New Zealanders landed at Anzac Cove, Gallipoli. They fought valiantly throughout the campaign until evacuated with the rest of the Allied forces at the end of the year and sent to Egypt, then on to France and the Western Front.

The New Zealand Scottish Regiment were lapsed at the time of the Second World War but were hastily re-formed as a battalion with detachments in four major cities, linked to the Black Watch and utilising the tartan. Like their Australian counterpart, the regiment were forbidden from going overseas for reasons of home defence, save for one company that represented the regiment in the New Zealand Expeditionary Force. This Scots Company joined the 27th New Zealand Battalion and took part in major events described in earlier pages at Greece, Crete, North Africa and Italy. Meanwhile, at home the New Zealand Scottish Regiment began a hefty training programme as the Japanese entered the war, and at Christmas 1942 the men prepared to sail to take up the defence of the island of New Caledonia, a hot, dusty and mosquito-ridden place where they were initially consigned to hard labour. They had to dig hundreds of defensive positions and work a quarry to build roads. In June 1943 the regiment learned that they were being disbanded because reinforcements were needed elsewhere in the Pacific theatre of operations, and most members were soon in active service on a number of fronts. The regiment were later re-formed. It is also of interest to note that New Zealand had the largest number of units in any Commonwealth nation that applied to use the Black Watch tartan, the full list being Dunedin Highland Rifle Volunteers, Wellington Highlanders, Auckland Highland Rifle Volunteers and the New Zealand Scottish Regiment.

SOURCES AND BIBLIOGRAPHY

***From the Black Watch Archive, Balhousie Castle, Hay Street, Perth.
(Official website www.theblackwatch.co.uk):***

A Brief Record of the Advance of Egyptian Expeditionary Force, compiled from official sources, 1919.

Anton, James, *Retrospect of a Military Life*, Edinburgh, 1846.

Barry, Major Gerald, war diaries, 1939–41.

Blair, Lt J. M., diary, Boer War, 1901.

Cameron, Capt A. R., diary, Boer War, 1899–1900.

Cochrane, Pte William, *Over the Hills and Far Away, reminiscences of the 2nd Battalion with the Chint Special Force, 6/1944–5/1945*.

Gerard, George, journal, 42nd Highland Regiment, 1814–15.

Gunn, James, personal account of the Peninsular Wars and Waterloo 1810–15.

Halkett, Lt P. A., *My Military Life: Memoirs, mainly relating to the Crimean War.*

Hill, Col W. F., *Scrap Book, 73rd Regiment circa 1859–1883.*

Historical Record, 1st Battalion, 1892–1908.

Historical Record of Egyptian Expedition Force, 1919.

Hopwood, Brig J. A., *Account of 1st Battalion, 1939–45.*

365

MacKenzie, Donald, *42nd in Penninsular War and Waterloo, 1808–16.*

MacPherson, Brig R. C., *Activities of the 4th Battalion, Black Watch, France, Gibraltar, Britain, Palestine, 1940–46.*

Madden, J. G., *Account of Retreat to Dunkirk by 6th Battalion, Black Watch, May 1940.*

Malcolm, John, *Reminiscences of a Campaign in the Pyrenees, 1822.*

Murray, Brig R., *Operations of 153 Brigade, Sicilian Campaign 1943.*

Notes on the activities of the 1st Battalion, Western Front, 1914–18.

Notes on the history of the Black Watch, Canada, 1939–45.

Notes, 1st Battalion, The Tyneside Scottish, 1939–45.

Notes, the New Zealand Scottish Regiment, 1939–43.

Notes, 30th Battalion, New South Wales Scottish, 1939–44.

Notes, the Black Watch of Canada, 1939–45.

Notes, 1st Battalion, Black Watch, France, 1940.

Operation Eclipse, 21 Army Group, The Occupation of North-West Europe, January 1945.

Operation Veritable, Account of Clearing the Area between the River Maas and the Rhine, 1945.

Papers relating to the 2nd Battalion, Black Watch at Tobruk, 1941.

Red Hackle, The, various editions

Robertson, Andrew, Diary of a Surgeon, 1733–5.

Rusk, Col G. A., file relating to Tobruk, 1941.

Sixth Battalion, Black Watch, war diaries, March–November 1944.

Stewart, Lt-Col J. G., *9th Battalion, Black Watch, France, 1915–16.*

The Times, 22/6/1815, containing an account of Wellington's despatches describing the Battle of Waterloo.

Ticonderoga: A digest of service, 1st Battalion, Black Watch.

Tobler, Major D. H., *A Brigade Intelligence Officer's Recollections, 1940–45.*

Tobruk, various papers relating to, 1941–2.

War diaries, 4th Battalion, Black Watch, Italy, September–November 1944.

Wheatley, Col John, diaries of service with the Black Watch.

Imperial War Museum Sound Archive:

Baron, John Frederick (Accession Number 23366), 1st and 2nd Battalion, including operations 1931–8 and 1939–48.

Dunn, George Willoughby (12594), 5th Battalion, military operations 1939–45, North Africa, Sicily, Italy, North-West Europe.

Ellis, Henry (19602), 1st Battalion, service operations 1945–1956.

Fairhurst, Joseph Levi (18347), 10th Battalion 1945, 2nd Battalion, India 1945–7 and beyond.

Grieve, John (23266), 1st Battalion 1939–40, PoW Germany 1940–45.

Gurdon, Robert (19604), officer 2nd Battalion, Germany from 1952, 1st Battalion, British Guiana 1956, Cyprus 1958 and beyond.

Hankins, Charles Aickman (17982), 6th Battalion 1937–43, wounded Tunisia.

Hilder, Richard Waterhouse (19599), Life Guards 1939–45, Chindit operations 1944.

Hopwood, John Adam (9698), British officer, 1st Battalion, operations in North Africa, Sicily and Commanding Officer for D-Day landings and beyond.

McGregor, John David (12572), British officer, 5th Battalion, military operations 1936–45 and beyond.

Nelson, Ian (25277), 5th Battalion, North-West Europe 1944–5.

Osborne, Gerald Michael (125730), 1st Battalion, North Africa, Sicily and beyond.

Paterson, George (19094), 1st Battalion, NCO, service operations from 1945, including Korea 1952–3, Kenya 1953–4.

Potter, Norman (18489), 1st Battalion, Germany 1951–2, Korea 1952–3, Kenya 1953 and beyond.

Simpson, Harry (18560), NCO 7th Battalion, service operations 1939–45 including UK, North Africa, Sicily and North-West Europe.

Stacey, Joseph (19603), 2nd Battalion UK, Germany, British Guiana, 1950–55, 1st Battalion, Cyprus 1958–9 and beyond.

Imperial War Museum, Department of Documents:

Bower, R. J. (4888), account of experiences as newly commissioned medical officer, Chindit operations, Burma 1944, and attached to 2nd Battalion Black Watch.

Donaldson, J. C. (1432), officer, 2nd Battalion Black Watch, Crete 1941 and beyond.

Macnaghten, A. C. R. S. (3696), captain, 3rd and 1st Battalions, Black Watch, extracts from letters home prior to 1914, before missing presumed killed.

Morrison, G. F. (11195), subaltern, 7th Battalion Black Watch, letters home, describing experiences with 51 Highland Division 1942, prior to his death on 24 October 1942.

Steven, S. H. (5525), and elder brother H. S. Steven, officers, 1/4th Battalion, extracts from letters home, prior to their deaths in First World War.

National Archives:

Files viewed: WO 26/20; WO 30/43; WO 71/125; WO 71/18.

Published sources:

Barker, A. J., *Fortune Favours the Brave: The Battle of the Hook*, Leo Cooper, 1974.

Brander, Michael, *The Scottish Highlanders and Their Regiments*, Seeley, Service and Co., 1971.

Calvert, Michael, *Chindits: Long-Range Penetration*, Ballantine Books, 1973.

Cannon, Richard, *Historical Record of the British Army*, London, 1845.

Craig, Neil and Jo Craig, *Black Watch, Red Dawn: The Handover of Hong Kong to China*, Brassey's, 1998.

Doyle, Sir Arthur Conan, *The Great Boer War*, Smith, Elder & Co., 1902.

Fergusson, Bernard (with Foreword by Field-Marshal Earl Wavell), *The Black Watch and the King's Enemies*, Collins, 1950.

Forbes, Archibald, *The Black Watch*, Cassell, 1910.

Fortescue, John, *A History of the British Army*, London, 1906.

Groves, Lt-Col Percy, *Illustrated Histories of the Scottish Regiments: Book One, The Black Watch Royal Highlanders, 42nd Foot,* W. & A. K. Johnston, 1893.

Harrison, Frank, *Tobruk*, Cassell, 1998.

Linklater, Eric and Andro, *The Black Watch*, Barrie and Jenkins, 1977.

MacWilliam, H. C., *A Black Watch Episode 1731*, W. & A. K. Johnston, 1908.

The Official Records of the Mutiny in the Black Watch, 1743, London 1910.

Moorehead, Alan, *Desert War*, Penguin, 2001.

Parker, John, *Desert Rats*, Headline, 2004.

Picken, Andrew, *The Black Watch*, (a novel roughly based on the story of The Fair Maid of Perth by Walter Scott), Richard Bentley, 1834.

Prebble, John, *Mutiny*, Penguin, New York, 1975.

Richards, Thomas B., *The Black Watch at Ticonderoga*, excerpt from Vol. X of the Proceedings of New York State Historical Association, reprinted by Heritage Books Inc, 1999.

Robinson, Jacob, *A Short History of the Highland Regiment*, London, 1743.

Rose, David, *Off the Record: The Life and Letters of a Black Watch Officer*, Spellmount, 1996.

Sterling, Lt-Col Anthony, *The Highland Brigade in the Crimea*, London 1895.

Stewart, Maj-Gen David, *Sketches of the Character, Institutions and Customs of the Highlanders of Scotland*, Inverness, 1885, reprint edn, Banton Press, Largs, 1993.

Wauchope, General Sir Arthur, *A History of the Black Watch in the Great War*, originally published in three volumes, reprinted in paperback by Naval and Military, 2002.

INDEX